Rethinking Merger Analysis

Rethinking Merger Analysis

Louis Kaplow

The MIT Press
Cambridge, Massachusetts
London, England

© 2024 Massachusetts Institute of Technology

All rights reserved. No part of this book may be used to train artificial intelligence systems or reproduced in any form by any electronic or mechanical means (including photocopying, recording, or information storage and retrieval) without permission in writing from the publisher.

The MIT Press would like to thank the anonymous peer reviewers who provided comments on drafts of this book. The generous work of academic experts is essential for establishing the authority and quality of our publications. We acknowledge with gratitude the contributions of these otherwise uncredited readers.

This book was set in Stone Serif and Stone Sans by Westchester Publishing Services. Printed and bound in the United States of America.

Library of Congress Cataloging-in-Publication Data is available.

ISBN: 978-0-262-04924-5

10 9 8 7 6 5 4 3 2 1

For Jody, Irene and Dave, Leah and Jared

Contents

Preface ix

1 Introduction 1

2 Framework 15

    A Decision Analysis and Information Collection 15
    B Mechanism Design 20
    C Rationality Constraint and Non-Neoclassical Merger Motives 22
    D Entry, Exit, Investment, and the Long Run 27
    E Distortions in Multiple Sectors 29
    F Social Objective 31

3 Price Effects and Market Definition 33

    A Market Definition 34
        1 *Diagrammatic Representation* 36
        2 *Composite Functions* 39
        3 *Reflections on Market Share Inferences* 43
    B Price Effects 48
        1 *Unilateral Effects with Homogeneous Goods* 50
        2 *Unilateral Effects with Differentiated Products* 61
        3 *Coordinated Effects* 68
    C Further Reflections 74
        1 *Questions and Concerns* 74
        2 *Origins, Evolution, and Inertia* 77

4 Efficiencies 81

    A Nexus between Efficiencies and Anticompetitive Effects 82
    B Merger Specificity and the Theory of the Firm 85

C Applications   95
    1 *Economies of Scale*   95
    2 *Economies of Scope*   101
    3 *Sharing Assets between Competitors*   104
 D Integrated Assessment of Efficiencies and Anticompetitive Effects   107
 E Efficiencies and the Long Run   113

5 Entry   117

 A Ex Post Entry   119
 B Ex Ante Entry   126

6 Priors, Predictions, and Presumptions   137

 A Overview   137
 B Structural Presumption   141
 C Priors and Predictions   149
    1 *Industry Studies*   149
    2 *Merger Retrospectives*   155
    3 *Merger Simulations*   159
    4 *Stock Market Event Studies*   163
    5 *Industry Expertise*   169

7 Institutions   171

 A Agency Expertise   171
 B Litigation Reform   177
 C Ex Post Merger Review   180
 D Competition Agencies' Domain   184

8 Objectives   187

 A Consumer versus Total Welfare   188
 B Short Run versus Long Run   194
 C Single-Sector Partial Equilibrium versus Multisector General Equilibrium   199
 D Competition as a Process   205
 E Other Objectives   209

9 Conclusion   213

References   221
Index   241

Preface

Why *rethink* merger analysis? Merger policy is unquestionably one of the most consequential domains of competition regulation throughout the world, and it has advanced greatly over the past half-century due in large part to advances in industrial organization economics. Merger analysis is thus quite important, and its broad features seem to be well settled.

But are they? And should they be?

When I contemplated launching this project in 2017, I had already written about fundamental defects in the market definition paradigm that underlies the so-called structural presumption (with recent efforts to reinforce and extend it) and other key features of modern merger guidelines and court precedents. But many of these ideas have not fully penetrated economic research, policy advocacy, and everyday merger practice, in part because it was not appreciated just how the key criticisms fit in and what their implications were. Hence the need to rethink, or at least to think some more. It turns out that the problems are worse than most imagine. An illustrative ΔHHI challenge threshold in a prominent, recent article would change by more than two orders of magnitude simply by varying the posited elasticity of demand within the range consistent with the HMT ratifying a narrow, homogeneous goods market. The pertinent formula also contradicts the use of the ΔHHI in the "relevant" market whenever the homogeneous market is broadened. Moreover, existing protocols can misorder mergers—presumptively challenging one and giving a pass to another—even when the latter merger would raise prices dozens of times more than would the former. Because defects in the market definition process are logical and absolute—market definition analysis can only degrade inferences, regardless of the information set—continued reliance on it, much less doubling down, has to be a mistake, and the errors can be large.

Existing analysis of efficiencies needs rethinking because so much has never been analyzed in the first place. Merger efficiencies must be merger specific, which usually means that they cannot be achieved through contractual arrangements short of a merger. Yet relevant research in industrial organization economics, including that applied to merger analysis, is almost entirely divorced from literature on the theory of the firm, contract theory, and organizational economics that directly addresses such questions (and, incidentally, is associated with several Nobel Prizes). Nor is relevant business and industry expertise consulted in analyzing merger efficiencies. Lacking an analytical framework and hence not examining much of the pertinent evidence, it is no wonder that efficiencies seem inscrutable.

Efficiencies (and entry) are also sequentially siloed in official merger protocols, relegated to the end of the inquiry, if one gets that far. But, taking a decision analytic formulation and using for concreteness the odds ratio formulation of Bayes' rule, how can one form the likelihood ratio for updating one's priors when there is no denominator? (Here, the likelihood ratio is the probability that the merger is anticompetitive given all the evidence divided by the probability that the merger is efficient given all the evidence.) Moreover, inferences from the merging parties' rationality constraint require an assessment of efficiencies even if one cares only about whether anticompetitive effects, in a vacuum, exceed some threshold. In this way and others, standard protocols are patently irrational.

Entry is also fundamentally misanalyzed. Inquiries into whether an otherwise anticompetitive merger will induce fully corrective entry are misguided except in extreme cases (some of which exist) because higher profitability, caused by higher equilibrium prices, is usually required postmerger to induce entry that was unprofitable beforehand. Instead, the prospect of (partially mitigating) entry may indicate that a merger motivated by anticompetitive considerations is unprofitable ex ante, shifting the appropriate inference to efficiencies—again reasoning from the merging parties' rationality constraint. Ex post entry also has important welfare consequences of its own, as established by famous but now neglected literature (associated with additional Nobel Prizes) from half a century ago.

Perhaps more importantly, entry that may be induced by the prospect of a subsequent buyout has been neglected until recently. And much contemporary analysis that does address such acquisitions takes entrants' existence and capabilities as given, whereas the most important impact of a merger regime in this domain involves effects on ex ante investment incentives. Reduced incentives from a more stringent regime can greatly reduce welfare—because many forms of innovation are undersupplied—but sometimes welfare rises because imitative investment and entry are often socially excessive. Hence, the direction of ex ante innovation is a first-order consideration in setting the relative stringency of merger regulation in important classes of cases.

In these ways and others, merger analysis needs substantial rethinking. This book seeks, often relentlessly, to ask all relevant questions without regard to where the answers may lead or whether they can directly be implemented in merger review. This course of investigation is the appropriate way to set research agendas, formulate policy, and determine how best to analyze proposed mergers. Proxies and shortcuts are necessary, but much contemporary policy debate puts the cart before the horse: How can one determine which protocols are better than others without first performing the underlying analysis correctly for broad classes of cases? That is, how can we know what counts as a good shortcut if we have not figured out where we should be going or checked whether the proposed shortcut takes us over a cliff?

This book also departs from much merger policy advocacy by analyzing how optimally to order mergers, from the most dangerous to the most beneficial, rather than advocating for more or less stringency. If we know, for example, that a certain population is underserved by the medical system, pulling out all the stops to give more drugs and perform more surgery on this population is not merely a blunt prescription but a truly dangerous one: additional, intrusive medical treatment on people who don't need it does not help offset but instead seriously adds to the harm from the failure to treat those who would actually benefit. The first-order problem is to figure out which mergers are more harmful or more beneficial, and to what degree. To address that problem, we need to rethink merger analysis.

* * *

When I started this project, I had not yet formulated a third of the questions addressed in this book. And for some of the questions already on my mind, I did not yet know the answers or even how best to go about finding them. Unsurprisingly, therefore, some of the results I present here modify or overturn notions I had previously accepted. Such is the nature of research, particularly when the focus is on rethinking that aims to identify relevant foundations and build afresh.

My inclination to start with foundations, focusing on central concepts and deriving their implications, was undoubtedly reinforced by my early education in economics. I was especially influenced by Hugo Sonnenschein, with his focus on microeconomic theory and welfare economics, and Michael Spence, whose teaching and writing emphasize core principles and clear connections between theoretical analysis and essential features of the world that one seeks to illuminate. In industrial organization, and antitrust in particular, I learned initially from Mike Scherer, Richard Caves, Michael Porter, Phillip Areeda, and, again, Michael Spence. My collaborators over the years—more recently, Aaron Edlin, Scott Hemphill, and especially Carl Shapiro—have deepened my engagement in the field and sharpened my thinking on many fronts. And, as always, my colleague Steven Shavell has provided a steady flow of criticism and encouragement that has contributed to this effort.

I am also indebted to myriad peers who have discussed various topics and my prior writing in ways that have illuminated and helpfully corrected my thinking on many issues addressed in this book. They include: Dale Collins, Mihir Desai, Joseph Farrell, Matthew Hammond, Oliver Hart, Michael Katz, John Kwoka, Francine Lafontaine, Robin Lee, Josh Lerner, Ulrike Malmendier, Leslie Marx, Douglas Melamed, Nathan Miller, Ariel Pakes, Joseph Podwol, Devesh Raval, Raffaella Sadun, Howard Shelanski, Daniel Sokol, Kathryn Spier, Michael Whinston, Abe Wickelgren, reviewers for the MIT Press, and conference and workshop participants at the Department of Justice Antitrust Division, the Federal Trade Commission, Harvard University, the Northwestern University Conference on Antitrust Economics and Competition Policy, the University of Southern California, and the USC-Cambridge Virtual Antitrust Workshop. I have also benefited substantially from the efforts of many talented research assistants (with apologies to any accidently omitted): Sebastian Becker, Alex Blutman, Samantha Carvalho, Angie Cui, Sumeet Dang, Niki Edmonds, Will Feldman, Dustin Fire, Ayako Fujihara, John Graham, Arka Gupta, Molly Gupta, Caitlin Hird, Peter Jen, Nick Juan, Kevin Lie, Betsy Lin, Jessica Ljustina, Andre Manuel, Kolja Ortmann, Matthew Pick, Bryan Poellot, Dina Rabinovitz, Ivan Reidel,

Preface

Micah Rosen, Parisa Sadeghi, Jessica Shung, Adam Spiegel, Désirée Stebler, Alexi Stocker, Patrais Strzelecki, John Sullivan, Joy Wang, and Adele Zhang. I have received financial support from Harvard's John M. Olin Center for Law, Economics, and Business and from my home institution, as well as the support of my dean, John Manning, and endless assistance from Molly Eskridge on many fronts. Thanks also to Matt Seccombe for the index and to Anne-Marie Bono, Judy Feldmann, Catherine Woods, and the rest of the team at the MIT Press for their help with editorial and production matters.

Disclaimer: I have consulted on antitrust matters, for both the government and private parties. As it happens, my work on mergers, all of it decades ago, was entirely for government agencies. In addition, my wife is a lawyer who has mostly represented the financial services industry.

1 Introduction

Why rethink merger analysis? Everyone appreciates that some methods (notably, market definition) are problematic and key subjects (efficiencies, entry) are underdeveloped. As I began to rethink these and other matters, I discovered some unsettling properties of conventional analysis and additional issues in need of attention. Further analysis identified encouraging directions for improvement and promising pathways for research.

Rethinking begins with foundations, the reexamination of which reveals deficiencies in basic elements of conventional analysis. Merger guidance from agencies, courts, and commentators often advances sequentially siloed protocols that contradict basic teachings of decision analysis and implicitly attempt to formulate likelihood ratios without denominators. If one uses the few formulas that are advanced to microfound merger guidelines' widespread use of changes in the Herfindahl-Hirschman Index (ΔHHIs), one finds that the relevant challenge threshold can vary by more than two orders of magnitude for homogeneous goods markets, even when confined to those consistent with merger guidelines' hypothetical monopolist test (HMT). And the HMT in these settings, when combined with U.S. Merger Guidelines' thresholds, would presumptively allow a merger that raises prices by one to two orders of magnitude more than another merger that would presumptively be challenged. Such properties are not mere rough edges or rounding errors.

Efficiencies need to be merger specific to count in favor of a proposed merger, which often requires that they cannot be achieved by alternative contractual arrangements. Yet neither the literature nor modern guidelines make use of the central ideas in the field of economics that directly address merger versus contract, those developed in research on the theory of the firm, which is associated with multiple Nobel Prizes.

Standard analysis of entry induced by otherwise anticompetitive mergers fails to leverage implications of market equilibrium and ignores direct social welfare effects of entry as such, which can reinforce or reverse the apparent undesirability of otherwise anticompetitive mergers. Moreover, guidelines and much analysis largely omit the most direct channel of relevance of such entry: inferences from the merging parties' rationality constraint—the reasons that the proposed merger is expected to be profitable—by contrast to whether postmerger entry would fully reverse price increases, which it generally would not. Additionally, another type of entry, that induced by the prospect of a subsequent acquisition, has been largely ignored until recently. Much policy discussion, particularly regarding large technology companies' acquisitions of nascent entrants, has begun to address this subject but typically takes entrants' presence and capabilities as given. Yet the most important effects of merger policy in this domain concern ex ante incentives to enter and for other investment, consideration of which reverses some suggested proscriptions but strengthens others.

Regarding overall methodology, merger review generally takes a short-run, partial equilibrium perspective for practical reasons. Yet long-run impacts and general equilibrium effects are sometimes of opposite sign and often are quite important for determining the overall social welfare impact of merger regulation. Merger protocols need to reflect these phenomena even if they cannot routinely be assessed in investigations of particular mergers. Doing so, however, does not uniformly favor more permissive merger review, as some have suggested.

These ideas illustrate what this book investigates and how it goes about doing so. When I began to rethink merger analysis, I was aware of some of these questions but more broadly was uneasy about much conventional wisdom because central foundational work had never been undertaken. Some of the conclusions presented here surprised me and conflict with my own prior writing and teaching. But often, before I began digging into a subject, I was unaware of the significance of some of the key questions, much less of what answers would emerge.

A guiding principle in this enterprise has been not to be deterred from asking hard questions by the possible lack of immediate, practical answers. I aim throughout to advance knowledge as far as I can, sometimes covering a good distance but other times coming up short. On some fronts, there are fairly direct implications for policy and practice. On others, research agendas are outlined.

Introduction

Another guiding principle has been to choose subjects in light of my own comparative advantage. Mostly, the analysis here is theoretical and conceptual, the realm of my prior work. On subjects where I could make progress, I did. On ones where I did not expect to have much new to say or that would have taken me too far afield to pursue, I abstained. Hence, even though this investigation covers most major questions relevant to the analysis of horizontal mergers, including many outside the conventional canon, the book is not comprehensive. Much of the analysis presented here is novel or involves significant excavation of mostly forgotten ideas, as well as cross-fertilization from other fields.

These two principles reflect a belief that better understanding will, in the present and in the future, inform research agendas and improve policy. We cannot answer questions we never ask. We cannot fix problems we have not identified. And we cannot design sound shortcuts and proxies to guide the everyday practice of merger review if we do not appreciate what a more complete analysis looks like and hence what the long-run effects of different protocols are likely to be.

The analysis in this book is complementary to an increasingly sophisticated body of applied research in industrial organization. That work has taught us much and, in combination with scholarship in related fields, can educate us even more going forward. Deploying valuable methods to address a broader set of questions can be expected to bear significant fruit. In recent years, this has begun to happen with respect to some of the topics explored here. The present investigation seeks to boost these efforts and instigate new ones. It proceeds as follows.

Chapter 2 presents the framework for merger analysis. Merger review poses important inference and prediction challenges associated with decision-making under uncertainty. It is important to make explicit the requisite analytical steps because some have been underutilized or skipped entirely in research and especially in practice. Proper analysis formulates concrete competing hypotheses, makes use of the merging parties' rationality constraint (which holds that only profitable mergers will be proposed), and triangulates across relevant factors and types of evidence.

Official protocols deviate from the correct approach by instead specifying sequential, siloed analysis of anticompetitive effects, efficiencies, and entry, although agency analysts no doubt may proceed in a more integrated fashion. At many points in the book, we will see how analysis of each of these issues informs the others, but how could it be otherwise? If we take the simple view that a merger is proposed because it is profitable, and that its profitability depends on anticompetitive effects and efficiencies, it is generically true that information about each of these components bears on correct inferences about the other. Under the odds ratio formulation of Bayes' rule, the ratio of the priors (the probability that the merger is anticompetitive versus efficient) is multiplied by the likelihood ratio associated with the relevant hypotheses to generate a ratio of posteriors. But if one considers anticompetitive effects in isolation, one is in a sense forming a likelihood ratio without a denominator. More broadly, basic teachings of decision analysis—and, where appropriate, mechanism design—are in tension with standard protocols and merger assessments.

This framework chapter also broaches the subject of competition policy's objectives and raises broader methodological issues. Key choices include those between consumer and total welfare, short- and long-run analysis, and partial and general equilibrium analysis. Pragmatic considerations and current practice tend to favor the former choice in each pair, whereas a more complete economic analysis and social welfare calculus point to the latter ones. The interim chapters highlight important differences along these axes, with more complete analysis deferred to chapter 8.

As a preliminary matter, it is worth recalling that long-run general equilibrium thinking, with free entry and exit, is central to the welfare properties of a market economy. Long-run effects often have the opposite sign of short-run effects. Cross-sector general equilibrium effects in the presence of imperfect competition in many sectors can significantly modify or reverse standard partial equilibrium prescriptions. Hence, although long-run general equilibrium analysis is infeasible in the review of particular mergers, broad contours of policy as well as practical protocols should be developed with these effects in mind.

Chapter 3 examines price effects and market definition. It begins with the market definition paradigm, which presents many conundrums for the economic analysis of mergers. To begin, the construct does not really exist in industrial organization economics. Moreover, when one attempts to examine the procedure carefully, fundamental defects become apparent: Any sensible attempt to define markets implicitly assumes that one already has a best estimate of market power in hand because such an estimate is needed to determine which market definition is superior. Hence, the process is unavoidably circular. Worse, short of crass reverse-engineering, market definition discards or distorts much of the information under consideration, introducing needless inaccuracy. No models or analysis have ever been offered that make use of market shares in redefined (broadened) markets, and no method exists to adjust interpretations of market shares in the manner that courts, analysts, and commentators have purported to do for over half a century.

Even basic questions of quantification have never been asked, much less answered. Suppose that a merger results in a postmerger HHI of 3000 and a ΔHHI of 300 in a properly defined HMT market—a merger regarded to be clearly in the danger zone. In whatever is imagined to be the benchmark, typical case, is such a merger thought to increase price by 18%? 1.8%? 0.18%? Do we know within an order of magnitude?

The bulk of chapter 3 directly analyzes the price effects of mergers in standard settings. Unilateral effects in homogeneous goods markets are typically examined using a Cournot model. This is the one setting where formulas containing the HHI or ΔHHI exist, but those formulas are applicable only in the homogeneous goods market, which is to say that market (re)definition undermines the ability to conduct the analysis. Furthermore, these simple formulations yield results that upend standard merger protocols. Under highly simplified assumptions, the combination of the HMT and the HHI/ΔHHI thresholds in the 2010 U.S. Merger Guidelines would safe harbor a merger that raises prices by *more than thirty-five times as much* as would another merger that would be presumptively challenged (an error that more than doubles under the 2023 guidelines). Using a more sophisticated analysis from the literature (but still for a simple, special case), in basic examples the critical ΔHHI threshold for challenging a merger varies by *more than two orders of magnitude* for market elasticities of demand consistent with the HMT being satisfied in the narrow, homogeneous goods market. The theoretical arguments that challenge the market definition paradigm are revealed to be not mere subtleties; rather, they indicate huge divergences from correct analysis—all in simple cases that abstract entirely from complications understood to be outside the standard market definition framework.

The Cournot model is also examined for its usefulness in merger assessment. Well-understood but often unmentioned limitations are highlighted. Notably, the best motivation for this model assumes capacity constraints, but these render problematic standard Cournot merger analysis, which in a sense compares two different long-run equilibria. Dynamic analysis is required to account for how a merger would change subsequent investment, with the result that horizontal mergers in this setting may be more profitable, and more anticompetitive, than they appear to be under static analysis.

The analysis of unilateral effects with differentiated products is the best developed and most often deployed technique in modern merger analysis. It has long been understood that the correct methodology does not employ market definition. Instead, mergers' price effects are determined primarily by the diversion ratios between the merging firms' products and by the firms' price-cost margins on those products. To be sure, the former are related to market shares in some standard models of demand, but the question to be analyzed is which if any of those models is applicable to a proposed merger. Any proper use of market shares is determined by that analysis, not by a generic formula using HHIs or ΔHHIs. Even in special cases in which equilibrium, endogenous, premerger market shares turn out to be probative of diversion ratios, the correct analysis uses those shares differently from their appearance in the HHI or ΔHHI and, moreover, necessarily employs additional information (about substitution) that is ignored in conventional market share tests of all kinds but is highly consequential for predicted price effects.

Coordinated effects require qualitatively different analysis. The greatest challenge is prediction of the extent to which a proposed merger will facilitate successful coordination. Unfortunately, little progress has been made on this difficult task. Usual market share measures are largely irrelevant, with one exception being that, for a given remaining number of significant firms, a larger postmerger HHI may indicate that coordination would be more (not less) difficult because, ceteris paribus, the HHI rises as firms are more asymmetric and greater asymmetry is typically thought to impede cooperation. In predicting coordinated effects, it is also necessary to determine how much prices would rise conditional on success. Here, standard tools of economics are quite helpful, but, again, they do not involve use of the market definition paradigm.

Chapter 4 turns to merger efficiencies. As a matter of logic and the law, proffered efficiencies must be merger specific if they are to serve as justifications for a proposed merger. Often this means that the efficiencies are not achievable by contract short of merger. Yet the economics literature on mergers and modern merger guidelines make essentially no reference to work on the theory of the firm that addresses precisely the question of the difference between bringing activities inside the firm versus relying on external contractual relationships. Also largely ignored is the work of organizational economists and others, mostly at business schools, that addresses related questions. A central aim of this chapter is to undertake cross-fertilization in order to generate new analysis of the subject as well as to apply that analysis to standard types of merger efficiencies: economies of scale, economies of scope, and the sharing of assets between competitors.

Another underdeveloped question concerns the nexus between a merger's anticompetitive effects and efficiencies. It is well understood that if, say, a retail merger promises significant economies in distribution but has some geographic overlap, a targeted spinoff may be appropriate, eliminating the anticompetitive effects but sacrificing little of the efficiencies. More broadly, however, this nexus question has not been examined systematically. For example, if an industry has ten symmetric firms of minimum efficient scale and technological change doubles that scale, it is generally regarded that mergers that pair off the firms (leaving only five) should be disallowed, relying instead on internal expansion and exit to solve the scale problem. Yet the latter also leaves the industry with only five firms, on the surface generating the same anticompetitive effects as when pairs of firms are permitted to merge. Many contractual alternatives to merger in other settings, such as ones involving the sharing of assets through a joint venture, may risk significant anticompetitive effects in the absence of intrusive regulatory oversight that is unlikely to be forthcoming. The chapter considers these issues and explains why some traditional instincts, such as that favoring internal expansion, may be correct after all but for more subtle reasons—in this instance, because disallowing mergers creates an endogenously exercised real option for society when scale economies are uncertain. In other settings, however, it is the efficiencies that may be merger specific whereas the anticompetitive effects are not.

The analysis of merger efficiencies also raises practical challenges due to difficulties of assessment. But this should not discourage best efforts, leaning instead on a one-size-fits-all efficiency credit. Efficiencies are quite heterogeneous, and the implicit current use of a rather high credit may inappropriately excuse many anticompetitive mergers. To address the informational challenges, competition agencies should enhance their reliance on in-house and on-call expertise of the sort held by individuals with significant experience advising, financing, or working in the industry. Their skills and knowledge bases would complement those of industrial organization economists at the agencies.

Chapter 5 analyzes entry, another underdeveloped subject in merger analysis. Merger guidelines focus on ex post entry, that induced by a merger's anticompetitive effects, and ask whether such entry would be sufficiently likely and rapid to nullify most or all of the price increases that would otherwise occur. Yet, short of fairly extreme cases (some of which exist), equilibrium analysis suggests that this is improbable because significant postmerger entry arises only when there will be increased postmerger profits that require sustained postmerger price elevation. Moreover, the direct social welfare consequences of induced postmerger entry are broadly ignored. Because entry tends to be socially excessive in homogeneous goods industries and in other settings with little benefit from product variety or spillovers, merger-induced entry may actually make a merger worse than if such entry did not occur. That result reverses, however, when entry brings highly valuable variety or other benefits that are external to prospective entrants.

The central relevance of postmerger entry to a proposed merger's price effects, however, lies elsewhere: in making inferences from the merging firms' rationality constraint. The prospect of significant postmerger entry, even when insufficient to restore the premerger price level, nevertheless reduces potential profits from anticompetitive price increases. This prospect shifts proper inferences toward efficiency explanations for the proposed merger because, the more that entry would suppress any price increase, the lower are predicted anticompetitive effects and hence the higher is the conditional expectation regarding efficiencies. Proper triangulation interactively considers evidence bearing directly on anticompetitive effects, efficiencies, and prospects for postmerger entry, in contradiction to conventional protocols that prescribe sequentially siloed analysis.

The chapter then examines ex ante entry, that induced by the prospect of a subsequent merger. Until fairly recently, this subject has received only modest attention in industrial organization research and even less in merger analysis and modern merger guidelines. The prospect of an acquisition raises the ex ante incentives for investment by entrants and other

Introduction

potential targets, and it also rechannels their activity in ways that can be socially beneficial or detrimental, depending on the context.

Because entry is socially excessive in homogeneous goods industries and others where entrants bring little value except their competition, acquisitions of such entrants—undertaken by dominant firms to extinguish their competitive threats—tend to be inefficient. The reason is not primarily the loss of competition, which may never materialize if the entry itself is discouraged by anticipation of a tough merger regime, but instead the wasted investment costs from excessive entry. By contrast, entry that adds variety, creates potential complementarities, or generates other positive spillovers tends to be undersupplied. Here, a permissive policy toward acquisitions of such entrants may be desirable due to the ex ante incentives it creates.

The central message is that ex ante entry and investment incentives are of first-order importance in the analysis of a significant subset of mergers that are subject to increasing attention, particularly regarding acquisitions by leading technology and pharmaceutical firms. Many current discussions take the nascent entrant's presence and capabilities as given, whereas the most important effects of merger policy in this setting are likely to be on ex ante incentives regarding activity earlier in the relevant timeline. Hence, it is important to undertake a dynamic analysis that accounts for the magnitude and direction of ex ante investment as a function of anticipated merger review, including its relative stringency across different types of acquisitions.

Chapter 6 shifts attention from methods of analyzing proposed mergers, the subject of the preceding chapters, to the empirical and practical challenges of predicting the effects of proposed mergers. Taking the prediction perspective that is associated with a decision-analytic approach, pertinent information consists of prior probabilities and the information in the case at hand, from which likelihood ratios are formed. In practice, these notions are not entirely distinct, and both are difficult to come by for many proposed mergers.

Because of these difficulties, the so-called structural presumption has had much allure. However, in light of chapter 3's analysis of market definition and its contrast with the correct ways to analyze price effects, this allure is really an illusion. Structural presumptions require the use of market shares, and one cannot determine market shares without defining markets. However, because market definition always destroys information and thus degrades inferences, this approach cannot help. For early screening, when information is particularly scarce, it is all the more important to use correctly whatever information an agency has. Analyses that might seem to lend some support to the use of the structural presumption do not, on inspection, actually do so. This failure should not be surprising because such attempts cannot escape the problem of defining markets—except by a form of reverse engineering that entirely eliminates any use of market shares as independent variables in triggering a presumption.

Most of chapter 6 addresses the main sources of information that may guide merger policy and the review of particular mergers. Internal and comparative assessments are offered for each type of information, both for purposes of forming prior probabilities and for understanding particular mergers under investigation. Industry studies of past mergers are the most useful but exist for a sufficiently large number of mergers in only a few settings. Also, caution is required because the market shares that appear in such studies generally are not those in the markets that are required under merger protocols (which, ironically, helps explain why these miscreant market shares can be useful for inference). Individual merger retrospectives sometimes illuminate particular settings, but their usefulness is often limited by difficulties in finding proper comparison firms for difference-in-differences analysis, brief time frames required for plausible identification and given data availability, and the idiosyncratic character of many mergers. Merger simulations are often a promising technique for prediction but typically require untestable modeling assumptions and are difficult to validate given the degrees of freedom in choosing specifications and performing subsequent analyses of mergers' effects. Stock market event studies potentially suggest broader patterns, but most such investigations do not isolate horizontal mergers, and they all require additional efforts to plausibly identify mergers' causal competitive effects and efficiencies. Industry expertise, from the merging parties themselves and other industry participants, provides valuable insights and helps place other information in context. Despite the limitations of each of these sources, they tend to be complementary and thus, taken together, can enhance predictions. Suggestions are offered for future research as well as how agency practice can, over time, enhance the ability to predict mergers' effects.

Chapter 7 considers the institutions that conduct merger review. The task of competition agencies is particularly difficult in light of resource constraints. The focus here is on the breadth of staff expertise, which currently is greatest regarding the assessment of anticompetitive effects, including empirical methods for estimating demand and conducting merger simulations. However, the analysis in the preceding chapters highlights issues, notably efficiencies, where the most relevant expertise may lie elsewhere: in understanding the theory of the firm, organizational economics, and contractual practices. And most issues, including the analysis of ex post and ex ante entry, would benefit greatly from industry-specific expertise of the sort that agencies only sometimes accumulate through experience. Broadening the scope of in-house and on-demand expertise is an important way to enhance agencies' capabilities, including when screening and investigating merger proposals. In complementary ways, reviewing courts might employ expert magistrates and court-appointed expert witnesses to increase their ability to adjudicate battles of experts and assess the credibility of business witnesses and other evidence. In addition to improving decision-making directly, the anticipation of more sophisticated assessments would induce agencies and merging parties to present more thoughtful analyses for courts' consideration and lead firms contemplating merger proposals to make more socially desirable decisions.

Agencies might also contemplate making greater use of ex post merger review in light of the challenges of prediction, which tend to be particularly great when nascent entrants are acquired. Although hindsight is often better than foresight, there are important limitations in reviewing consummated mergers, including the perverse incentives that may be created in the interim and the difficulties of unscrambling the eggs. The merging parties also have incentives to exacerbate these problems as well as to behave in ways that obscure subsequent assessments of what would otherwise have become of the target's assets and opportunities. Finally, brief attention is given to competition agencies' appropriate domains in light of their comparative advantages relative to other government entities that often employ other policy instruments and focus on different problems.

Chapter 8 addresses the appropriate objective of a competition regime as a matter of optimal policy, exploring a number of dimensions implicitly set to the side in conventional thinking. It recasts the familiar and much-debated choice between consumer and total welfare standards as one of optimally matching instruments to policies. Drawing on literature in public economics, it explains how, for any distributive target, a consumer welfare standard is Pareto dominated by a total welfare standard: one can move from the former to the latter in a manner that makes every income group better off. An important and intertwined choice concerns whether to focus on short- or long-run effects of merger decisions and of merger policy as a whole. This question is pressing because long-run welfare ultimately matters most. Moreover, consumer and total welfare prescriptions tend to converge in the long run, casting that choice in a different light. Relatedly, many important effects of mergers—on competition, efficiencies, and both ex ante and ex post entry—do not arise immediately. Therefore, a short-run focus omits important anticompetitive effects as well as other welfare consequences of merger regulation. Another largely neglected dimension involves the use of a single-sector partial equilibrium approach in most industrial organization research as well as in scholarship on competition policy and in agency practice. Accounting for multisector general equilibrium effects of competition enforcement may substantially amend or upset conventional enforcement protocols and priorities in light of the presence of significant competitive imperfections in many sectors of the economy.

Considered next is the notion that competition rules should aim to protect competition as a process rather than seeking directly to obtain good outcomes. This objective points to important ways that competition regulation can influence welfare, but it cannot directly be made operational in the context of merger review. Finally, brief attention is given to some other objectives that have been advanced as appropriate goals of competition regulation, including with regard to horizontal mergers.

As discussed in the concluding chapter, the aim throughout this book is to improve the analysis of horizontal mergers in order to better guide overall policy and the practice of merger review. I advance no broad argument that current merger review in one jurisdiction or another is too lax or too stringent. To take a medical practice analogy: Some procedures—whether surgery, chemotherapy, or drugs—may be used too often or not enough, but the most important task is to make accurate diagnoses so that the right patients get the right care. Providing unnecessary and dangerous treatments to some patients does not offset but rather compounds the harm of failing to provide needed treatment to others. Likewise for merger review.

Better understanding must be our guide. Many ideas developed here involve the identification of ways in which anticompetitive mergers may now be missed, and others suggest respects in which some mergers may be beneficial due to unrecognized or misunderstood effects. A number of these considerations are new or are cast in a different light, and many would benefit from further study. Researchers should ask hard questions, begin to answer them as best as they can, identify where further work appears promising, and present findings along the way, wherever they may point. We cannot know the best policy a priori. And we cannot design sensible proxies and protocols that embody the unavoidable simplifications required for merger review without appreciating the relevant effects of our choices.

* * *

As this book was being finalized, the U.S. Department of Justice Antitrust Division and the Federal Trade Commission issued draft, and then final, revised Merger Guidelines (2023). This book retains numerous references to the 2010 U.S. Merger Guidelines along with the 2023 Guidelines, which are offered primarily for concreteness. The 2010 U.S. Merger Guidelines also are more similar to those in the rest of the developed world than is the 2023 revision. But most important in light of this book's focus on analysis rather than the law, the 2023 guidelines do not substantially advance or amend the proffered means of economic analysis of most of the issues addressed here. Adjustments to the text and additional footnotes throughout the book note many similarities and highlight the most relevant differences.[1]

---

1. A notable change is the Merger Guidelines' (2023) introduction of legal analysis, in the process advancing bases for merger challenges that do not purport to be tightly grounded in the economic analysis of mergers' likely effects on welfare. The 2023 guidelines also address subjects not in the 2010 guidelines, particularly vertical mergers, which are not considered in this book.

2 Framework

Merger decision-making needs to be grounded explicitly in fundamentals in order to guide analysis, reduce errors, and avoid omissions. This chapter's framework is partly familiar but also contains important pieces that have been underemphasized or omitted in research as well as in merger review by competition agencies and courts. Sections A through C elaborate building blocks from decision analysis, mechanism design, and reasoning from the merging parties' rationality constraint. These uncontroversial foundations have important implications, some of which contradict protocols in modern merger guidelines, as will emerge in subsequent chapters on price effects, efficiencies, and entry.

Sections D and E turn to core features central to the analysis of imperfect competition—entry, exit, investment, and multisector distortions—which have received even less attention but can have significant consequences, even reversing the sign of a merger's welfare effects in important settings. Section F remarks briefly on the social objective, focusing here on consumer versus total welfare. Further analysis of these subjects is deferred to chapter 8. Nevertheless, many of these elements are applied in interim chapters. For example, much of chapter 5 on entry uses these ideas to identify first-order considerations that are entirely missing from EU and U.S. Merger Guidelines. Throughout, it proves useful to have these principles clearly in mind.

A. Decision Analysis and Information Collection

Merger analysis conventionally adopts a decision analytic perspective: What will be the (consumer or total) welfare effects, going forward, if the merger is allowed rather than blocked? This framing will be developed here and then extended to a mechanism design approach in section B. A full analysis combines the two, for welfare depends on both the ex ante effects of the anticipated stringency of merger review and the ex post effects of merger decisions. Most of the ideas developed in this section are applicable in a mechanism design framework, mutatis mutandis.[1]

Despite their familiarity, some of the basic principles do not appear to be reflected in official protocols embodied in merger guidelines or in many court decisions, although some are nevertheless followed behind the scenes in agency practice.[2] An obvious but important point is that expected values should guide decision-making even though, for example, U.S. legal rules are sometimes interpreted to hinge on probabilities alone (Katz and Shelanski 2007a). For example, a merger associated with a modest probability of significant anticompetitive effects and a high probability of negligible effects is optimally prohibited, whereas a merger with a larger probability of modest anticompetitive effects and a somewhat smaller probability of significant benefits is optimally allowed. By contrast, a rule that prohibits mergers if and only if they are more likely than not to be nontrivially anticompetitive would err in both of these cases.[3]

---

1. The formal relationship between the two approaches can be gleaned from the general analysis of proof burdens in Kaplow (2011c). A central difference is that, in deciding whether to allow a proposed merger based on its predicted effects, one updates one's priors in light of the signals in the case at hand, whereas in a pure mechanism design setting, one asks how a marginal change in the signal threshold for prohibition would influence ex ante behavior, which itself has welfare consequences. For either (or a combination), the problems of information collection and interpretation are similar, even though the familiar Bayesian formulation that emphasizes the determination of posterior beliefs is inapt for mechanism design.

2. The analysis here draws on Kaplow (2019, 2021a, 2022). The most extensive application in this book appears in section 4.D on the efficiency credit. Note as well that appearances can be deceiving. Many (but not all) economists familiar with agency practice have told me that agencies follow something closer to optimal protocols in many respects. And court opinions that appear to the contrary may implicitly embed reverse engineering to some degree, wherein conclusions on early steps of the analysis are in fact driven by considerations formally relegated to later steps.

3. The U.S. standard of proof in civil cases, which includes mergers, is the preponderance rule, often interpreted as requiring that the pertinent proposition be more likely than not true, without regard to actual impacts. On the other hand, Section 7 of the Clayton Act employs the verbs "may" and "tend," and it is obscure what is meant by a greater than 50% probability that something "may" happen. One suspects that actual decision-makers sometimes take a more pragmatic approach. Courts' references to a "reasonable" probability may reflect this.

Greater confusion may arise from a failure to think clearly about prior probabilities and updating based on information in the case at hand. For example, regarding both anticompetitive effects (chapter 3) and efficiencies (chapter 4), various presumptions are often advanced. A natural interpretation is that these reflect Bayesian prior probabilities—or, in a more thorough analysis, they would be derived from them in fairly direct ways.[4] But any such approach raises the problem of choosing the applicable priors. Are we referring to the prior for all horizontal mergers? Those in a given sector? At a given level in the supply chain (manufacturers versus wholesalers versus retailers)? Of a given size? Using a certain technology? Independent of the genre of efficiencies that are claimed? And so forth. The choice of applicable priors quickly becomes entangled with the consideration of information pertinent to the case at hand, which is normally seen as falling in the realm of updating. Note further that if a presumption is to have any ultimate force rather than serving merely as a heuristic that guides early thinking, then one might have to expend as much effort to adjudicate which is the correct presumption (prior) as would be required to determine the best estimate, taking all the evidence into account.[5]

Another set of problems arises from the use of sequential siloing of the following sort, which variously appears in merger guidelines, court opinions, reform proposals, and commentary: One first considers only anticompetitive effects. If they are not sufficiently demonstrated, the merger is allowed. If they are, one next considers efficiencies. If these are not sufficiently high, the merger is prohibited. But if they are large enough, then one finally considers the totality of effects. Entry analysis might come in between, at the end, or be undertaken in parallel with or instead of efficiency analysis.

To be sure, it can be helpful to divide labor among investigators and, at times, to focus one's analysis on certain pieces of the puzzle. And because

---

4. To illustrate the latter point, if one were setting an efficiency credit (see chapter 4), one might set it equal to mean efficiencies if it is to equal one's priors. But if there are costs to considering the matter further, or if one will allow the merging parties to show that actual efficiencies are higher but disallow the agency from showing that actual efficiencies are lower, the optimally set credit might differ substantially from its expected value.
5. As suggested in sections 3.A and 6.B, market definition disputes—which must be resolved to determine whether market-share-based presumptions are triggered—can have this character.

written expression is linear, agencies' closing statements, filed complaints, and court opinions may naturally be organized sequentially, addressing interconnected subjects in separate segments. Nevertheless, such a template is a poor guide for information gathering and analysis.

In commonsense terms, focusing on only one side of a scale is not a good way to determine which way it tips. After detailed analysis of one side, one may have little idea of the answer, but even a quick peek at the other side may often be decisive and in any event should inform how much effort is appropriate and how that effort is best directed.

Closely related, there are foundational problems of logic with a siloed approach to inference. For concreteness, consider the odds ratio form of Bayes' rule: posterior odds equal prior odds times the likelihood ratio (the likelihood of seeing the signal given the truth of one hypothesis relative to the likelihood under the other hypothesis). Obviously, one cannot evaluate a ratio without a denominator. Even before considering merging parties' rationality constraint (deferred to section C), signals need to be interpreted with regard to all hypotheses under consideration in order to know even the direction in which priors should be revised.

Moreover, as a practical matter, much information in merger investigations pertains directly to multiple factors. For example, better understanding the merging firms' cost functions illuminates competitive interactions, helps to identify demand, informs efficiencies, and bears on entry. (Formal estimation, of course, can succeed in identification only by examining some of these factors together.) Once substantial information has been collected for the purpose of analyzing anticompetitive effects, one has already learned much about these other considerations, so it would be irrational not to consider and revise those estimates as well. To take a rather different example, agencies and courts often attempt to infer merging parties' motives and hence likely merger effects from internal evidence, particularly that which firms generate in the ordinary course of business. Conflicting interpretations will often be advanced, and it is obviously impossible to resolve disputes about ambiguities while contemplating only one hypothesis (interpretation) in isolation.[6]

---

6. One might contrast an abstract null hypothesis that encompasses a broad range of possibilities, but it would be better to crystalize the most relevant explanations and assess their relative consistency with the evidence under consideration. In assessments of monopolization or abuse of dominance, or of horizontal restraints (other

Consider next the related question of the optimal order of information gathering and analysis. Agencies have finite resources and time, and even in cases worthy of careful review, one could investigate and analyze ad infinitum. As a useful heuristic, such efforts should be guided by the ratio of diagnosticity to cost: collect first the information that, for a given cost, is most diagnostic and, for a given diagnosticity, is the cheapest. Particularly as an investigation proceeds—and in light of inevitable diminishing returns to particular avenues of inquiry—the optimal next steps will often alternate between different issues, say, anticompetitive effects and efficiencies. Moreover, the optimal next steps are endogenous to what has been learned thus far. No one-size-fits-all rubric makes sense, much less one that purports to front-load anticompetitive effects, consider them exhaustively, and only then (if they are sufficiently established) turn to efficiencies. Recalling that much information pertains to both (and to entry), and that many individual pieces can be understood only with multiple considerations in mind, we can see that optimal information collection and decision-making are inherently intertwined processes that depart substantially from a sequential, siloed approach. These points will be reinforced by the explicit consideration of the merging parties' rationality constraint in section C.

As a final note, these basic lessons are important at the early screening stage, where the urge to use shortcuts is greatest. It may well make sense to begin with anticompetitive effects to the extent that one is simply identifying which mergers are horizontal or have horizontal elements. Once past that point, however, the foregoing becomes operative. For example, in substantial mergers, it is common (at least in the United States) for the merging parties' early proffers to include substantial information on and analysis of many aspects of the proposed merger, including the business case for the deal, which tends to involve efficiency claims. If those efficiency justifications seem likely to be pretextual or in any event almost surely insubstantial or not merger specific, that tentative conclusion usefully informs how carefully to examine anticompetitive effects. Likewise, significant uncertainty about efficiencies may suggest prioritizing the identification of industry

---

than price fixing), analysts have long emphasized the virtues of articulating more precisely, at the outset, both anti- and procompetitive explanations for the practices under consideration because greater concreteness helps guide information collection and focus analysis. The text here elaborates these benefits for merger assessment.

players or experts who could be consulted about such matters.[7] Or, to take another familiar example, if entry seems likely to be especially easy, it may be possible to resolve an investigation quickly. The lesson is simple: the need to make screening decisions under time constraints with limited information does not suspend the laws of economics or inference but instead elevates their importance, with the understanding that a leading role will be played by priors, fragmentary signals, and basic theory rather than sophisticated, data-driven assessments.

B. Mechanism Design

Section A and much that follows in this book examine the effects of permitting a proposed merger, going forward: direct anticompetitive effects, merger-generated efficiencies, and entry that may be induced by the merger. But ex ante effects are also important; notably, they constitute the focus of section 5.B on ex ante incentives of firms to enter or otherwise invest that arise from the prospect of subsequent buyout premiums. This section briefly considers some channels of (mostly ex ante) influence that are relevant in setting the stringency threshold, where it will be assumed that the competition regime is capable of commitment.[8] That is, as in mechanism design more broadly, we will ask how an agency would optimally set approval rules in light of the anticipatory behavioral responses they will generate and the welfare effects thereof.

---

7. This observation foreshadows the discussion in section 7.A about institutional capacity: if a competition agency is heavily staffed with industrial organization economists who can perform sophisticated analysis of anticompetitive effects, but the agency lacks on-staff or on-call industry experts who can aid in the assessment of efficiencies, there will be a tendency to defer and demote analysis of the latter.

8. Commitment seems plausible in many legal systems through legislation, treaties, regulation, precedents, binding guidelines, budgets, and reputation (repeat play), but the matter is not analyzed further here. Interestingly, some literature assumes that agencies cannot commit to pursue, say, a long-run total welfare standard but can nevertheless commit, say, to a short-run consumer welfare standard, which they might rationally adopt rather than a short-run total welfare standard because the former is more conducive to long-run total welfare, their actual objective. Analysis at various points in this book explores the different implications of short- versus long-run objectives and of consumer versus total welfare standards, seeking to illuminate the possibilities without advancing a particular one as more realistic in one jurisdiction or another.

The most-studied channel concerns the influence of agency stringency on merger proposals. The set of firms and their capabilities are taken as given. From this set, merger proposals are selected. If all welfare-increasing mergers would be approved (as they would be under a decision-analytic approach associated with no commitment), firms would propose the mergers that would be most profitable to them, subject to that approval constraint. An agency would do better, however, by making its approval standard at least somewhat more stringent (Besanko and Spulber 1993; Nocke and Whinston 2013). For marginal mergers (under the pertinent welfare standard), prohibition involves no social cost but sometimes induces acquirers to choose different targets and thereby propose mergers that clear the higher hurdle. Those substitute mergers raise welfare by a strictly positive amount rather than zero, so some increase in toughness beyond the posited threshold is desirable.[9]

Another angle concerns subsequent merger proposals in the same industry. Permitting or prohibiting a merger today will influence which merger proposals will be profitable in the future and their associated welfare effects if such future mergers would be approved. Hence, a threshold different from a myopic one that considers only the direct effects of the merger at hand may well be optimal (Nocke and Whinston 2010).[10] This adjustment, examined in isolation, can be understood in the decision-analytic framework without requiring commitment. What is necessary is that the agency's decision on the present merger proposal consider not just the merger's direct effects but also the indirect, longer-run effects through changing the trajectory of future merger proposals. That analysis also requires consideration of which future proposals should be accepted, which in a dynamically consistent formulation feeds back on the current decision.

The discussion thus far focuses on merger proposals by existing firms with given capabilities. Probably more important are the broader ex ante effects of a merger regime on entry and investment. In some settings, the prospect of buyout premiums generates socially excessive ex ante incentives, so that

---

9. This perspective can usefully be applied to inquiries into the merger-specificity of efficiencies, the subject of chapter 4. As noted there, one potentially relevant alternative means of achieving efficiencies associated with a merger proposal is a different merger proposal that generates smaller anticompetitive effects.

10. Motta and Vasconcelos (2005) examine and reach a skeptical conclusion about the possibility that approval of an efficient merger may cause less efficient competitors to exit, thereby reducing competition in the future.

a stricter regime raises welfare in large part because it discourages entry and investment (Rasmusen 1988; Gowrisankaran 1999; Mermelstein et al. 2020). But in others, incentives to create new varieties, develop complementary capabilities that can produce merger synergies, or undertake other innovation would be socially too low if subsequent buyouts were prohibited, so a more lenient regime may be optimal. Although these factors are often difficult to analyze, they may be the most important effects of merger policy in some domains, such as those involving rapid technological change. This subject is analyzed in section 5.B.

C. Rationality Constraint and Non-Neoclassical Merger Motives

Begin with neoclassical merger motives and the merging firms' rationality constraint. Firms are assumed to propose only jointly profitable mergers, and profits are understood to arise from some combination of anticompetitive effects and efficiencies.[11] The rationality constraint has two important implications for how inferences should be made under these assumptions.

First and most obviously, the relevant priors when making the sorts of inferences discussed in section A should be conditional ones that reflect expected profitability. Most simply, one truncates the distribution, removing the part that involves unprofitable mergers. Further adjustments are implied by section B's analysis recognizing that there is an interaction between which proposals merging parties would expect an agency to approve and proposal selection.[12]

---

11. One can incorporate proposal costs—which might include interim financing costs and disruption costs to planning and retention when the future is in limbo—and integration costs, which can be treated as negative efficiencies. A more complete analysis when there is uncertainty about the approval decision would reflect, for example, that proposal costs are incurred regardless. Moreover, it may matter how quickly a merger is expected to be approved, which can vary depending on the time a reviewing agency takes and whether one must also pursue the matter in court if the agency seeks to block the merger but the parties expect ultimately to prevail.
12. Taking the decision-analytic framework without commitment, this consideration can be complex and generate surprising conclusions: a clearly anticompetitive merger would not be permitted, hence would not be proposed, so an agency should not believe that a proposed merger is actually very anticompetitive. When one adds that parties incur proposal and disruption costs, as mentioned in the preceding

Second, the rationality constraint importantly informs updating. If the information on the specific merger indicates that efficiencies are likely to be small, perhaps not even enough to cover proposal and disruption costs, then nontrivial anticompetitive effects are likely. In this respect, any evidence bearing on efficiencies affects inferences about anticompetitive effects.[13] And vice versa: if the information suggests that anticompetitive effects are probably insufficient to make the merger profitable, then our posterior on efficiencies should accordingly be higher. Note that this interdependence reinforces section A's criticism of sequential siloing because merging parties' rationality constraint is one of the channels through which the analysis of anticompetitive effects and efficiencies is interdependent. This basic logic is absent in most merger guidelines and court opinions, although it undoubtedly influences agency investigations and merger decision-making and, because of its commonsensical nature, it may have some impact on courts' assessments of contested mergers as well.

For concreteness, consider briefly one important setting in which reasoning from the merging parties' rationality constraint is central. Anticipating section 5.A, modern merger guidelines misanalyze one of the most important effects of entry that may be induced by the immediate anticompetitive effects of a merger: that anticipation of postmerger entry may render unprofitable a merger proposal motivated primarily by the prospect of anticompetitive effects. As will be explained, it may often be true that ex post entry would not be sufficient to counteract the price increase but would nevertheless sufficiently reduce the merging parties' anticompetitive profit potential to substantially alter the appropriate inferences about efficiencies in a manner that, taken together, is favorable to approval.

The foregoing discussion, like much that follows in this book, accepts the neoclassical paradigm. However, there is substantial empirical support

---

footnote, and that the parties can only predict the distribution of noise in the agency's signals, one suspects that the resulting conditional priors may have standard properties. By contrast, if one takes a mechanism design perspective that assumes commitment, the analysis is more straightforward.

13. This point, developed further in section 4.D, implies that even a decision-maker that cared only about anticompetitive effects and thus not at all about efficiencies would examine—and not back-load or ignore—the efficiencies involved in a proposed merger. This elementary logic seems entirely missing in modern merger guidelines and much merger analysis.

for other merger motives, although most of that evidence, unfortunately, does not isolate horizontal mergers but instead reflects a diverse set of acquisitions that, for the most part, are not horizontal.[14] Merger proposals can arise as a consequence of agency problems (empire-building: Baumol 1959; Marris 1964; Jensen 1986), behavioral infirmities (optimism bias and hubris: Roll 1986; Malmendier and Tate 2008), market pricing imperfections (an underpriced target or overvalued securities used to finance an acquisition: Shleifer and Vishny 2003; Savor and Lu 2009), or tax savings (Butters, Lintner, and Carey 1951; Auerbach and Reishus 1988). There also exist negative versions of many of these phenomena that will not be separately explored here: agency slack may lead a manager to forgo modestly profitable acquisitions to save effort, an overly optimistic manager may be excessively bullish about internal growth or other means of going it alone, securities mispricing may be in the opposite direction, and the triggering of taxes may discourage otherwise efficient mergers.

As usually advanced, such explanations tend to reduce the profitability threshold for merger proposals to a net negative expected value. That would call for adjustments to priors conditional on seeing a merger proposal and also different updating. If less profitability is required, expected anticompetitive effects and efficiencies are both lower. Evidence that anticompetitive effects are unlikely to be sufficient to make the merger profitable still points, but less strongly, toward efficiencies. And evidence that efficiencies are likely to be low still suggests, although more weakly, that anticompetitive effects are larger than otherwise.

These observations raise practical and conceptual questions. As a practical matter, consider whether decision-makers should employ a common shift to their priors and inferences or undertake more case-specific adjustments. For example, one could consider the merging firms' governance characteristics, indicators of CEO optimism (like those in Malmendier and Tate 2008), or details of how the proposed merger would be taxed in order

---

14. Many decades ago, empire-building, hubris, and other such motivations for firms' behavior, including merger decisions, were more commonly discussed. After an interim period featuring advances in neoclassical analysis, these dimensions are receiving renewed attention. As subsection 6.C.4 explores, empirical research in finance has devoted more attention to the question of merger motives, motivated by findings that many mergers seem to be value reducing or, at a minimum, seem to be unprofitable for acquiring firms.

to tailor the adjustments, at least approximately. Or in reviewing the merging parties' documents, one could look for indicators of such explanations rather than confining interpretations to ones bearing on anticompetitive effects or efficiencies.

There are also conceptual questions going to competition agencies' and tribunals' jurisdiction, expertise, and role. Put sharply: If an agency regarded most merger proposals to be overall inefficient, say, due to managerial problems, should it adopt a strict threshold that prohibits many more mergers? On one hand, such priors may well indicate that a wider range of proposed mergers would reduce welfare.[15] On the other hand, they also imply that fewer merger proposals would be anticompetitive. In that event, much of the welfare gain from a tougher merger regime may arise from the reduction in wasteful manifestations of firms' agency costs, normally in the domain of markets, contracting, and corporate law. Taking an even sharper case, a competition agency would not plausibly challenge an unrelated acquisition because the best evidence is that most of these are value-destroying or because market analysts view the particular acquisition as value-destroying. That conclusion, however, does not decide the question of how this consideration should factor into the analysis of a plausibly anticompetitive merger.[16]

---

15. Different non-neoclassical motives have qualitatively different implications. Agency and behavioral problems can induce unprofitable mergers that reduce the merging firms' value and, as a consequence, social welfare, ceteris paribus. By contrast, a simplistic interpretation of securities mispricing and tax savings is that the merging firms do not lose value but third parties (other shareholders or the Treasury) do. In some respects, one can analogize these to internalities and externalities, respectively, in literatures that consider Pigouvian corrections.

16. Some have suggested that agencies focus on anticompetitive effects and conventional efficiencies, ignoring these other considerations, but it is obscure what it means to ignore hypotheses that are plausible and may be directly supported by the information under assessment. (For example, if business documents indicate that the acquirer believed the merger would produce large synergies, but the primary basis for the belief is that "we are just so much better than everyone else," does "ignoring" that evidence suggestive of hubris mean that we assume the efficiencies are instead real, that we ignore that efficiencies in fact motivated the merger, or something else altogether?) The inference question is conceptually distinct from the question of an agency's objective function and jurisdiction. To illustrate the latter, "ignoring" managerial self-serving motivations could mean omitting the efficiency costs therefrom in the welfare calculus and hence permitting more mergers, whereas "ignoring" tax savings could mean omitting them from the merging firms' profits, implying a

Consider as well how such possibilities could arise if merger-specific inquiries into these matters were allowed. Suppose that an agency claims, reasoning neoclassically from the merging parties' rationality constraint, that the merger is likely to be anticompetitive because efficiencies are negligible. May the merging parties rebut this claim by asserting empire-building, hubris, mispriced securities, or tax savings as justifications? Or if the merging parties respond to a demonstration of modest anticompetitive effects by arguing they are insufficient to render the merger profitable and hence there must instead be substantial efficiencies, may the agency respond that it is not efficiencies but hubris that led to the proposal, so the small, net anticompetitive effects are plausible after all?

For concreteness, let us examine the implications of some particular non-neoclassical merger motives. If managers overestimate their own abilities, are they more likely to exaggerate the potential of a contemplated merger to raise prices (perhaps by overly discounting the threat of postmerger entry), which may call for downward revision of anticompetitive effects in particular? Or might they underestimate anticompetitive effects because their optimism about their own firm's products leads them to underestimate premerger diversion to the target's products? Are they more likely to exaggerate potential synergies or underestimate the challenge of integrating the two firms, both of which imply that efficiencies are likely to be lower than may appear, for example, from internal documents? That may favor blocking more mergers because expected efficiencies are lower, although, as noted, the resulting inference of anticompetitive effects may also be weaker. Or, as suggested briefly above, might overconfident managers overestimate their ability to succeed through internal growth—such as by making rather than buying capabilities they currently lack—which implies that only especially attractive mergers are pursued? (This possibility does not in itself indicate whether such a particularly profitable merger is so because of anticompetitive effects or efficiencies.)

Non-neoclassical merger motives seem broadly prevalent, are of uncertain importance regarding horizontal mergers in particular, and have multiple

---

reduction in producer surplus and hence a more stringent regime. Despite the distinction between these types of questions, note that they inevitably overlap, such as in setting enforcement priorities, which includes screening merger proposals to determine which ones warrant further analysis and thus possible prohibition.

and sometimes conflicting implications for inferences about anticompetitive effects and efficiencies. For other reasons as well, it is unclear how these motives should be factored into a competition agency's merger assessments. The subject, therefore, raises numerous questions for further analysis and empirical research.

D. Entry, Exit, Investment, and the Long Run

An economy's equilibrium is determined by the interaction and balance of many forces that, if examined in isolation, yield a partial and sometimes misleading understanding of their effects and the welfare consequences thereof. This section briefly elaborates the dynamic dimension of the problem, with details variously pursued throughout the book, particularly in chapter 5 on entry. By contrast, most merger analysis, both in economic research and agency practice, is static. The premerger constellation of firms, including their capabilities, is taken as given. The merger proposal under consideration is viewed as a one-off, unanticipated event. And the postmerger world typically envisions no subsequent mergers, no changes in firms' investment behavior—except for possible integration efficiencies in the merged firm—and only occasional attention to entry or product repositioning. The motivation is tractability, particularly for an agency with a limited budget that must review myriad merger proposals quickly. Nevertheless, it is important to understand what is missing, to formulate proxies and shortcuts with an eye to how omitted factors typically affect outcomes, and to develop a sense for when further inquiry in a given case might be warranted.

Entry, exit, and investment are central to the economy's functioning and, accordingly, are the focus of important literatures in industrial organization and other fields (Hopenhayn 1992; Ericson and Pakes 1995; Melitz 2003). When these decisions are undertaken in a profit-maximizing fashion, with rational expectations not only about other firms' behavior but also about the stringency of merger review, additional effects of merger decision-making emerge, as mentioned in section B on mechanism design. Notably, much entry and investment may be undertaken precisely because actors expect to be subsequently acquired. After mergers, if a sector indeed has fewer competitors going forward for a substantial period of time, investment incentives will be different. For example, in the two-stage instantiation of the Cournot model with homogeneous goods (in which firms choose capacity in stage one and produce at capacity in stage two), a merger after capacity is set may have no short-run effect on price, and mergers can readily be unprofitable in the short run. However, the merging firms' post-merger investment will ultimately fall, leading to higher prices and greater profits for the merging parties (Berry and Pakes 1993). A recently expanding literature on product repositioning suggests further modifications to static analysis (Fan 2013; Fan and Yang 2020; Gandhi et al. 2008; Li et al. 2022; Mazzeo, Seim, and Varela 2018; Wollmann 2018).

Other welfare effects become apparent when a dynamic view is adopted. Entry and exit decisions generically involve externalities in imperfectly competitive environments (Spence 1976; Dixit and Stiglitz 1977; Mankiw and Whinston 1986). Similar analysis applies to many investment decisions. On one hand, any firm's action that raises its profits by taking customers from other firms imposes a negative, business-stealing externality to the extent that the forgone sales by others were at prices in excess of marginal cost. On the other hand, firms do not realize the full returns on many investments, such as when they contribute to variety (much of the consumer surplus being inframarginal) or generate spillovers through innovation that is not fully appropriable. A central implication is that, even if a merger's effects on such decisions are small enough to be approximated locally, the welfare effects are first order because the preexisting equilibrium is distorted. Hence, many effects that are traditionally omitted from analysis or are recognized but examined only with regard to their impact on price may have additional welfare consequences. Furthermore, these effects are sometimes of opposite sign and a priori may be as or more important than what is traditionally analyzed. For example, merger-induced entry in a homogeneous goods industry tends to reduce welfare from the fixed costs thereby incurred more than it raises welfare through mitigating the merger's price increase.

A long-run analysis with more endogenous variables is far more difficult to conduct. Nevertheless, in some respects it may be easier because equilibrium forces may be clear whereas the particular steps different firms (including potential entrants) may take along the way can be harder to predict, particularly as to their timing. The transition path is relevant due to discounting: hence, knowledge that eventually a more competitive outcome will ultimately arise is understood to be insufficient to justify lenient competition policy. But long-run effects of particular mergers and of merger policies more broadly are significant, so ignoring them is likewise unsatisfactory.

Note further that many sources of uncertainty about the long run have short-run analogues that complexify even more limited analysis. When a dominant incumbent firm acquires a startup, predicting whether the merger primarily provides an ex post reward to valuable ex ante investment while creating distinctive synergies, or instead extinguishes nascent disruption, will be difficult to ascertain without some understanding of the dynamic forces surrounding the merging firms' activities. More broadly, some anticompetitive effects, many efficiencies, and perhaps most consequences regarding entry, exit, and investment materialize only in the medium to long run. Because static analysis may offer limited and potentially misleading clues, a short-run approach to horizontal merger analysis can be quite problematic in many settings.

Accordingly, some of the analysis in this book, particularly in chapter 5 on entry, adopts a longer-run, dynamic perspective. This dimension of merger analysis would greatly benefit from further research. More effort should also be devoted to drawing implications for the practice of merger review. Some tentative suggestions will be presented along the way.

E. Distortions in Multiple Sectors

Along with entry, exit, and investment within a sector, the flow of resources across sectors, along with concomitant entry and exit in other sectors, is central to an economy's functioning and the welfare properties of the resulting equilibrium. Nevertheless, as is familiar, both theoretical and empirical work in industrial organization typically examines a single sector. Sometimes the sector that is the focus of the analysis is implicitly modeled as if it were the entire economy. Often, an outside good is introduced in order to isolate the sector under investigation (Lancaster 1980; Mankiw and Whinston 1986; Berry 1994). These features are employed for tractability and, for many purposes such as estimating demand, they may be fairly innocuous. But these simplifications are highly consequential, particularly for welfare assessments, in light of evidence suggesting that there are significant distortions in many sectors of the economy. See, for example, De Loecker, Eeckhout, and Unger (2020) and Hall (2018), as well as the discussions in Basu (2019) and Syverson (2019).

In the history of economic thought, this concern once loomed large. Lerner's (1934) famous article—the origin of the Lerner index—asserted that the level of markups in an economy is irrelevant to social welfare; only their deviations matter.[17] The simple intuition is that deadweight loss from price in excess of marginal cost arises from too few resources being consumed in the distorted sector; they flow instead to other sectors where marginal utility is lower relative to marginal production costs. However, if every sector is marked up by the same proportion, resources have nowhere else to go. Put another way, distortion arises when price *ratios*, which determine consumption allocations, differ from marginal cost ratios. But when all markups are proportional, these price ratios are the same as they would be in an undistorted economy. In their famous article on the general problem of the second best, Lipsey and Lancaster (1956) featured the problem of "degrees of monopoly" (markups in many sectors), which was so well known that they felt no need "to review the voluminous literature on this controversy." Subsequently, however, this concern about the implications of markups in nontargeted sectors largely vanished from industrial organization economics, including its application to competition policy.[18]

This problem is analyzed in section 8.C, drawing on Kaplow (2023a). It explains how a broad range of results is possible once one accounts for entry and exit in all sectors along with the cross-sector resource flows and general equilibrium price effects. This book nevertheless sets these important issues to the side, focusing instead on how best to analyze merger policies' effects in the targeted sector in which the proposed horizontal merger occurs. In principle, one would wish to combine analyses in all sectors of the economy to determine optimal policies for each. Somewhat less ambitiously but more practically, one can imagine developing an approximation of the effects across sectors of an economy that would then factor into the customized analysis of a targeted sector, perhaps through a standard allowance or shadow cost. Such an adjustment factor might reflect markups across the economy as well as the degree to which entry in various sectors confers positive rather than negative externalities. In addition, if intervention in

---

17. An important qualification, which Lerner noted parenthetically, concerns the distortion of labor supply, which is elaborated in section 8.A and examined in Kaplow (2021b), which analyzes a model with heterogeneous individuals, profits with income-dependent incidence, endogenous labor supply, and income taxation (but with markups exogenous), showing that results of the sort discussed in the text here go through.
18. It is, however, reflected in a recent strand of literature on international trade and macroeconomics (Bilbiie, Ghironi, and Melitz 2019; Epifani and Gancia 2011; Holmes, Hsu, and Lee 2014).

some particular sector was understood to result mainly in outflows from or inflows to certain closely related sectors (strong substitutes or complements), one might weight those sectors' features much more heavily in making the rough adjustment. Given the dearth of research on these matters, no such program is currently feasible. Nevertheless, in light of the likely magnitudes of markups in many sectors of the economy as well as distortions associated with entry and exit, research on these phenomena would be quite valuable.

F. Social Objective

No decision-making framework is complete without specification of the objective function. This is the subject of chapter 8, but it is useful to offer some preliminary remarks that illuminate the analysis throughout this book. The focus will be on conventional notions of consumer and total welfare.[19] Where relevant, the analysis will distinguish these objectives, often without mentioning them because overlapping or differential implications will be apparent.

Merger guidelines in many jurisdictions (including the European Union and United States, but not, for example, Canada) seem to embrace a consumer welfare standard. This stance is primarily reflected in merger guidelines' crediting of efficiencies only to the extent that they are passed through to consumers. Nevertheless, there is much to be said for economists' traditional focus on total welfare.

First, these two standards tend to converge over time, with long-run consumer welfare often better proxied for by short-run total welfare than by short-run consumer welfare. For example, costs that are fixed in the short run are variable in the long run, and long-run equilibrium prices tend to equal average costs, implying that consumers do ultimately bear costs that may be fixed in the short run.[20] Note as well that distortions in

---

19. As is familiar, "consumer" welfare is a shorthand for counterparty welfare; hence, mergers that increase monopsony power most directly reduce suppliers' (including possibly workers') welfare.

20. A suggestive empirical analysis by Hall and Woodward (2010) finds that entrepreneurs funded by venture capital approximately break even on an ex ante, risk-adjusted basis, from which one might infer that, even in rapidly changing parts of the economy, long-run properties tend to govern. It does not follow, however, that substantial anticompetitive effects from a merger will promptly be erased.

investment incentives often have opposite effects depending on the time frame because, by definition, investments involve short-run costs that are incurred to generate long-run benefits. Such considerations will be central in chapters 4 and 5 on efficiencies and entry, respectively. It should be noted, however, that a longer-run perspective that emphasizes total welfare does not systematically favor weaker merger regulation, as is sometimes supposed, because many adverse effects of mergers materialize only in the future (recall from section D the example of reduced postmerger investment in the Cournot setting).

Second, a major rationale for emphasizing consumer welfare over total welfare concerns the differences in the distributive incidence of effects on consumer surplus versus profits, the latter being much more favorable to the rich. Interestingly, economists and regulatory agencies of many sorts do not generally take this consideration to be a central guide to policy. For example, this orientation may favor significantly weaker environmental and safety regulations than otherwise dictated by conventional, unweighted cost-benefit analysis because the willingness to pay for health and safety as well as for environmental amenities is notably greater as income rises, relative to the incidence of the costs of much regulation. A central justification for agency specialization that employs a total welfare standard is that taxes and transfers tend to be dominant distributive instruments, enabling all income groups to receive larger slices of a greater social pie when regulations are set to maximize efficiency (total surplus). The analysis that supports this conclusion is sketched in section 8.A.[21]

---

21. The superiority of using the tax and transfer system for redistribution (rather than skewing regulations in inefficient ways) is familiar but may not be immediately obvious due to distortions associated with redistributive taxation. The seminal paper in public economics that analyzes this interaction is Atkinson and Stiglitz (1976). A formal extension to competition policy is developed in Kaplow (2021b), which accounts as well for indirect effects of both markups and the receipt of profits on labor supply and shows that the optimal (indeed, Pareto dominant) policy is that which maximizes total welfare. The optimal taxation literature elaborates numerous qualifications, but most tend to be sector specific as to their direction and are also orthogonal to conventional redistributive notions. For example, the incentive constraints in the second-best redistribution problem are relaxed by taxing leisure complements and subsidizing substitutes. Markups that differ across sectors might have such an effect (or the opposite), making them less (or more) detrimental than otherwise, with the sign determined by the complementarity of consumption in that sector to labor supply.

3 Price Effects and Market Definition

The prediction of price effects is central to the determination of whether a proposed horizontal merger should be prohibited. This chapter's analysis of the subject abstracts from efficiencies (chapter 4), entry (chapter 5), and other important considerations. Moreover, it follows convention in focusing on price effects as such, often taken as a stand-in for additional dimensions like quality (one can contemplate quality-adjusted prices) and innovation (future prices and quality). It also examines potential anticompetitive effects downstream—higher prices charged to buyers—rather than upstream effects borne by input suppliers. These latter expositional simplifications are employed throughout the book.

The analysis of price effects draws on the methods of industrial organization economics applicable to particular settings in which horizontal mergers may result in higher prices, such as unilateral effects with homogeneous or differentiated products and coordinated effects. Section B examines these methods. This chapter begins, however, in section A with an extensive treatment of market definition. Although this concept does not really exist in formal economic analysis, it has been central to antitrust analysis of horizontal mergers (and more) for over half a century. Accordingly, it is important to appreciate the underlying nature of the market definition paradigm, which reveals why it has no real role in economic models of mergers and indicates how its dictates diverge from those models' analytical prescriptions. Section B's examination of the correct economic analysis of mergers' effects will reinforce this contrast with approaches that attempt to rely on market definition. Section C offers some reflections on how these discrepant paths emerged and how it can be that, in respects, both continue to be followed.

A. Market Definition

The market definition paradigm holds that one way—perhaps the only legally permitted way, or a useful way, or a crude proxy—to infer price effects is through a two-step process. First, one defines a market, often called the "relevant" market in antitrust parlance, in which one then computes each firm's market share. Second, one infers a merger's price effects from those market shares. In the words of the 1963 U.S. Supreme Court decision in *Philadelphia Bank*, "a merger which produces a firm controlling an undue percentage share of the relevant market, and results in a significant increase in the concentration of firms in that market, is so inherently likely to lessen competition substantially that it must be enjoined in the absence of evidence clearly showing that the merger is not likely to have such anticompetitive effects."

Modern merger guidelines, launched in the United States and followed in much of the developed world, often employ the Hypothetical Monopolist Test (HMT) for step one and then examine the (naively computed) postmerger Herfindahl-Hirschman Index (HHI) and the ΔHHI (the difference between the post- and premerger HHIs) for step two.[1] Sufficiently high levels of the two measures trigger a presumption of anticompetitive effects, whereas sufficiently low levels indicate that the merger is benign.[2] Many

---

[1]. In practice, the HHI and ΔHHI are computed under the unrealistic assumption that the merged firm's market share will equal the sum of the premerger shares of the merging firms and that the shares of nonmerging firms remain the same. The ΔHHI corresponds to *Philadelphia Bank*'s second prong ("a significant increase in concentration"), but the HHI, which receives much attention in guidelines, court opinions, and academic literature, is quite different from *Philadelphia Bank*'s first prong (which refers to the combined share of the merged firms, making no reference to any notion of concentration in the market as a whole). See Kaplow (2022) for further discussion.

[2]. For example, the U.S. Merger Guidelines (2010, p. 3) state: "Mergers that cause a significant increase in concentration and result in highly concentrated markets are presumed to be likely to enhance market power, but this presumption can be rebutted by persuasive evidence showing that the merger is unlikely to enhance market power." The EU Merger Guidelines (2004), drawing on EU Commission Notice on the Definition of Relevant Market (1997), employ a similar framework to indicate that challenges are unlikely when concentration or the increase in concentration is low, but they do not affirmatively dictate a likelihood of challenge when both are

court opinions are written as if this paradigm is mandatory, and its output appears to be decisive in many merger cases.[3]

Despite the proclaimed foundational status of the market definition paradigm, economists and many competition lawyers have long been queasy about its all-or-nothing character due to the lumpiness of admissible definitions that are implicitly taken to include only colloquial ones. Yet the problems go far deeper, rendering the methodology worse than useless in all applications. The seriousness of the shortcomings should hardly be surprising in light of the method's absence from the formal economic analysis of price effects.[4]

This section elucidates the market definition paradigm through two complementary depictions. First, it diagrams the underlying approach, which makes the core logic explicit. Second, it characterizes the process as involving the use of two functions—one mapping the available information set to a market definition and another mapping that definition (really, the resulting market shares) to an inference about price effects. The composition of these two functions is contrasted to unconstrained analysis and

---

high. It is unclear the extent to which practice within the agencies—regarding the analytical approach or ultimate decisions to challenge mergers—adheres to these dictates. Many current and former staff in the U.S. agencies have told me (and some have said publicly) that the thresholds have little effect on internal analysis but do influence which cases are brought to court and how those cases are presented, but the range of opinions I have heard is somewhat mixed. It remains to be seen what will become the practice under the U.S. Merger Guidelines (2023), including the extent to which the U.S. agencies and courts will draw on an alternative trigger for the presumption (closer in form, even if tighter in levels, to that in *Philadelphia Bank*) based on a high postmerger share for the merging firms (30%) combined with a significant increase in concentration (ΔHHI of 100 in the 2023 guidelines, compared to what seems to be approximately 600 in the case).

3. Kaplow (2022) discusses whether these appearances may be deceptive, noting the possibility of reverse engineering—whether subconscious or intentional—wherein a market definition is chosen to ratify a conclusion based on direct consideration of price effects. The U.S. Merger Guidelines (2023) confusingly state that the preferred way to define markets is through the use of direct evidence, which is widely understood to be a substitute for market definition rather than a means of choosing a particular market (Kaplow 2024).

4. A few more recent articles—some discussed in section B of this chapter or in chapter 6—may appear to give a different impression, but those discussions will explain why this is not the case.

inference. The section concludes with reflections on key elements that help explain why the methodology cannot aid in the prediction of a merger's effects.[5]

The analysis in this section encompasses all means of defining markets and drawing inferences from the market shares therein, whether using modern merger guidelines' methodology (HMT, HHI, and ΔHHI) or otherwise. Additional limitations that inhere in modern merger guidelines' particular approach are identified in section B. The ultimate conclusion is that, whatever is the available information set—whether that available to an agency conducting early screening or to a tribunal making a final decision—the market definition paradigm is strictly dominated and hence cannot serve as a basis even for rough presumptions about mergers' effects.

1. Diagrammatic Representation

To visualize the thought process embodied in the market definition paradigm, consider the following representation of a stylized setting involving a choice between two proffered market definitions, Broad and Narrow.

Starting from the left, some set of information is used to make a decision on market definition. If Broad is chosen, shares (and thus, for example, the HHI and ΔHHI) will be low, so the inferred price increase will be low, so the merger would be (presumptively) allowed. Conversely, if Narrow is chosen, shares will be high, so the inferred price increase will be high, so the merger would be blocked (or subject to further analysis).

Inspection of figure 3.1 raises some fundamental questions. First, what is the nature of the information feeding into the market definition decision and how is that information analyzed? Either the information and analysis pertain to the prediction of anticompetitive effects (price increases) or they do not. The latter would be bizarre and thus is not pursued here. But the former is strange in a different manner: Why analyze information regarding the predicted price increase in order to use that information instead to define a market, in order to obtain market shares, in order to use them to

---

5. The criticisms in this section build on those first advanced in Kaplow (2010, 2011a). For references to and discussions of some of the subsequent debate (which does not directly address the logical claims most relevant to the present analysis), see Kaplow (2012a, 2013b).

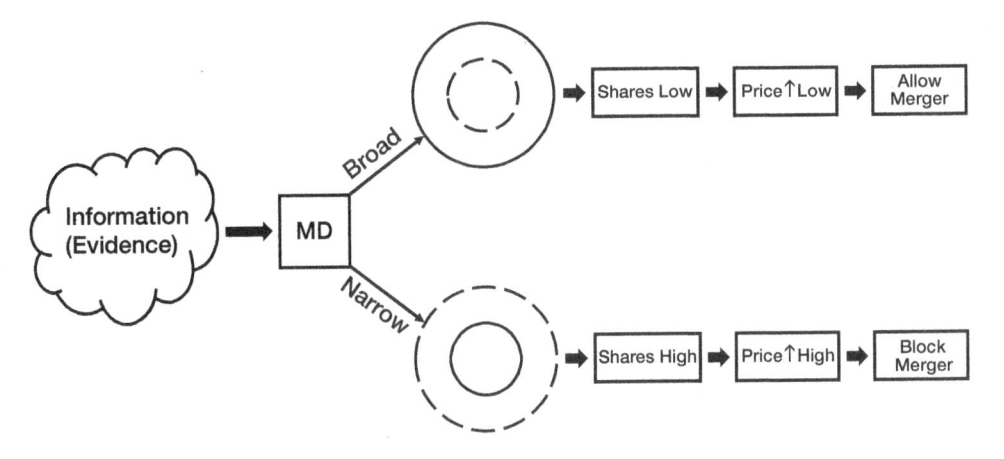

Figure 3.1
Market definition.

draw crude inferences about the likely price increase? This construction is patently circular.[6]

Unfortunately, reflection immediately reveals that this method is actually worse. If the process were entirely circular, we would at least end up where we started. Instead, we distort and discard information along the way and thus make needless error. The nature of the loss is suggested by the foregoing statement: we start with a predicted price increase (however noisy that may be) but end up with some sort of crude inference about the likely price increase based on market shares in one or another market. To develop this idea more precisely, it is helpful to consider a second, rarely asked question.

What is the *criterion* for defining the market?[7] That is, when we deem one market definition to be better than another, what do we mean? Here

---

6. Moreover, as will be developed in section 6.B, this methodology is oxymoronic under the so-called structural presumption in the United States, wherein anticompetitive effects are presumed (not even inferred) from market shares—explicitly to avoid the need to have to predict these effects—when one must first define the market, which is done by weighing conflicting evidence and resolving battles of experts on anticompetitive effects in some fashion.

7. As will emerge in section B, the HMT is not an answer to this question. The HMT is an algorithm, whereas the question addressed here is different: What is the loss function that is taken to be (perhaps approximately) minimized by use of the HMT? That question has never been answered or, really, even asked.

we will take the criterion for the best market definition to be that which generates the best inference about the matter at hand: the predicted price increase. Put another way, one market definition is deemed to be better than another if the expected inference error is smaller under it than under the other market definition.

Once we state this criterion, two problems are evident in light of the fact that we must somehow determine the expected error associated with each market definition. That determination requires that we have: (1) an estimate of the predicted price effect (that is derived without reliance on the shares in the not-yet-defined market), and (2) an understanding of what price effect would be inferred from each of the market definitions that we might choose.

The first requirement encapsulates the circularity of the market definition process: we must already have an estimate of the price effect in order to choose the best market definition, yet the whole point of the market definition exercise is to aid in estimating the price effect. Moreover, we can now see more clearly the nature of the avoidable error. Our criterion first asks that we estimate two errors, ξ^{Broad} and ξ^{Narrow}, each measured by reference to our best estimate. Then, our criterion chooses Broad if and only if $\xi^{Broad} < \xi^{Narrow}$. Hence, our error (relative to our best estimate) equals $\min\{\xi^{Broad}, \xi^{Narrow}\}$. But if instead we eschew market definition altogether and stick with our best estimate, we avoid this error—error that is *in addition* to the inevitable error inhering in our best estimate. Why choose the market with the smaller supplemental prediction error when we can avoid that error entirely by abandoning market definition? Note further that we would also save the effort involved in determining the prediction errors.

The second requirement presents a further conundrum. To measure these prediction errors, we not only need to have our best estimate already in hand, but we also have to figure out what price effect we would infer conditional on each market definition that we might choose. Yet it has never been explained how those inferences are to be made. The best one can do is to make no inference whatsoever in any such market and instead assign our best estimate for each of these; then we would draw the same (and best) inference regardless of the market definition that is selected. But no one imagines that this is what intense market definition disputes have been about for the past half-century—or that this degenerate solution has any correspondence to the protocols in merger guidelines or anywhere else.

Price Effects and Market Definition

Section B will explain that we can sometimes make an inference of sorts—essentially, our best estimate—in Narrow because it may correspond to representations embodied in some models used in merger analysis. But there is no basis whatsoever for formulating an independent inference in Broad because it does not correspond to any model. Hence, this pointless, information-destroying market definition paradigm is also fundamentally unspecified.

2. Composite Functions

The foregoing critique is general in that it does not focus on a particular market definition algorithm (like the HMT), particular uses of market shares (like the HHI or ΔHHI), or particular thresholds (like those in various jurisdictions' merger guidelines). This subsection presents a complementary, similarly general, and somewhat more formal statement of the market definition paradigm. Specifically, it formulates each of the two steps—market definition (the left portion of figure 3.1) and inference of price effects from market shares (the right portion of the figure)—as a separate function and then compares the output of the composition of these two functions to that of the function that directly infers price effects from the information inputs used by the market definition function.

Begin with the function that captures whatever might be our best possible inference of a proposed merger's effects, considering all the information at hand:

$\Delta MP = h(\sigma)$,

where σ is the signal vector representing the available information and the function h is our best mapping from that information to an estimate of ΔMP, the predicted change in market power (price increase) from a proposed merger. This representation is taken to capture the best an analyst could do with the information at hand; familiar methods of making these predictions will be examined in section B. Note that the information set is arbitrary and hence might correspond to the limited information available when an agency screens mergers at an early stage. That is, nothing in this construction, or in the previous figure, depends on the quantity, quality, or nature of the information set. Moreover, the information inputs are taken as given, so that all differences between the use of the function h and the market definition functions presented next will be attributable to how that information is processed.

Contrast this function to what is done under the market definition paradigm, which has two steps. It begins by defining a market:

$$s = g(\sigma),$$

where the function g is some mapping from the same signal vector σ to a relevant market with associated market share vector s. That is, g is our market definition algorithm (perhaps, but not necessarily, the HMT), and because the pertinent output of the market definition decision is firms' shares in the relevant market, it simplifies exposition to take as the function's output those shares rather than the "market" as such (in which those shares would then be measured).

Next, we have:

$$\Delta MP = f(s),$$

where the function f is some mapping from the market share vector s to an inference about the effect of the proposed merger on market power, ΔMP. For example, merger guidelines' thresholds provide crude categorizations. Note, however, that they do not articulate, even approximately, what market power effects are thought to be associated with each category. For example, if the postmerger HHI is 3000 and the ΔHHI is 300, is the typically imagined price increase 18%? 1.8%? 0.18%?[8]

Finally, define the market definition paradigm's composite function:

$$\tilde{h}(\sigma) = f(g(\sigma)).$$

It is natural to inquire about the relationship between our best inference function, h, and this composite function, $\tilde{h}$, which indicates the ultimate

---

8. This omission is seriously problematic, particularly under the U.S. structural presumption examined in section 6.B but similarly under that embodied in the U.S. Merger Guidelines (2010, pp. 3, 19) and others, existing and proposed. After triggering a presumption that a merger is "presumed to be likely to enhance market power," what happens if the merging parties then demonstrate annual marginal cost efficiencies of $75 million that will be passed on to consumers? Do they win (or at least shift the burden back to the government)? Or may the government concede this and assert that the parties lose because that is not large enough to outweigh the presumed market power enhancement? Or does this demonstration now require quantifying, for the first time, the predicted price effects? If that is the implication, does demonstration of $1 annual savings suffice to require the quantification of price effects, rendering moot the implication of any presumption from the market definition exercise?

prediction arising from the market definition process. We should also consider how one might choose the market definition function, g, and the market share inference function, f, so as to minimize the misalignment. In addition, we can ask how wide is the gap if g is taken to be the HMT and f the thresholds in some merger guidelines. Observe that neither those guidelines nor commentary ever state these questions explicitly, much less attempt to answer them.

It is obvious that there has to be a gap between h and $\tilde{h}$ and that it is likely to be substantial unless one engages in crass reverse engineering. Illustrations of huge divergences are offered in section B. For the present, let us consider the matter analytically and qualitatively. Before proceeding, however, consider this extreme implementation: define g not as a market definition function in the ordinarily understood sense but rather as a function that outputs as the first element of the vector s the value ΔMP from the correct function h, and then define f as the identity mapping of that same element of s to its own output.[9] Setting this sort of circumvention to the side, let us now examine the two market-definition-associated functions, f and g, as they are ordinarily understood.

Begin with $\Delta MP = f(s)$. Obviously, s is not a sufficient statistic for the price effects of a proposed merger. This function does not consider the elasticity of demand, the nature of competitive interaction, and other obviously relevant factors. Indeed, the typical need for the demand elasticity is ironic. The entire market definition exercise—in particular, consideration of broadening initially narrow markets—is motivated by the relevance of substitution and, in particular, the concern that high market shares

---

9. A related and similarly crass mode of reverse engineering, which may correspond to what agencies and courts sometimes do, focuses on the final decision. First, determine whether to block or allow the merger based on one's best understanding of the merger's likely effects—without regard to market definition. Then choose the market definition that rationalizes that decision. That is, if the decision is to block, choose Narrow, where the shares are high, and if the decision is to allow, choose Broad, where the shares are low. As discussed in chapter 6, this creates a serious difficulty in studying agencies' (or courts') actual decision-making processes. For example, using agency-generated market share data, it may appear that large shares and/or significant increases in shares raise the probability that a proposed merger is challenged, but those shares are typically recorded by agency staff after a recommendation has been made whether to challenge the merger (or along with it), using an undisclosed market definition process.

in narrow markets may give a misleadingly high impression of market power by ignoring the constraining effect of substitutes. Yet the elasticity of demand embodies an expenditure-share-weighted sum of all the cross-elasticities and hence already measures substitution correctly, both substitution to goods that would be added to the market if it is redefined and also to all other goods that will remain outside the broader market. Not only does broadening a market fail to capture substitution correctly, but (either way) the analyst will still need the substitution information embodied in the demand elasticity, which is ignored in the standard process of inferring effects from market shares.

Given that price effects depend very much on the type of setting and on key features of costs and demand, we cannot imagine that any such function $f(s)$ could provide a plausible guesstimate over any significant domain of cases (no matter how well chosen is the function $g(\sigma)$ that determines the market in which the share vector s is calculated). Note further that this function f needs to be the same regardless of whether the share vector s arose from a narrow market or a broader, redefined one. Anticipating section B, we can also ask, for whatever is the best f we might envision, whether HHI and ΔHHI are the correct summaries of the input vector s. That is, setting aside that s is not itself a sufficient statistic for price effects, we can ask whether HHI and ΔHHI are sufficient statistics for whatever information in s might be relevant. As we will see, they are not, and for reasons that differ across contexts and between models in a given context.

Next, examine $s = g(\sigma)$ and consider what might be the best market definition function. The question itself is highly problematic precisely because of the aforementioned point: the function's output is restricted to being a share vector s. Indeed, the notion of a "relevant" market is fundamentally confused because it presumes that such a share vector is the thing we need to know. Note as well the additional, familiar restriction entailed by the convention that only colloquial market definitions and their implied values of s are permitted to be in the range of g: because the actual range of competitive effects is a real number (taking a one-dimensional setting), restricting the range of g—and, accordingly, the domain and range of f—to a few discrete values is additionally and needlessly restrictive.

As explained in subsection 1, the best we can hope to do in defining the market is to minimize (avoidable) prediction error. To further develop that idea, begin by defining $\Delta MP^{Broad} \equiv f(s^{Broad})$ and $\Delta MP^{Narrow} \equiv f(s^{Narrow})$, that is, the market power inferences one would choose to draw (the price effects one would predict) conditional on each market definition in a given case. Then our earlier two error measures are $\xi^{Broad} = |\Delta MP^{Broad} - \Delta MP|$ and $\xi^{Narrow} = |\Delta MP^{Narrow} - \Delta MP|$, where $\Delta MP = h(\sigma)$, that is, our best estimate of the merger's effect, given the available information. Then, under this framework, we can choose whichever market definition minimizes the supplemental error, which yields an avoidable error of $\min\{\xi^{Broad}, \xi^{Narrow}\}$. This is the partially reverse engineered, circular result that was discussed in subsection 1. As explained there, we need ΔMP, out best estimate of the merger's effects, which in turn requires use of the correct inference function, h, to undertake the exercise. The present reformulation therefore reaffirms both the circularity of the market definition process and that the method is actually worse than a purely circular one due to the loss of information.

This is, in a sense, the least bad we can do—short of complete reverse engineering that renders the entire market definition process devoid of content. But the foregoing is not what we purport to do. Instead, the market definition process required under merger guidelines (the HMT) and suggested by looser discussions of the subject (such as in prominent court opinions) contemplates protocols that do not even claim to minimize the prediction error (subject to the severe constraints of the envisioned two-step process). When we consider as well that intuitively plausible markets are finite, lumpy, and will involve share vectors that in any given case can take just about any form, and when we further recall all the key information that is omitted from the share vector s—the only input to $f(s)$—we can expect that the errors would often be quite large. The problem, it should be emphasized, has nothing to do with the inherent difficulty of predicting proposed mergers' effects. However noisy such predictions may be, that limitation is reflected in the function $h(\sigma)$. The market definition process instead substitutes two highly constraining subfunctions—the composite of which, $\tilde{h}$, differs markedly from h—thereby introducing additional and often substantial error. This incoherent market definition overlay has never been given an economic foundation and, we now can see, cannot be given one.

3. Reflections on Market Share Inferences

Most prior discussion of the market definition paradigm—and much of the battle of experts in contested merger (and other antitrust) cases—focuses on the market definition function itself, $s = g(\sigma)$, corresponding to the left portion of figure 3.1. It is useful to supplement the preceding analysis by reflecting further on the second function, $\Delta MP = f(s)$, corresponding to the right portion of the diagram, wherein an inference about price effects is made from market shares. Under modern merger guidelines, levels of concern are stated in terms of thresholds that depend on the HHI and ΔHHI. Court cases like *Philadelphia Bank* and a second structural presumption in the U.S. Merger Guidelines (2023) make pronouncements using just the market share information of the merging firms. And other realms of competition regulation, such as monopolization under Sherman Act Section 2 and abuse of dominance under TFEU Article 102, likewise are associated with market share threshold tests, ones focused on a single firm's share. Even setting aside the aforementioned criticisms, it is worth considering further this use of market shares to infer or presume something about market power, particularly in light of the fact that it has never been explained where any of the market share figures used to trigger various consequences come from or what they are imagined to imply.[10]

First, as will be developed in section B, there are some economic models in which certain market share information plays a role. Most familiar are the appearance of the HHI in a markup formula in certain simple models of Cournot competition with homogeneous goods, and the relevance of the dominant firm's market share in a basic model of a dominant firm with a competitive fringe, likewise with all firms selling homogeneous goods. Notice, however, that there are no formulas that use market shares in redefined, broader (nonhomogeneous goods) markets, such as are ordinarily contemplated to be plausible relevant markets after undertaking the market definition exercise.

Suppose that a merger of two apple growers was contemplated and that the applicable market definition protocol broadened the market to include orange growers along with apple growers. What then? One could compute a "market" elasticity of demand for the apples and oranges market, perhaps

---

10. More broadly, competition analysis often focuses on market power without always being clear on the channels by which market power is relevant to the understanding of particular competitive effects in a given context, which in turn makes it unclear what the best measure of market power is (and thus the best way to infer it), or even whether market power as such rather than some of its determinants is what is most probative (Kaplow 2017).

the value-weighted fall in the quantity demanded of apples and oranges combined if the price of both were increased by the same marginal proportion. But what would one do with that value? Specifically, how would it help predict the price effect of the merger of the two apple growers, particularly once one already has the market elasticity of demand for apples? Moreover, that elasticity already includes, as an appropriately weighted component, the cross-elasticity of demand for oranges. There is no need to include oranges in the market for that channel of substitution to be registered; moreover, doing so sets aside the correct information about that substitution and much more. In all, it gives us a "market" that does not facilitate a proper understanding of the question at hand. That is, the redefined market is not actually "relevant" to any sensible economic analysis.

The mystery of how one is to make valid market power inferences from market share information in redefined markets is another foundational question regarding the market definition paradigm that has rarely been asked. The matter is considered in Kaplow (2010, 2011b), where it is explained that the only way to make inferences in such a broadened market is in essence to undo the market redefinition, return to the homogeneous goods market, and proceed as one would if market (re)definition was never contemplated.

Second, the widespread understanding that the market definition process is at best an imperfect proxy is associated with the recognized need to interpret market shares in whatever is deemed to be the relevant market in light of any factors that indicate that the ordinary inference of market power may over- or understate relevant competitive forces. This necessity was recognized at least as early as the U.S. Supreme Court's 1962 decision in *Brown Shoe* and was strongly advanced in *General Dynamics* in 1974. Related suggestions appear in merger guidelines and commentary.

Yet the very idea of adjusting our standard market share inferences upward or downward is mysterious. To begin, the benchmark inference, from which we are to make these adjustments, has never been stated in the first place. Recall the above query: If the postmerger HHI is 3000 and the ΔHHI is 300, is the typically imagined price increase 18%, 1.8%, or 0.18%? We do not know even within an order of magnitude.[11]

---

11. As developed in Kaplow (2010, 2011b), one could attempt to address this part of the puzzle through the adoption of a standard reference market (or, really, a

Moreover, how are we to understand a suggestion, say, by the merging parties that the ordinary inference should be adjusted significantly downward because, in the case at hand, factor F has a value of only 3.5? We do not know the baseline inference. We do not know what factors are thought to underlie any such inference. And we do not know what the "ordinary" levels of any such factors are imagined to be. Indeed, for all we know, 3.5 is not an unusually low value of F but actually is atypically high, so the direction of adjustment should be upward. Nor do we know the size of the case-specific differential or the magnitude of the derivative of the predicted price effect with respect to that factor. Hence, although agencies, experts, other analysts, and courts have been purporting to contemplate all manner of such adjustments for over half a century, it seems impossible to provide a foundation for this activity.

There is a third, qualitatively different concern with making inferences about market power from market shares, one associated with the demise of the structure-conduct-performance paradigm. Market shares are endogenous, rendering such inferences conceptually problematic (not just noisy). Thinking of the function $\Delta MP = f(s)$ as corresponding to a regression equation, we have market shares on the right side as independent variables and market power effects on the left side as the dependent variable. Demsetz (1973) and associated writing postdates *Philadelphia Bank* but predates the emergence of modern merger guidelines (usually taken to commence with the 1982 and 1984 versions in the United States).[12] Nevertheless, merger guidelines and subsequent practice appear to proceed as if this paradigm shift never happened. We can also ask how we are to understand subsequent

---

continuum of such markets), in which certain market power inferences are simply stipulated to be associated with stated market share vectors *s*. This solution of sorts does not, however, answer the questions that follow in the text. Kaplow (2011b) further explores the subject, including a detailed discussion of the meaning of—really, the impossibility of affixing any meaning to—the famous pronouncement in *Alcoa* that ninety percent "is enough to constitute a monopoly; it is doubtful whether sixty or sixty-four percent would be enough; and certainly thirty-three per cent is not."

12. An additional problem with endogeneity (related to the so-called *Cellophane* fallacy) arises with imports in the geographic market definition context. Ceteris paribus, if market power is greater (say, because the demand elasticity is lower), prices will be higher, drawing in more imports and thus reducing the market shares of domestic firms. Under the structural presumption, a merger between two domestic firms would thus look less dangerous the greater was actual market power.

modeling efforts and empirical work that involves the use of market shares to predict the price effects of mergers.

As elaborated in the specific applications in section B, the core reconciliation, when the analysis is done correctly, is as follows. First, even if market shares are endogenous, an act of merging two previously separate firms can be taken to have a causal role in both changes in resulting market shares and changes in market power (price effects). Second, formulas derived for certain models that do feature market shares implicitly account for their endogeneity. To elaborate, the primitives of these models are typically features of demand and of firms' costs, as well as the nature of competitive interaction (typically taken to be exogenous and unaffected by the merger). One can derive the equilibrium and undertake comparative statics to indicate how the equilibrium would change due to a merger. In such equilibria, prices and quantities are endogenously determined. From those quantities, one can determine firms' market shares as a function of the model's primitives (particularly, firms' marginal costs) in the "market" that corresponds to the model. Finally, if the model is sufficiently simple, there may be a closed-form solution for price effects and, furthermore, one might be able to use (invert) the expressions for firms' (endogenous) shares to substitute for firms' marginal costs, yielding an expression for a merger's effect on price as a function of some premerger market share information and other parameters.

Appreciating the origins of such formulas immediately yields an important cautionary note. One might be inclined to ask, as is often done, how the price effect of a merger would change if the market share of one firm was higher and that of another firm was correspondingly lower, ceteris paribus. But this question is not well posed. Because the shares are endogenous rather than being parameters, they cannot change in the hypothesized manner when everything else is held constant. Instead, the implicit comparative statics exercise is something like the following: Imagine changes in marginal costs such that the premerger market shares would (endogenously) change in the stipulated fashion, and assume that no other parameters in our formula would be altered. Then, determine how those changes in marginal costs would alter the price effects of the merger as indicated by that formula. When using such lessons in practice, it will generally be necessary to ascertain the underlying parameters responsible for the particular market share configuration in the case at hand in order to predict the merger's price effects.

B. Price Effects

This section offers only a highly abbreviated treatment of the extensive economics literature on the prediction of price effects from horizontal mergers, for anything more would be disproportionate to the contours of this book and redundant of existing treatments.[13] In the spirit of this book's theme of rethinking merger analysis, this section focuses on stress points: unanswered questions, additional challenges, and divergences between the methods of industrial organization economics and the dictates of official protocols, notably those regarding market definition and the use of market shares in markets so determined. Empirical work that bears on these issues is discussed in chapter 6.

The discussion to follow briefly states how analysis is conducted in standard settings, with an emphasis on whether and how any market share information might sometimes be relevant. That emphasis, however, raises a foundational question: Given the incoherence of market definition (via the HMT or otherwise), just how is it that economists have been able to undertake analyses that use market shares and even sometimes assess, for example, whether the ΔHHI is a helpful indicator of mergers' anticompetitive effects in some settings? The answer, usually implicit, is that those analyses are not conducted using what competition law regards to be "relevant" markets but instead using what economics regards to be useful models. As will emerge, these models depict what competition regulators would view as narrow markets, that is, the markets one would start with before applying the HMT. The analysis in a sense sticks with that starting point without regard to what the HMT or any other market definition algorithm would require. Hence, investigations that might seem to bear on modern merger guidelines and court decisions do nothing of the sort. They instead explore implicit replacements that eliminate market definition entirely.[14]

---

13. See, for example, Whinston (2006, 2007), Kaplow and Shapiro (2007), and Asker and Nocke (2021).
14. Some recent applied work suggests that the use of HHIs and ΔHHIs may have some predictive power even though best practice is otherwise. See, for example, Garmon (2017), Kwoka and Gu (2015), and Nocke and Whinston (2022). For analysis based on simulations or predictions, it is important to recognize that claims about the relative superiority of different methods have a partially tautological character

The U.S. Merger Guidelines (2010) themselves are enigmatic. The 1982 version launched the HMT and made standard the use of HHIs and ΔHHIs. Yet the 2010 guidelines confine nineteen of twenty mentions of "HHI" to the sections on market definition and market share threshold tests. The only (twentieth) mention that appears in the sections that actually analyze price effects is a *disclaimer* of the HHI's importance.[15] Stepping back, we can see a growing appreciation among industrial organization economists and antitrust experts of all sorts that there is a sharp disconnect between proper analysis and official protocols, although actual practice (at least inside the agencies) may be closer to the former.

This section analyzes this chasm explicitly in each of the three now-standard settings: unilateral effects with homogeneous goods, unilateral effects with differentiated products, and coordinated effects.[16] In each instance, we will see how market definition can only lead analysis astray. The HMT in particular is misconceived, market shares are never sufficient statistics, and the HHI and ΔHHI are usually the wrong market share metrics when such are relevant (and sometimes they even enter with the wrong sign).[17] Finally, it will become clear that many of the errors inherent in use of merger guidelines' protocols are qualitatively different across the three settings, rendering unsound any quest

---

in that the benchmark for predictive accuracy is a particular model (so using that model to predict necessarily yields the most accurate results). The point in the text is entirely different: that such research does not in fact use HHIs and ΔHHIs in so-called relevant antitrust markets (whether the HMT-defined market or otherwise), a matter discussed further in section 6.B.

15. "The Agencies rely much more on the value of diverted sales than on the level of the HHI for diagnosing unilateral price effects in markets with differentiated products." U.S. Merger Guidelines (2010, p. 21). The U.S. Merger Guidelines (2023) remove this exception that proves the rule, leaving the HHI entirely unmentioned in its analytical discussions. That said, the 2023 guidelines contain many more invocations of the relevance of "concentration," presumably measured by the HHI.

16. As is familiar (e.g., U.S. Merger Guidelines 2010, §6.2), adjustments are necessary to analyze settings with auctions or bargaining, but for present purposes it is sufficient to explicate the problems in more basic settings. A recent line of work develops tools for bilateral oligopoly bargaining, with applications often focusing on the health sector (Chipty and Snyder 1999; Gowrisankaran, Nevo, and Town 2015; Ho and Lee 2017).

17. The U.S. Merger Guidelines (2023) advance a second structural presumption that substitutes a high (over 30%) postmerger share of the merging firms for a high postmerger HHI (but using a ΔHHI of 100 for both). This alternative fares no better, for essentially the same reasons, and hence will not be discussed separately.

for a common algorithm and market share template—which court opinions and guidelines have employed since the 1960s. The final section of this chapter addresses how the present state of affairs arose, why market definition and inferences from market shares retain appeal despite their infirmities, and what implications arise for understanding current merger decision-making and improving the process going forward.

1. Unilateral Effects with Homogeneous Goods

When two or more firms produce homogeneous goods and compete on price—that is, play a one-shot game in which other firms' prices are taken as given—it is familiar that the equilibrium price will equal firms' marginal costs. If there are at least three firms, then a merger of any pair leaves at least two, so the same result obtains, although the merged firm may have marginal costs that differ from those of the merging firms, so there could be price effects on that account.

Unilateral effects could arise when instead there is a dominant firm that chooses its quantity but all other firms behave as a competitive fringe, choosing their quantities to equate their marginal costs to price. If the dominant firm acquires a fringe firm, or if a merged firm acts as a dominant firm when previously all firms were price takers, the merger will increase price. Such straightforward unilateral effects are not, however, the focus of standard merger analysis of the subject.

It is conventional to posit Cournot quantity competition to analyze unilateral effects with homogeneous goods. Firms choose their quantities simultaneously, taking the quantities of the other firms as given, in a static, one-shot game. This assumption—to which we will return—is not easy to support conceptually in many settings and has not received broad empirical support. For now, we will maintain this assumption that is employed in prominent literature on horizontal mergers and proceed to examine its implications.

One first determines firms' behavior and the resulting equilibrium, taking the number of firms as given. In a simple model, using firms' first-order conditions and re-expressing their optimal quantities using their equilibrium market shares, one can obtain the familiar result that the industry-wide, average, output-weighted markup (share-weighted Lerner index) equals HHI/$|\varepsilon|$, where ε is the market elasticity of demand for the homogeneous good. (There is some abuse of notation in that the HHI in this formula uses 1.00 rather than 10,000 for a monopolist; similarly, a 10% share is represented as 0.1, so 10% squared yields 0.01 rather than 100).

Before proceeding, note that this formula and the elaborations to follow assume that one sticks with the narrow, homogeneous goods market when determining which firms to include when computing the HHI and their corresponding market shares. Importantly, this must be done regardless of whether the HMT or any other market definition procedure dictates otherwise. The first-order conditions that ultimately allow us to make use of firms' market shares—as well as the market elasticity of demand—are all predicated on analysis of the homogeneous goods market. There is no modified formula that would use market shares in a broader market or some notion of a market elasticity of demand in such a composite market. Market redefinition would make it impossible to undertake the analysis. By contrast, in the homogeneous goods market, we can proceed. Furthermore, as noted in section A, the elasticity in this market fully and properly incorporates substitution to all other goods, including any that one might imagine including in a broader market via some market definition exercise.

Let us turn now to the determination of the effect of a merger of two firms in this homogeneous goods market on price. Although this analysis, elaborated below, is more involved, preliminary insight can be obtained by proceeding quite naively, using the HHI/|ε| formula (and other assumptions elaborated in the footnote) to compare the markup after the merger to the markup before the merger in order to predict the effect of the merger on the markup. This highly oversimplified exercise uses the formula ΔHHI/|ε|, following the (incorrect) convention in merger guidelines and court decisions of using premerger market shares to compute ΔHHI.[18]

---

18. This formula would be correct if the assumptions behind our original HHI/|ε| formula held both before and after the merger and, importantly, ΔHHI was calculated using the equilibrium levels of the HHI before and after the merger. However, the general practice, followed in the examples below, is to build from the market shares and HHI before the merger, computing the ΔHHI and the HHI level after the merger mechanically, assuming that the merged firm's postmerger share is the sum of the merging firms' premerger shares and that the shares of nonmerging firms do not change. As developed below, because the merged firm (setting aside merger efficiencies) reduces output and the nonmerging firms increase output in the new equilibrium, the actual, equilibrium ΔHHI will differ. If the merging firms are relatively small, output tends to be reallocated toward larger firms, implying a larger ΔHHI, and conversely if the merging firms are relatively large.

An immediate implication is that, in this one (and only) setting in which HHIs play a central role in a formula for markups, it is the ΔHHI alone that indicates the price effect of a merger; the level of the HHI is irrelevant. Moreover, the ΔHHI, even in this simpleminded formulation, is not a sufficient statistic, for we also need to know the demand elasticity. Because that can vary widely, any threshold in this setting based only on market shares—even if it used the ΔHHI (or more sophisticated functions of the merging firms' market shares, examined below) while appropriately ignoring the HHI—would be significantly misleading.

To illustrate this point and develop the analysis further, let us stick with this naive formula and consider the important but until-now omitted task of market definition. Merger guidelines insist that, before computing the HHI or ΔHHI, one must first choose the correct market. For concreteness, we will here employ the HMT. Consider two cases, one where the HMT passes, so we stick with the homogeneous goods market, and one where the HMT fails, so we broaden the market.

For case one, consider a merger that—in the narrow, homogeneous goods market we have been considering—is associated with a naively computed (postmerger) HHI of 2501 and a ΔHHI of 201, just over the U.S. Merger Guidelines' (2010, p. 19) thresholds that put a merger in the range that is "presumed to be likely to enhance market power." Suppose, moreover, that this narrow market barely passes the HMT using a 5% threshold, which is to say that a hypothetical monopolist would raise prices just over 5%. Making some additional, crass assumptions for this back-of-the-envelope exercise, the magnitude of the implicit demand elasticity is approximately 16, which implies a price effect of approximately .0013 (0.13 percentage points).[19] Recall that this merger is presumptively challenged.

For case two, consider a merger to monopoly in a homogeneous goods market. Moreover, let us suppose that in this case the 5% HMT barely fails for

---

19. This crude calculation can be understood roughly as follows. If the premerger HHI were 0, a hypothetical monopolist (HHI of 10,000, but actually 1.00 in the formula) facing a demand elasticity with a magnitude of 21 would raise prices 5% (a price 5% above marginal cost is associated with a Lerner index of .05/1.05 = 1/21). Because the premerger HHI is 2300 (0.23) rather than 0, some simple algebra can be used to show that the associated elasticity has a magnitude somewhat above 16. The merger's actual (naive) ΔHHI of 201 (0.0201) divided by this elasticity generates a price effect of somewhat above 0.0012, which the text rounds up to 0.0013.

Price Effects and Market Definition 53

the narrow market, which is to say that the hypothetical monopolist would raise prices slightly less than 5%. Of course, that hypothetical monopolist is, after the merger, an actual monopolist, so that is the price effect of this merger. However, because the HMT fails, this fact is ignored and instead the market must be expanded, and we will assume that this broader market is unconcentrated, meaning that this merger, per the U.S. Merger Guidelines (2010), is "unlikely to have adverse competitive effects and ordinarily require[s] no further analysis."

Let us now juxtapose these two cases: In the former, the guidelines' methodology—considering the HMT and the HHI and ΔHHI thresholds—presumptively challenges a merger raising price by 0.13 percentage points. In the latter, this same machinery gives a pass to a merger that raises price by almost 5 percentage points, *more than thirty-five times as much.*[20] Hence, in a simple, plain-vanilla setting, we can see that straightforward application of the market definition paradigm, as embodied in modern merger guidelines, gets backwards two mergers with price effects that are more than an order of magnitude apart.[21] Nor is this designated outcome close, for the guidelines' middle region is leaped over. Worse, this extreme malfunction arises in the one setting (homogeneous goods, unilateral effects, Cournot competition) in which there exists a formula in which the HHI is central. Nor does this simple example slip in efficiencies, entry, or other complications: it is the most basic case, which should be in the bull's-eye of the merger guidelines' machinery.

---

20. If we had substituted the 1800/100 thresholds in the U.S. Merger Guidelines (2023) for the 2500/200 thresholds in the U.S. Merger Guidelines (2010) in constructing case one, this difference would become more than eighty times as much. The main reason is that requiring a ΔHHI of 100 rather than 200 cuts by half the effect of the merger and thus doubles the multiple. Substituting the HHI of 1800 for 2500 somewhat raises the implied elasticity for case one, further increasing the multiple.

21. Note that, as stated, the guidelines are only positing a presumption in the first case and the ordinary manner of proceeding in the second. However, the other considerations—entry, efficiencies, powerful buyers, and failing firms—are posited to be absent in the stated examples. On the other hand, if one supposes (as is no doubt actually true to some extent) that economists in agencies largely ignore both the HMT and the thresholds using HHIs and ΔHHIs, and instead are guided by the direct analysis of price effects, then we would have less of a problem in practice.

Having used a naive formula (and supplemental crude assumptions) to illustrate how the market definition paradigm in general and merger guidelines' implementation thereof in particular lead us badly astray, let us return to the Cournot model to provide some further illumination when one undertakes a more complete analysis of a merger's effects. An immediate challenge is that one needs to specify what happens to the merging firms' cost functions when they combine into a single firm. This important matter, which is addressed to the efficiencies inquiry undertaken in chapter 4, is ultimately empirical, the answer depending on the nature of the merger under consideration. It also raises questions of the applicability of the Cournot model, a subject to which we shall return.

For this reason—and others relating to tractability—the literature often instead addresses the following question: How much lower would the merged firm's marginal costs have to be in order for the merger's effect on price to be neutral?[22] The literature formulates answers in different ways, each of which helps us appreciate the subtleties of the problem. Farrell and Shapiro (1990) show that the marginal cost of the merged firm (at the premerger combined output) must be lower than the marginal cost of the more efficient merging firm (at its own premerger output) by an amount that equals the difference between the price and the marginal cost of the smaller, less efficient merging firm prior to the merger.[23]

Nocke and Whinston (2022) offer a complementary representation that is partly in terms of market share measures, under the simplifying assumption that every firm, including the postmerger firm, has constant marginal cost. They offer expressions for how much the merged firm's marginal cost must be below the weighted average of the merging firms' premerger marginal costs. Their expression for a price-neutral merger, even with these simplifying assumptions, is a bit messy: it features the market elasticity of

---

22. In addition to taking a hypothetical approach to the merged firm's cost function, this way of putting the question avoids the need to make nonmarginal predictions of price effects, which depend on the curvature of demand (Werden 1996). Moreover, under the posited experiment, the merged firm will produce the same total quantity as did the two firms premerger, and all other firms will thereby be induced to keep their quantities constant as well. This further simplifies the analysis because the result will be independent of the shape of firms' cost functions.

23. Goppelsroeder, Schinkel, and Tuinstra (2008) present formulations of the requisite marginal cost reduction in a wider range of settings.

demand; the ΔHHI appears twice, each time as a square root; and an expression for the within-merger HHI (the premerger HHI computed as though the market had only the two merging firms) appears three times, sometimes as a square root.

A key lesson is that, even setting aside the demand elasticity, ΔHHI is not close to a sufficient statistic for assessing these mergers. Moreover, as illustrated in the accompanying footnote, the demand elasticity has a huge effect: because the ΔHHI appears as a square root, the critical ΔHHI rises with the square of the elasticity, so moving the magnitude of the elasticity from 1 to 10 (which is well within the range for the HMT to validate the homogeneous goods market) raises the critical ΔHHI by a factor of 100 in Nocke and Whinston's (2022) first formulation.[24]

We can summarize these results for unilateral effects with homogenous goods under the further assumption of Cournot competition. The market definition process can result in wildly inaccurate inferences. Within the narrow, homogeneous goods market (which corresponds to the model at hand), market share information is not nearly sufficient to indicate price effects. The HHI level is not even part of the relevant market share information. And the ΔHHI, which is the relevant market share information using a naive formulation, is no longer the sufficient summary of the two merging firms' premerger market shares once one undertakes the correct analysis, even for a simple case with constant marginal costs. Taken together, even simple formulations that have been developed to come as close as possible to validating any use of the ΔHHI in any market produce wildly varying thresholds for the critical ΔHHI.

---

24. Nocke and Whinston (2022) offer an illustration (with symmetric merging firms) that has a critical ΔHHI of ~45 (to overcome merger efficiencies of 5%) when the magnitude of the elasticity is assumed to equal 1, but their same formula with an elasticity of 10 yields a critical ΔHHI of ~4500. One might direct attention to some small range of elasticities, perhaps with magnitudes between 1 and 3 (which still entails an order of magnitude range in the critical ΔHHI), but such would be problematic. As discussed earlier, even with the HMT, one would stick with the narrow, homogeneous goods market with elasticities as high as (roughly) 16 for mergers with market shares at the beginning of the range indicating a presumptive challenge. Moreover, a number of merger challenges have focused on fairly narrow markets (consumable office supplies sold through office superstores in *Staples*, premium natural and organic supermarkets in *Whole Foods*), where it is hardly apparent that extremely low elasticities are appropriate.

Stepping back from these analytics but before considering the applicability of the Cournot model, we should consider as well the implication of the merging firms' rationality constraint, examined in section 2.C. Salant, Switzer, and Reynolds (1983) show that, in the absence of efficiencies, mergers in the Cournot model may well be unprofitable, particularly when they do not result in a market that approaches monopoly.[25] The intuition is that the model involves the merged firm reducing its output, leading nonmerging firms to raise theirs, dampening the price increase resulting from the merger. Most of the increase in industry profits from the merger accrues to the nonmerging firms, a positive externality (the opposite of business-stealing), whereas the full brunt of the sacrifice (quantity reduction) is borne by the merging firms themselves. Other work relaxes various of the assumptions of Salant, Switzer, and Reynolds (1983), showing that Cournot mergers can be profitable at lower levels of concentration, but the core point remains.[26]

This analysis reminds us of the importance of reasoning from the merging firms' rationality constraint. When the upward pricing pressure created by a merger is insufficient to make it profitable, neoclassical analysis implies that there must be nontrivial efficiencies to carry the day that in turn need to be incorporated into the assessment. Proposed mergers are a selected sample; if a notable subset of Cournot mergers would be unprofitable when ignoring efficiencies, the implied (conditional) distribution of efficiencies associated with such merger proposals is correspondingly higher. This point contrasts with mergers in settings with differentiated products and price competition, examined in the next subsection. There, under common (but not universally valid) assumptions, the merged firm's price increases are sufficient to make the merger profitable (ignoring efficiencies) and other firms' optimal responses are ordinarily taken to involve higher prices (with lower quantities), reinforcing that effect. Such mergers would be profitable even if efficiency fell somewhat, so the distribution of efficiencies implied by selection under the rationality constraint is lower in that setting.

---

25. One of the many insights in Stigler (1950) concerns the profitability of mergers, implicitly in homogeneous goods industries. He noted the incentives of firms to stay out of mergers in order to benefit from higher prices, including through increases in their own output.

26. See, for example, Perry and Porter (1985), Levin (1990), and McAfee and Williams (1992).

Another point about all mergers, including those properly analyzed in a Cournot framework, is that price effects are not the same as total welfare effects, a subject analyzed in Farrell and Shapiro (1990). Among the lessons is that a merger of smaller firms—which, in the Cournot model, will be those with higher marginal costs—tends to increase productive efficiency because these relatively inefficient firms contract after a merger whereas larger, lower-cost firms expand. This output reallocation can raise total welfare even though consumer welfare falls and there are no production efficiencies for the merging firms. Note further that in this sort of case, the equilibrium postmerger HHI will rise further (because market share is reallocated from small firms to large firms), which is to say that a higher equilibrium (rather than naively computed) HHI is, on this account, associated with higher, not lower social welfare.

Let us now consider the applicability of the Cournot model ot one-shot quantity competition to mergers in homogeneous goods industries, continuing to defer to subsection 3 the possibility of coordinated pricing. In a sense, this model can be understood as one in which firms' simultaneous quantity choices are associated with commitment for the duration of the period that the one-shot game covers, which would not be instantaneous in the real world. But it is not clear why this should be. As is familiar, in the imagined Cournot equilibrium each firm's output is sold at a price in excess of its marginal cost, so a firm would profit by reducing its price a moment later. By similar reasoning, other firms would do the same, which is more akin to Bertrand competition in prices, with the result that price would be driven down to marginal cost. Or one might suppose that the firms appreciate that they are in a repeated game, in which case equilibria with coordinated pricing may arise, which is also outside the model.

A leading rationalization for the Cournot model is that, under appropriate assumptions, it can be interpreted as the reduced form of a two-stage game (Kreps and Scheinkman 1983).[27] In stage one, each firm chooses a capacity—perhaps the size of its plant or production run—and in stage two all the firms sell the entirety of their homogeneous quantities in a conventional market wherein price is determined so as to equate this fixed supply to market demand. It is common to briefly mention this rationalization

---

27. Davidson and Deneckere (1986) show how relaxing various assumptions of this model have important implications for the results.

before proceeding to analyze the Cournot model, but often without assessing whether the assumptions employed or the applications envisioned are consistent with this formulation. Tirole (1988) emphasizes both the choice of the right model more broadly and, in particular, the need for the application to justify the two-stage framework. He suggests that indeed the most compelling uses require that the quantities correspond to capacity or other investment decisions.[28]

Additional questions posed by the two-stage formulation concern the first-stage choices. First, they are regarded to be simultaneous, but once they are viewed as involving investments, such as the size of one's plant or the number of plants to construct, this assumption seems questionable in many settings. In a simplified, sequential alternative, the firm moving last would naturally take other firms' capacities as given, but early movers would anticipate how their choices would influence those moving subsequently. In the simple case with two firms (the Stackelberg model), the first mover chooses a higher-than-Cournot quantity because it knows that the second mover will react by reducing its quantity somewhat, with the result being a higher total quantity and a lower equilibrium price than under Cournot.[29]

Second, consider the role of buyers, particularly large buyers that are often present in intermediate goods markets where homogeneous goods are more common. Such buyers often engage in elaborate negotiations and enter into long-term contracts, rather than buying in a spot market as supplies are needed. Any such buyer would anticipate the Cournot outcome

---

28. Stating the matter as a simple choice between Bertrand and Cournot, it is sometimes suggested that the former may be more apt when marginal cost is nearly constant whereas the latter is more indicative when marginal costs rise steeply (with a capacity constraint being an extreme version). Nevertheless, for tractability, it is common to assume constant marginal costs when working with the reduced-form, one-stage, quantity-setting game. That assumption is plausible if understood to be applicable to the creation of the capacity or to firms' production up to their capacity constraints, but it can be problematic otherwise. For example, as discussed below, it is typically assumed in Cournot analysis of mergers that nonmerging firms react by increasing their output in such models at the same, constant marginal cost, even if in the application their plants were previously constructed and are assumed to already have been operating at capacity before the merger.
29. Maskin and Tirole (1987) examine a model in which two symmetric firms in alternative periods make capacity decisions that last for two periods, with the result that each is induced to choose quantities higher than in a standard Cournot model to influence the other firm's choice in the next period.

and realize that it has an incentive to bargain at stage one with one of the firms in order to obtain a lower price. The counterparty producer likewise stands to gain from striking a deal that removes the buyer from the market and then engaging in the quantity game with the other firms as to the remaining part of the demand curve. When such behavior occurs, the two-stage game operates differently—there is an unraveling of sorts—and the reduced-form, one-stage Cournot game is no longer rationalized.

Finally, and particularly important for present purposes, consider the applicability of this two-stage model once a merger is contemplated. Cournot analysis of mergers, when thus situated, is often best understood as applicable to a merger that occurs at a stage zero, before the capacity choices of any of the firms are made. That is the implication when one is comparing equilibrium solutions of the reduced form with and without the merger. Yet actually proposed mergers are typically in established industries, wherein firms already have plants, supply chains, distribution systems, and so forth. It has been noted, for example, that in some settings—viewing the merger as occurring after stage one, perhaps before stage two or amidst repeated one-shot play in stage two when capacity is durable—a merger would have no effect. If starting afresh, the merged firm would build less capacity (and the nonmerging firms more), but with the plants already in place, they would be utilized to full capacity as long as price exceeds marginal cost, which it would after the merger (unless the price fell rather than rose, and by a sufficient amount).

Static Cournot analysis, in abstracting from any dynamics, is difficult to apply to mergers in such settings. Building on this idea, Berry and Pakes (1993) briefly examine a highly stylized dynamic incarnation that allows for investment, depreciation, entry, and exit. They indeed find that some mergers have no immediate impact due to preexisting capacity that would continue to be utilized fully. Another important lesson of their simulations relates to the merging firms' rationality constraint. They find that many mergers are unprofitable in a static sense. Nevertheless, the present discounted value of many statically unprofitable mergers is positive because the merged firms would achieve substantial savings over time from their optimally reduced levels of investment.[30] Chen (2009) examines a dynamic

---

30. See also section 5.B, discussing dynamic models with entry in more recent literature that likewise employs Cournot models.

Cournot model in which firm size asymmetries are not due to differences in underlying production functions but instead to stochastic investment and depreciation. He finds that mergers reduce welfare more in the long run than in the short run and that welfare falls more in his model than when the same size asymmetries are rationalized by differences in firms' technology, as conventionally assumed.

These comments on the applicability of the Cournot model are merely meant to be suggestive. Returning to Tirole (1988), one indeed needs to be careful when using Cournot models to understand competitive interactions in homogeneous goods industries. The present discussion counsels further caution when extending them to analyze horizontal mergers. Although many models are useful despite their obvious lack of complete realism, two caveats are important here. First, the reason to use the Cournot model rather than, say, the Bertrand model is that equilibrium price and quantity determinations are thought to be better understood under the former. Therefore, if the Cournot model's limitations pertain specifically to the price-setting process—and sometimes suggest modifications in the direction of Bertrand—the gap between model and application is central. Second, models are used to train intuition. But it is familiar that many features of the Cournot model are opposite to those of Bertrand, so we need to be careful about what lessons we learn from the exercise.

As a final note, despite the frequent use of Cournot models in industrial organization economics and their central role in prominent academic analyses of mergers in homogeneous goods markets, it is unclear how often competition agencies actually use Cournot models to determine unilateral effects in this setting. This observation reflects informal conversations, occasional remarks in the literature by individuals in a position to know, the U.S. Merger Guidelines' (2010) omission of Cournot analysis when discussing unilateral effects with homogeneous goods, and the relative inattention to this case in the Commentary on the U.S. Merger Guidelines (2006).[31] The latter devotes only half a page to presenting a single instance of unilateral effects with homogeneous goods—and it is one involving a merger creating a dominant firm rather than Cournot competition—by contrast to the

---

31. The U.S. Merger Guidelines (2023) include discussion of Cournot analysis, but it is unclear the extent to which this signals greater use thereof in light of the other considerations noted in the text.

Price Effects and Market Definition

presentation of a wide variety of examples in other settings. If this is so, it is unclear whether this situation reflects concerns about the inapplicability of such analysis, the fact that such mergers are indeed often unprofitable and hence not proposed, or something else. In any event, there is a significant gap between the Cournot model's apparent unimportance in practice and its significant role in economic modeling of competition and of the effects of horizontal mergers in particular.

2. Unilateral Effects with Differentiated Products

When firms produce differentiated products and compete on price, taking other firms' prices as given, the resulting equilibrium prices exceed marginal cost. It is conventional to posit Bertrand, one-shot price competition to analyze the unilateral effects of mergers in this setting. As with the use of the Cournot model with homogeneous goods, this too is an assumption, one that is also subject to reservations and that is usually maintained rather than tested when performing empirical work. Notably, demand estimation typically leverages firms' first-order conditions that themselves are predicated on the supposition that other firms' prices are taken as given.

For purposes of analysis and for demand estimation, including that feeding merger simulations, it is also common to impose further structure on preferences. Taking some standard formulations, it is supposed that consumers choose between goods in some cluster of related, differentiated, substitute products and an outside good.[32] There are variations and refinements, such as allowing nests within the cluster or imposing particular functional forms; these are mostly set to the side here. On the production side, the exposition here follows the common convention wherein each firm (premerger) produces a single variety of the good.

One might associate such a model's cluster of related goods with a narrow market. Likewise, the market elasticity of demand might be understood as the fall in demand for the cluster—switching purchases to the outside good—as the prices of all goods in the cluster are increased proportionately.

To assess unilateral market power in a merger between two firms that each produce a single good in the cluster, we also need to consider consumers' willingness to substitute among goods within the cluster. Although

---

32. In many empirical implementations, the outside good is taken to generate separable, constant marginal utility, which removes income effects.

loosely associated with cross-elasticities, this substitution is more usefully measured by diversion ratios that weight these cross-elasticities by quantities in order to indicate what portion of the fall in demand is diverted to another good when the price of a single good rises.[33]

Whether a particular firm's markup is high or low clearly depends on both this market elasticity (substitution to the outside good) and the diversion ratios (substitution to other goods in the cluster), although some posited demand systems mechanically connect these two phenomena. There are immediate implications for the use of market shares to assess market power. Consider a perfectly symmetric cluster of a given number of firms. Higher or lower magnitudes of either form of substitution, each of which implies potentially great differences in market power, are all associated with the same HHI, taking this cluster as the market in which shares are computed. One might redefine the market if the former elasticity is large, as the HMT commands, but neither analytics nor empirics are aided by combining our posited cluster of goods with some other subset of goods in the economy if our model's structure is correct; doing so would only confound any use of market shares within the expanded group of goods. Nor can such an exercise address the potentially large variation in the magnitudes of the diversion ratios. For these reasons, standard analytical and empirical methods do not engage in the paradigmatic market definition exercise but instead attend to the pertinent structure and magnitudes of the parameters of the demand system, along with firms' marginal costs.

Under convenient assumptions that may or may not approximate reality in a given application but serve as a benchmark for thinking, diversion ratios can be taken to be proportional to market shares in the cluster. Under others, some goods may be particularly close substitutes for each other whereas others are more distant. For example, two brands of compact cars may be close substitutes for each other whereas a luxury brand probably is not a close substitute for either one. And even vehicles in a similar price range, perhaps a pick-up truck and a sports car, may be distant substitutes.

---

33. As Kaplow (2010) discusses, antitrust's early focus on cross-elasticities, which continues in court opinions today, is yet another confusion associated with (but not necessarily implied by) the market definition paradigm. The U.S. Merger Guidelines (2010) do not mention cross-elasticities and use the phrase "diversion ratio" more often than the term "elasticity." The U.S. Merger Guidelines (2023) are similar, mentioning "cross-elasticity" only once.

For these reasons and others, notably differences in firms' cost functions, markups generally differ across goods.

The simplest analysis of mergers in this framework considers a merger of two firms, with the merged firm now setting the prices of both of the products that were previously determined independently. For now, efficiencies are set to the side. We might imagine that each type of good was produced in its own specialized plant, with the merger having no effect on either operation.

Such a merger internalizes part of the positive externality on other sellers from raising either of the two goods' prices. Some fraction of the lost sales from raising the price of either good is now captured by the same firm, which owns the other good after the merger. Hence, there is upward pricing pressure. For each good, this effect is stronger the higher is the fraction of lost sales that go to the other good—the diversion ratio—and the greater is the relative markup on that good, because the product of these two factors indicates the magnitude of the profit recapture (Farrell and Shapiro 2010). That said, one must be careful in making these assessments due to endogeneity, recalling our earlier discussion of comparative statics with market shares, wherein standard ceteris paribus assumptions are violated. Here, when all goods in the cluster are closer substitutes for each other, diversion ratios will be higher but markups will be lower.

Moving from the analysis of what may be regarded as the first-round upward pricing pressure for a single good, note first that the merged firm has an analogous incentive to raise the price of the other good. The magnitude of that incentive typically will differ from that for the first good both because diversion ratios are not generally symmetric (consider a good that is many consumers' second choice, after one or another of the many other niche products in the cluster) and because the markups on the two goods generally differ.[34]

One can also take the analysis further. For concreteness, suppose that the prices of all goods in the cluster are strategic complements.[35] Regarding the

---

34. A common further step in the analysis of upward pricing pressure, which was noted in subsection 1 on Cournot models, is to determine the compensating marginal cost reduction required for the merger to be neutral. In addition to the two-way feedback between the merging firms' products, it is necessary to account for the fact that marginal cost reductions themselves affect pricing incentives.

35. It is sometimes forgotten that this standard formulation is an assumption and not a generic property of Bertrand competition with differentiated products. As

two goods taken alone, for each price increase on one good, the firm appreciates that this will make profitable further price increases on the other, and so forth. Other firms will react to the price increases on the goods sold by the merged firm, here by raising their own prices, generating further positive feedback. These reactions imply, ceteris paribus, a greater increase in prices in the resulting equilibrium.

It has long been accepted that market definition is unnecessary to analyze unilateral effects with differentiated products in the Bertrand model. Indeed, we have just discussed how price effects are properly analyzed. But given the continued and widespread insistence on market definition, at least in formal protocols and court opinions, even when analyzing this type of merger (which seems to cover most challenged mergers), further elaboration is in order.

As developed in section A, market definition here is not merely unnecessary but also seriously counterproductive. As with the Cournot model, it is not even clear what it would mean to conduct analysis within the contours of a redefined market. The diversion ratios are the diversion ratios and the markups are the markups. For example, if demand is estimated assuming substitution within a cluster of goods and also between that cluster and an outside good, one does not perform a different analysis on a much broader cluster if the estimation reveals that substitution to the outside good exceeds some threshold. Moreover, if one wishes to use the sorts of formulas discussed below that express the effects of mergers in these settings using equilibrium premerger market shares, those shares are those within the cluster being analyzed, not in some broader, hybrid cluster. Likewise for any demand parameters that relate to elasticities. If one redefined the market, the formulas would become useless, and there really would be nothing one could do with market shares and other features of this broadened market.[36]

---

developed by Bulow, Geanakoplos, and Klemperer (1985), strategic complementarity is favored by rising marginal costs and firm demand elasticities that fall in other firms' prices. In the case sometimes used to illustrate the analysis, which features constant marginal costs and linear demand, prices are indeed strategic complements.

36. There is the usual qualification regarding reverse engineering in that one could appropriately redefine all relevant factors to generate the same result, essentially nullifying the broadening of the market, thereby rendering market redefinition merely pointless rather than destructive.

Focusing on the HMT in particular, it should always have seemed strange that we would assess the price increase of a hypothetical *monopolist* for the purpose of predicting the price effects of a horizontal merger, notably, in the typical case in which we do not have a merger to monopoly. In our present setting, however, we could apply the HMT to a contrived and particularly narrow market consisting solely of the two merging firms' products. The key is that, once we undertake the first step of the HMT, which determines how much our hypothetical monopolist would profitably raise price, we must stop, ignoring the rest of the machinery altogether. After all, that hypothetical monopolist is our merged firm. Whether that price increase is above or below some arbitrary HMT threshold, say, 5%, should not affect how we conduct our analysis. In particular, we should not, when it is above 5%, then consult the HHI thresholds (which would be exceeded in any event). Nor, when it is below 5%, should we somehow broaden the market, repeat the HMT, and ultimately consult the HHI thresholds in whatever market we then find ourselves. It is obvious that this official methodology discards the direct answer to our central question—how much the merger would raise price—and substitutes meaningless answers to different, obscure questions. These observations reinforce the point that the market definition paradigm does not merely generate a noisy, imperfect proxy but rather throws away information and, more broadly, leads us astray.

Consider further whether, if we do stick with our original cluster, deeming that to be our relevant market, market shares in that market are meaningful. As already explained, the upward pricing pressure created by a merger depends on the diversion ratios between and the markups on the two products. One can consider particular structures of demand under which diversion ratios are proportional to market shares, so in those cases one of our two factors will be proportional to shares in that particular market. But we also need to know the factor of proportionality. More broadly, as with the Cournot model, one can solve special cases of differentiated products models and, where sufficiently tractable, derive formulas for a merger's price effects as a function of model primitives. Furthermore, one can substitute equilibrium market shares for quantities and thus derive an expression in which market shares appear, along with other parameters.

Nocke and Whinston (2022) present such an analysis for firms with constant marginal costs where demand takes either the constant elasticity of substitution or multinomial logit form.³⁷ Their formulas show how much a particular measure of the merged firm's efficiency (captured by a notion of firm "type") must improve in order for a merger to be consumer-surplus neutral. In both cases, the formulas make no use of the HHI. Only the market shares of the two merging firms enter, and these shares appear in a number of places and ways, none corresponding to the ΔHHI. In both cases, the formulas also include substitution parameters, so the market share information is clearly insufficient. Moreover, the formulas for the two special cases are qualitatively different from each other. Finally, one should keep in mind that the merging firms' shares in these formulas are endogenous, rendering simple comparative statics exercises problematic (one must consider ceteris paribus changes in the model's primitives, not in equilibrium market shares). Taken together, we can see that there is a wide gulf between these formulas and the market definition paradigm as instantiated in merger guidelines and otherwise.³⁸

This analysis, like that for mergers in the Cournot model with homogeneous goods, often follows Werden (1996) in examining what efficiencies are necessary for a merger to be consumer-surplus neutral because otherwise, to predict price effects, one needs to know the curvature of demand (and of the cost function, when not setting that problem aside by assuming that all firms' marginal costs are constant).³⁹ Note further that a consumer-surplus-neutral merger in these analyses is total-welfare increasing because the merging firms' costs fall. Also, as with Cournot mergers, when prices do change there may be effects on productive efficiency due to reallocations

---

37. For an earlier analysis using logit demand, see Werden and Froeb (1994).
38. Explorations of the relationship between, say, ΔHHI and price effects—through simulations, regressions, or otherwise—may find a positive correlation, but the text suggests that this can be misleading. It would be natural to include the two merging firms' market shares (which are the determinants of ΔHHI) independently—or, better yet, in the manner that pertinent formulas suggest is appropriate—which one suspects would undermine or at least alter any findings regarding the ΔHHI. Some analyses, moreover, use HHIs or ΔHHIs (or other indicators that depend on market definition) drawing on information from agency documents or court filings. These indicators, however, reflect market definitions chosen by the agency, presumably to support positions that may well have been predicated on other, more direct analyses. These independent variables are thus endogenous in a different, more worrisome sense than usually confronted. Section 6.B elaborates this problem.
39. For further exploration of demand curvature and pass-through, see Jaffe and Weyl (2013) and Miller et al. (2016, 2017).

across firms with different costs. In basic cases, when relatively small firms merge, production tends to shift to larger firms that, ceteris paribus, have lower marginal costs (which explains why, in equilibrium, their output is greater), and conversely when relatively large firms merge.

Moreover, as mentioned in the Cournot analysis, Deneckere and Davidson (1985) show that all mergers are profitable when we have Bertrand competition with differentiated products (and production costs are unaffected)—under constant marginal costs and linear demand, which are sufficient to imply that prices are strategic complements, as we have been assuming here. Hence, the implication of the merging firms' rationality constraint is that the admissible range of efficiencies conditional on seeing a merger proposal includes a negative segment, and a fortiori it includes the case in which the effect on production efficiency is zero.

Finally, consider the applicability of the Bertrand model in the present setting. It is often regarded to be more plausible than the Cournot model with homogeneous goods for two reasons. First, as discussed in the next section, the alternative assumption of coordination is typically regarded to be less plausible with differentiated products because the coordination task is more challenging.

Second, with respect to unilateral effects themselves, it often seems more natural to view firms as setting prices rather than quantities. On reflection, however, this is hardly clear.[40] As stated above, if capacity is fixed, even for a modest period (say, after completion of a production run), the Cournot formulation regarding what other firms hold constant seems more appealing. More broadly, both assumptions seem questionable. Under Cournot, quantity cannot be adjusted at all (which requires rigid capacity constraints, no inventories, and limits on advance contracting in the two-stage formulation). Under Bertrand, other firms are regarded to be able, in principle, to supply infinite quantities at their given prices. Under both, firms repeatedly experience their assumptions being violated—if not instantly, often fairly quickly and in predictable ways. Finally, a maintained assumption of both formulations is that the merger under investigation will not itself change the nature of firms' competitive interactions. In all, we should be uncomfortable with our analyses of these cases—a more typical stance in the 1970s and 1980s—and devote greater attention to testing these assumptions

---

40. As Friedman (1988) elaborates, this is unclear even in one-shot games.

rather than confining our attention mainly to empirical analysis that leverages them to identify parameters of demand and cost functions. See section 6.C. This is a challenging task, in part because it requires the introduction of dynamics that these familiar one-shot games omit.

3. Coordinated Effects

The analysis of coordinated effects requires a qualitatively different approach from that applicable to unilateral effects.[41] Here, we wish to predict how mergers may influence firms' propensity to play and their success at playing certain strategies in a repeated game rather than how they influence play in a one-shot game in which each firm takes as given other firms' actions of a specified type. As a legal matter, a merger raising the danger of coordinated effects is deemed to be anticompetitive regardless of how success in this repeated interaction may be accomplished postmerger—in particular, whether or not it would involve the sort of "agreement" that might itself be illegal.[42]

It is useful to decompose the analysis of coordinated effects into two questions: the extent to which a proposed merger would facilitate coordinated price elevation and how much prices would increase conditional on success. We will begin with the latter question because of its closer relationship to the foregoing analysis.

Suppose that a merger would raise the probability of the firms coordinating perfectly rather than competing (as they are assumed to be doing before the merger). This common assumption itself raises an interesting paradox.

---

41. For discussion and extensive references on coordinated effects generally, see Marshall and Marx (2012), Kaplow (2013a), and Harrington (2017). For applications to horizontal mergers, see Harrington (2013) and Porter (2020).

42. As a practical matter, if most coordination inevitably had to be achieved in a manner regarded to be illegal and, moreover, if such coordination were readily detected and capable of being proved before a tribunal, then predicted but uncertain coordinated effects would be a weak basis for disallowing mergers. The alternative policy of allowing such mergers and subsequently challenging coordination if and when it arose would be more attractive. However, challenges of detection (and, relatedly, of sufficient deterrence) as well as quandaries regarding when successful coordination is itself illegal have long led competition policy to favor blocking mergers posing significant risks of coordinated effects. Nonetheless, to the extent that there is some deterrence of coordination, the predicted likelihood of coordinated effects should be discounted accordingly.

Anticipating some of the later discussion, the more a setting is conducive to coordination, the more the firms may already be engaged in coordination, so the smaller would be any coordinated effects of the merger.[43]

Turning back to the question at hand, note that it directly corresponds to the first step of the HMT, but only to that step. After all, perfect coordination entails firms acting as if they were a monopolist (abstracting from the efficient allocation of production across firms, which might also be accomplished if side payments were feasible). However, as with the previous subsection's examination of unilateral effects with differentiated products (when we took the market to consist of only the two merging firms' products), here too it is necessary to truncate the analysis immediately upon completion of the HMT's first step. That is, we determine (by whatever methods and using whatever information is available) how much we think the hypothetical monopolist would profitably raise price, and that is our answer. Period. If the answer is high, say, above a 5% benchmark, there is no need to determine the HHI and ΔHHI in our initial market and then to consult HHI thresholds in order to obtain a fuzzy answer regarding the level of danger involved.[44] And if the answer is below 5%, we again would be throwing away that answer and ultimately deriving useless HHI and ΔHHI measures in some broader market, all in order to obtain some fuzzy (and incorrect) answer instead.

It should also be noted that, when contemplating coordinated effects, the initial, narrow market is indeed the relevant one (even though we will

---

43. Yet another paradox can arise. Often it is assumed that, in the supergame that might give rise to equilibrium strategies that support coordinated price elevation, punishment involves reversion to a Cournot quantity game rather than to Bertrand competition. In that event, a horizontal merger's enhancement of unilateral effects in the absence of coordination (that is, an increase in the Cournot reversion equilibrium price) makes punishment less effective, which in turn inhibits collusion (Davidson and Deneckere 1984). In light of the questions raised in subsection 1 about the domain of the Cournot model, it is probably more helpful to consider explicitly the effects of capacity constraints on the success of coordination, and then the effect of the merger, which combines the capacities of the two merging firms. Literature that addresses this dimension is noted briefly below, when considering how a proposed merger may affect asymmetries.

44. Likewise, under the U.S. Merger Guidelines' (2023) second structural presumption, which substitutes a threshold share of the merged firms (30%) for the postmerger HHI (1800), we again receive no illumination of the magnitude of the danger involved.

not, at this point, pay attention to the market shares therein). We are typically concerned with coordinated effects in homogeneous goods settings, or ones that are nearly so. Coordination is difficult enough, and product differentiation adds to the complexity.[45] Therefore, the initial market, often regarded as a narrow one consisting (only) of homogeneous goods, is indeed the relevant context to examine. It would be unusual that a merger would substantially boost the likelihood and success of coordination in some broader, hybrid market (although if such a fear were plausible in some particular case, it would be appropriate to analyze that possibility).

At this basic, conceptual level, the market definition paradigm's quest for what it regards to be the relevant market is fundamentally misguided in this setting. This observation is ironic in light of the fact that application of the paradigm arose in the merger context—and the HMT and use of HHIs became prevalent—at a time where the primary focus of merger regulation was on coordinated effects. Only later, as formally embodied in the 1992 version of the U.S. Merger Guidelines, did unilateral effects enter the picture, and they have now come to replace coordinated effects as the central if not nearly universal concern.[46] Nevertheless, modern merger guidelines continue to use the original framework, one that we now see is dysfunctional in all applications.

Consider next our question concerning the extent to which a proposed merger would contribute to the likelihood and success of coordination.

---

45. Most prosecuted price-fixing cases, whether involving global cartels or local bidding rings, involve homogeneous goods, many of which are intermediate goods, not differentiated consumer products. Interestingly, because coordination with differentiated products should require more detailed and frequent communications due to its greater complexity, one might expect such cases to be overrepresented in the sample of successful prosecutions—yet they are, as noted, largely absent, suggesting that their underlying frequency is quite low.

46. It is unclear the extent to which modern merger challenges are motivated by concerns for coordinated effects. On one hand, the Commentary on the U.S. Merger Guidelines (2006) devotes a number of pages and examples to coordinated effects. On the other hand, some inside and outside the agencies have suggested to me that allegations of coordinated effects are often included for good measure but are not really the focus of the agencies' analysis or most of the government's litigated cases. Even so, court opinions often discuss and sometimes emphasize coordinated effects. In the European Union, there have been relatively few cases focusing on coordinated effects in the decades since an important loss in 2002, but perhaps some revival has occurred more recently.

Predicting coordinated effects is a daunting task, even before attempting to assess the impact of a merger thereon. Lacking better tools, it is conventional to examine structural features of markets in order to determine whether they suggest that the merger arises in a setting that is conducive to coordination and, if so, to see whether the merger seems likely to materially facilitate coordination. Among the factors considered are market structure, firms' production functions (notably, their capacities), and the nature of transactions, including their observability (pertaining to pricing, quantities, and buyer-seller pairings) and, relatedly, the behavior of buyers, including how they structure auctions or engage in negotiations (Stigler 1964; Fabra and Motta 2018). Of particular interest is how readily firms can somehow coordinate on a target price and their ability to detect and punish cheaters, which in turn determine firms' incentives to cheat, the focus being on coordinating firms' incentive compatibility constraints (Green and Porter 1984).[47]

Regarding the effect of a proposed merger itself, most mergers are not regarded to have much impact on many of these factors. Mergers do affect market structure and may affect the merging firms' production functions. Perhaps the most systematic effect that facilitates coordination is that a merger of two firms reduces the number of firms by one, which lightens the coordination burden and reduces the number of possible sources of disagreement. Once one determines the premerger number of significant competitors and knows the postmerger reduction (here taken to be one), the HHI and ΔHHI provide no further illumination. A merged firm may also receive a better signal of demand than that received by either firm separately, so it may be more able to determine whether lost sales are due to a fall in demand or some other firm's cheating, which relates to Stigler's (1964) suggestion that concentration can thereby aid coordination.

Mergers may also influence the extent of asymmetries that might make coordination more difficult. Differences in costs may generate more disagreement on price, or differences in capacities may affect deviation incentives and punishment abilities in ways that make it harder to support as high a price or, indeed, any coordinated price elevation at all (Compte, Jenny, and Rey 2002; Vasconcelos 2005). Here, the HHI is somewhat relevant, but

---

47. See also Loertscher and Marx (2021) on firms' decisions to participate in a cartel rather than remain outside of it.

with a sign opposite to conventional interpretations. Holding constant the number of firms (and, relatedly, the reduction in that number caused by a merger), the HHI is higher the greater is the asymmetry in market shares (which tend to be related to firms' costs). Indeed, perfect symmetry minimizes the HHI for a given number of firms. Hence, in this atypical instance in which the HHI may be independently probative of price effects through an identifiable channel, its indication is opposite to the standard inference reflected in merger guidelines and court opinions.

Turning to the ΔHHI, it is hard to draw systematic implications. A given ΔHHI could be generated by the merger of two firms in a group of firms that were previously symmetric, reducing symmetry to that extent. Or it could be generated by a merger of two firms that were previously asymmetric with each other or with the other firms, potentially increasing overall symmetry to that extent. Or it may involve the elimination of asymmetry between the merging firms but increased asymmetry with other firms. If symmetry seems important on some dimension, whether the dimension is well proxied for by market shares or not, it makes more sense to directly examine how a proposed merger influences that factor. Examining the ΔHHI or HHI is not worth the albeit negligible effort.[48]

Sometimes attention is focused on so-called maverick firms (Baker 2002). Although often only loosely defined, this notion is generally a shorthand for a firm that is likely to disrupt coordination for some reason. But that reason needs to be identified and analyzed. Perhaps a maverick firm is smaller, has a different cost function, is a recent entrant that is rapidly expanding, has a steeper discount rate because it is near bankruptcy, or has an idiosyncratic manager. A merger that absorbs a maverick is often thought to facilitate coordination, although that may depend on whether the merged firm dampens or magnifies the maverick's distinctive traits. And sometimes a merger, perhaps of two small firms, is thought to beneficially

---

48. Consider the following simple examples of "6 to 5" mergers. Suppose first that all 6 firms are symmetric prior to the merger. Then the premerger HHI is 1667, the naive postmerger HHI is 2222, and the naive ΔHHI is 555. Now suppose instead that, premerger, 4 of the firms each had a 20% market share and that the two merging firms each had 10% market shares. Then the premerger HHI is 1800, the postmerger HHI is 2000, and the ΔHHI is 200. Here, the former case has a larger postmerger HHI and a much larger ΔHHI than the latter, but the former merger destroys symmetry whereas the latter merger creates symmetry.

create a more viable maverick. On the other hand, mergers of small firms may reduce asymmetry and thereby create a firm that would join a coordinating coalition rather than remain outside of it. Relatedly, because smaller firms may be more inclined to cheat (they have more to gain from deviation and less to lose from possible disruption), it may be that mergers of smaller firms (associated with a lower ΔHHI) contribute more to effective coordination than do mergers of larger firms (associated with a higher ΔHHI)—really another instance of greater symmetry being favorable to coordination. Stepping back, a central difficulty with the examination of mavericks for insight into a merger's effects on coordination is that the maverick label is often the conclusion of analysis rather than something directly observed.

At the opposite end of the spectrum from mavericks, it has been traditional to focus on the potentially facilitating role of a firm that serves as the price leader.[49] This emphasis focuses more on the challenges of choosing a target price on which to coordinate rather than on the incentives to deviate and the ability to detect and punish cheaters. To the extent that this coordinating function is particularly important, a merger that creates a firm that might better serve this role could have an anticompetitive effect. Note here that a particular sort of asymmetry is regarded to facilitate coordination rather than undermine it, although it may do that as well through other channels.

Note finally that the merging parties' rationality constraint is relevant, as always, in making appropriate inferences. Mergers in settings where coordination is plausible but merging would make it more difficult are less likely to be proposed than mergers that facilitate coordination. Of course, mergers may also be motivated by efficiencies—which, depending on the context, may facilitate or undermine coordination. Relatedly, a merger that might seem to make coordination more difficult may be most likely to arise in a setting in which coordination is not very likely regardless.

---

49. Byrne and de Roos (2019) suggest that an asymmetric price leader was important in their study of coordination by retail gasoline stations. A focus on price leadership might explain why one of *Philadelphia Bank*'s requirements was whether "a merger . . . produces a firm controlling an undue percentage share of the relevant market," which does not appear in modern merger guidelines (but is introduced in the U.S. Merger Guidelines 2023) and is largely ignored in modern literature addressing the use of market shares to infer mergers' price effects.

C. Further Reflections

1. Questions and Concerns

The market definition paradigm is internally incoherent and interferes with the ability to determine the likely price effects of any type of horizontal merger. This subsection highlights some additional shortcomings, particularly those associated with modern merger guidelines.

First, why should one use a hypothetical *monopolist* test to analyze mergers that ordinarily are not mergers to monopoly? We have learned that the HMT misfires even when we do have mergers to monopoly or mergers that might appropriately be analyzed as such. In the toy examples for unilateral effects with homogeneous goods, the posited merger to monopoly that would raise prices almost 5% is presumptively allowed whereas the other merger (not to monopoly) is presumptively challenged even though it would raise prices only ~0.13%. For this merger to monopoly—and also in the differentiated products setting if we start with a market having only the two merging firms' products, and in the coordinated effects setting if we wish to determine the extent to which fully successful coordination would raise prices—application of the HMT and subsequent use of the HHI and ΔHHI in merger guidelines' thresholds is patently wrong. In each of these applications, the correct action is to take only the first step—asking how much the contemplated monopolist would raise price—and just stop. That is our answer. The HHI and ΔHHI in that narrow market are of no use, and it certainly makes no sense to examine them in any broadened market if the first step of the HMT fails and thus market redefinition is supposed to be triggered. It is remarkable that these obvious, simple points that render the HMT market definition methodology flatly and obviously incorrect have gone unnoticed for decades. Such is the confusion induced by the market definition process, including the apparent rigor of the HMT algorithm.

Second, just how much of a price increase should merger guidelines contemplate as being sufficient to challenge a merger? Many write and speak as if the answer is something like 5%, referring to the focal-point figure often associated with various guidelines' SSNIP tests. But this is not even approximately correct. Our toy examples with unilateral effects suggest that, in one case, ~0.13% is enough, but in another, nearly 5% is not enough. It is hardly clear how to interpolate from those figures given that their outcomes are backward. More broadly, the former case showed how the HMT can confirm a narrow market despite very high elasticities (~16 in that example) and very small price effects. But not always, as the latter example shows. Consulting the grids rather than the HMT itself, we asked whether a postmerger HHI of 3000 with a ΔHHI of 300 is imagined typically to raise prices by 18%, 1.8%, or 0.18%. We also noted (using a simple formula in the literature) that the ΔHHI necessary to hit a specified upward pricing pressure threshold can vary by more than two orders of magnitude using elasticities in narrow markets that survive the HMT.[50]

One can also approach this question from a different direction. Suppose that the government agreed with the merging parties' experts that, whatever the HMT, HHI, and ΔHHI might indicate, the merger would raise prices (absent efficiencies or entry) by some stated level. Would that merger be blocked or allowed?[51] Court opinions and agency guidelines have almost universally avoided this basic question through use of the market definition approach. One can see why a nonexpert court might prefer to make a dichotomous choice between Broad and Narrow, based on a loose discussion of a range of factors, rather than to opine on the magnitude of the predicted price effect, but it is hard to defend this approach as sound policy.

Third, just what are economic expert witnesses doing when they write reports and testify about what constitutes the "relevant" market? As a matter of economic fundamentals, there really is no such thing, and the accepted ways of correctly (if highly imperfectly) predicting mergers' price effects do not undertake the market definition exercise in any setting, as elaborated in section B.[52]

---

50. This example was given in the footnotes for the Cournot case using Nocke and Whinston's (2022) formula, wherein the critical ΔHHI was ~45 with a demand elasticity of 1.0 but ~4500 with an elasticity of 10.0—whereas merger guidelines' thresholds and those appearing elsewhere give no regard to the elasticity in setting cutoffs. Of course, the analysis would be quite different yet again if one used any of Nocke and Whinston's differentiated products merger formulas (and also different depending on which of those formulas were used).
51. If any positive elevation suffices, why is any analysis necessary since horizontal mergers generically create positive (even if possibly small) upward pricing pressure via unilateral effects?
52. This point has interesting potential implications for U.S. merger litigation because rules for the admission of expert testimony require that experts employ methods supported by their discipline.

Fourth, what can be said about what market is "relevant"? We have seen that, as a matter of proper economic analysis, it is usually going to be what is regarded as a narrow one (always eschewing market redefinition). The reason is that this so-called market sometimes corresponds to representations in models that may be useful in the different settings, whereas there are no models that characterize effects in broad, hybrid markets. This is not a "pro-government" view but rather merely a statement as to how best to analyze horizontal mergers. If even large merging firms cannot raise prices very much, correct analysis of price effects should reveal that instead of rendering it more obscure. In such narrow markets, market shares (understood to be endogenous) are sometimes useful, but the manner in which this is so differs qualitatively across the standard settings and, even in a particular one (notably, unilateral effects with differentiated products), the formulas are quite different depending on the demand system. Hence, the one-size-fits-all approach that is officially stated in modern guidelines is nonsensical. Moreover, when shares are relevant, the HHI and ΔHHI are not the correct summaries.[53]

Finally, how can so many defend the market definition paradigm, and merger guidelines' instantiation thereof, as useful proxies, shortcuts, screens, rules of thumb, or guides for nonexpert courts? Any such tools must at some level be anchored in sound analysis and evidence. But that foundation was never laid and, as is now clear, cannot be provided. As emphasized in section A, market definition always does strictly worse, taking as given the information at hand, however limited that may be. Nor is it clear how a generalist judge can make better use of evidence bearing on price effects—including estimates of the price effects themselves—to choose what is in essence a metaphor, using either fuzzy criteria or an algorithm (the HMT) that is not well connected to the problem at hand.

---

53. The HHI in particular is not even loosely correlated with relevant market share information in those formulas in which (endogenous) shares of the merging firms appear. As suggested in footnotes in chapter 8, however, the HHI is sometimes taken as a proxy for the level of market power (by contrast to any change induced by a proposed merger), and a given price increase has a greater impact on deadweight loss (total welfare rather than consumer welfare) when prices are initially more elevated.

2. Origins, Evolution, and Inertia

A century ago, economists were a long way from formally extending Cournot's and Bertrand's notions of competitive interaction to analyze the unilateral effects of horizontal mergers. Also not yet in sight were developments regarding coordinated effects—whether Stigler's (1964) seminal analysis or Friedman's (1971) supergame framework—and even less understood was how any such analysis might illuminate which mergers would facilitate price elevation by groups of firms. Even today, the former can be difficult to implement empirically so as to derive reliable predictions, and the latter is a conceptually challenging enterprise where little headway has been made. Both subjects are elaborated in chapter 6.

In such a world, it is perhaps unsurprising that something like market definition and the use of resulting market shares to make inferences about market power would emerge. Some of the origins in U.S. antitrust law are found in the development of monopolization doctrine. Sherman Act Section 2's reference to monopolization literally suggests a 100% share—of something—which readily leads to inquiries that ask, "of what," as well as to relaxation of the notion that only literal monopoly was encompassed.

Against this backdrop, Lerner (1934) advanced what is now called the Lerner index of market power. Long forgotten is that this famous article was motivated by his desire to put an end to the then-emerging but in his view contemptuous practice of using market definition and market shares when addressing matters relating to market power. He even used scare quotes to emphasize the vacuity of attempting to define "commodity" and "industry."[54] Although Lerner's index is often used, his warnings have been forgotten.

There is another interesting feature of the evolution of the market definition paradigm and its associated inferences or presumptions from market

---

54. After mentioning a variety of problems with using market shares, Lerner (1934, p. 166) states: "there is one that interests us particularly here, and that is the relatively simple one of defining the commodity." In his subsequent discussion, he refers (p. 168) to market shares as "irrelevant statistics" and emphasizes the need to "[put] an end to attempts . . . to find a measure of monopoly in terms of the proportion of the supply of a commodity under single control." "It is quite unnecessary, for this purpose, to say anything at all about the 'commodity' which the 'industry' produces. . . . All the difficulties of definition of 'commodity' or 'industry' are completely avoided" (Lerner 1934, p. 171).

shares in the context of assessing horizontal mergers. At the time of *Brown Shoe* and *Philadelphia Bank*, the first U.S. Merger Guidelines in 1968, and the modernized guidelines in 1982 and 1984 that resemble those in use today in much of the developed world, market definition and market share thresholds were understood to illuminate the danger of coordinated effects, implicitly in homogeneous goods markets. Subsequently, as reflected in the 1992 guidelines and later iterations, much contemporary analysis focuses instead on unilateral effects, most often with differentiated products.[55] Hence, even if the methodology had provided a helpful proxy in the context in which it was initially developed, it would be quite a coincidence if the same methods and similar targets likewise provided sensible answers in the qualitatively different setting in which it is now usually employed. In fact, we have seen that it does not work in either. The actual stages of development, rooted more in legal discourse than in economics, help to explain how we arrived where we are today.

There is, however, more to the current situation than neglect or idiosyncratic path-dependence and institutional conservativism. The latter surely has influence, as agencies may be reluctant to promulgate revised merger guidelines that sharply contradict not only long-standing court precedents but also their own established methodology.[56] Moreover, the irreducible

---

55. It is natural to consider why such an important shift occurred. One explanation would be new empirical evidence documenting either the unimportance of coordinated effects or the importance of unilateral effects, but the discussion in chapter 6 casts doubt on this explanation. Schmalensee (2012) suggests that part of the answer may lie in economists' toolkit. As explored in section B, tools for analyzing the unilateral effects of mergers were newly developed and refined, including more sophisticated empirical methods for demand estimation that can feed merger simulations. By contrast, there has not been comparable development for coordinated effects, and the demise of the structure-conduct-performance paradigm reduced confidence in the view that coordinated effects were pervasive. Juxtaposing these two sets of observations, the use of more sophisticated techniques for unilateral effects may have raised courts' expectations regarding what constitutes sufficient proof, expectations that could not readily be met in cases challenging coordinated effects.

56. The U.S. Merger Guidelines (2023) continue to reflect this reluctance and, indeed, rely more heavily than before on market shares rather than analysis of mergers' likely effects. On the other hand, the 2023 guidelines advance the examination of direct effects, but somewhat mysteriously as a means to market definition (perhaps implicitly embracing the reverse-engineering approach to market definition discussed in section 6.B, addressing the structural presumption) (Kaplow 2024).

fact remains that the best direct methods of predicting mergers' effects are subject to significant limitations in the best of circumstances. In addition, the press of time and resource constraints on agencies in screening merger proposals and the need ultimately to convince nonspecialist courts enhances the allure of simpler methods that might serve as proxies or provide metaphors for communicating more refined analysis.

Complementing these forces, there is intuitive appeal to some basic notions: surely competition tends to be weaker in more concentrated markets and, relatedly, mergers that significantly increase concentration should be expected to weaken competition more than those that do not, ceteris paribus. Elements of these intuitions appear variously in the preceding subsections' analyses.

Nevertheless, it did not take long for economists, legal specialists, and courts to realize that not all "markets" are created equal. The fix (or fudge) involved market definition: if we confine our market share inferences to shares computed in the *relevant* market, all should go well, or at least not too badly.[57]

Unfortunately, as this chapter demonstrates, these intuitions are far too limited—and their ultimate applications' dependence on market definition far too destructive—for this approach to be helpful. It always rested on wishful thinking. No one points to seminal papers that purport to ground this approach because it never was grounded. Upon inspection, we can see that there is no way to avoid the circularity and loss of information inherent in any market definition process. The valid fragments reflected in the foregoing intuitions about concentration and competition are retained—and given neither more nor less weight than they deserve—when one instead undertakes direct analysis of mergers' anticompetitive effects using the tools apt for the situation at hand. This is, by definition, the best we can do given the state of existing knowledge, the difficulty of predicting firms' future behavior, and the inevitable limitations on the information available to analysts and decision-makers at any given stage of merger review.

Economists and many of the lawyers in competition agencies, and those otherwise involved in merger review and litigation, are to varying degrees

---

57. As mentioned, *Brown Shoe* and *General Dynamics* emphasized from the outset the need to interpret the resulting market shares in context in making inferences about proposed mergers' anticompetitive effects.

aware of the shortcomings of the market definition paradigm. Agencies undoubtedly—at least some of the time and to some extent—undertake the correct analysis as best they can. If they decide not to challenge a particular merger, that may be the end of the story. And if it is thought that a merger should be blocked, then a case can be brought that may embody, at least to some extent, a reverse-engineered approach to market definition. Specifically, a narrow market will be advanced, in which the market shares are high, satisfying merger guidelines' thresholds and court precedents. And judges deciding cases may, at least implicitly, proceed likewise, finding a narrow market definition more convincing when they believe (based on other evidence) that the merger is indeed anticompetitive, but adopting a broad market definition when they are unconvinced of the merger's alleged anticompetitive effects. Nevertheless, attempting to operate such a system—some of the time, to some degree, and largely sub rosa—undermines transparency and accountability, distorts analysis and decisions in individual cases, interferes with attempts to improve the regulatory regime, and provides a misleading guide for further research.

4 Efficiencies

Efficiencies may be regarded as sufficiently ubiquitous to justify permitting most horizontal mergers, which is in fact done. Yet they are also said to be considered only occasionally and to rarely tip the balance in favor of a merger. These understandings are difficult to reconcile, for there is no plausible joint distribution of anticompetitive effects and efficiencies such that virtually always one or the other is clearly larger. Regardless, efficiencies have long been subordinated in horizontal merger analysis. Part of the reason is the underdeveloped state of the conceptual framework.

The core subject is merger specificity. Section A examines the nexus between efficiencies and anticompetitive effects of proposed mergers, motivated by the observation that some nonmerger alternatives that might achieve proffered efficiencies may also produce some or all of the anticompetitive effects. Section B draws on the theory of the firm and other literatures that address the challenging questions of when and how bringing activities inside a firm may differ from alternative contractual arrangements. Although directed to the question of what mergers can accomplish that contracts cannot, and thus going to the heart of merger specificity, this research has had little penetration in horizontal merger analysis. Section C provides applications to basic types of merger efficiencies: economies of scale, economies of scope, and the sharing of assets between competitors. Section D elaborates the need to integrate the analysis of efficiencies and anticompetitive effects, contrary to the often advanced approach of sequential siloing wherein efficiencies are examined only after a determination that anticompetitive effects are likely to be substantial. Section E offers a long-run perspective on merger efficiencies, which bears on pass-through as well as the choice between consumer and total welfare standards.[1]

A. Nexus between Efficiencies and Anticompetitive Effects

Merger guidelines intuitively and uncontroversially credit only efficiencies that are specific to the proposed merger (EU Merger Guidelines 2004; U.S. Merger Guidelines 2010, 2023). The familiar rationale is that, for efficiencies to justify allowing an otherwise anticompetitive merger, it must be that the merger is a necessary condition for achieving those efficiencies. Otherwise, the merger should be blocked, avoiding the anticompetitive effects without sacrificing the efficiencies. Further analysis and possible balancing are appropriate only with respect to merger-specific efficiencies.[2]

This logic, however, is incomplete because it takes for granted the merger specificity of anticompetitive effects. If a merger is necessary for efficiencies but the anticompetitive effects are not specific to the proposed merger—they would transpire regardless—then the merger should be allowed even if the efficiencies would not otherwise be sufficiently large. This possibility will be illustrated below, in an example involving economies of scale.

A more complete view of merger specificity is obtained by focusing on the nexus between efficiencies and anticompetitive effects in a proposed merger. To see the basic idea, suppose that the various activities of a proposed merged entity are completely separable; that is, the pieces can be severed from each other without the separation itself having any effect on efficiency or competition. Perhaps manufacturing and distribution are separable, or it may be that plants or retail outlets in different locations are

---

1. Much of this chapter draws on Kaplow (2021a), which contains a more intensive exploration of many of the subjects considered here. An important omission in this chapter—and in the literature more broadly—is the ex ante effect on efficiency associated with an active market for firms, such as the enhancement of managers' incentives due to the threat of being acquired as well as the pressure provided by competitive intensity. Another neglected channel, ex ante inducement of entry and other investment, is examined in chapter 5.
2. This point, like most of the analysis in this chapter, does not depend on whether a consumer or total welfare standard is adopted, although the requisite magnitude and nature of efficiencies that suffice to outweigh or mitigate the anticompetitive effects may differ. The relevance of welfare standards to the assessment of efficiencies is considered further in section E.

operationally and competitively distinct. In such circumstances, we should allow any part of the merger necessary to achieve the efficiencies but disallow those that generate anticompetitive effects. For example, if the efficiencies arise from combining one part of two firms' operations but the anticompetitive effects are confined to an unrelated area of geographic overlap in distribution, imposing conditions that require spinning off assets to avoid combination of the latter is appropriate. Sometimes efficiencies may be highly concentrated, perhaps confined to a single department of each of two merging hospitals, in which case prohibiting the merger but allowing a limited joint venture might be optimal. At the other extreme, if the very assets whose combination creates the efficiencies are also responsible for the anticompetitive effects, then the merger (to that extent) should be allowed if the efficiencies dominate under the relevant welfare standard but prohibited if they do not. We face the conventional trade-off precisely when there is a complete nexus between efficiencies and anticompetitive effects.

Similar analysis applies to mergers that are not fully modular in the sense just described. For example, a spinoff in the case of limited geographic overlap may sacrifice only a fraction of the efficiencies, in which case the spinoff should be required unless that portion of sacrificed efficiencies is sufficient to outweigh the associated anticompetitive effects that would be averted. But perhaps distribution economies are generated precisely where there is geographic overlap. Or with a proposed merger of two pharmaceutical companies that overlap only in certain therapeutic categories, it may be that the synergies lie precisely in those lines of research, not the unrelated ones. Then we are back to the case of a direct trade-off because both the efficiencies and anticompetitive effects are not only merger specific but, more importantly, arise in the same part of the proposed combination. This nexus-based perspective dictates that efficiencies be specific to whatever part of the merger generates the anticompetitive effects if the proffered efficiencies are to justify those anticompetitive effects.

Yet another important dimension that has received little attention in this regard concerns the alternatives to merger, whether they involve internal expansion or contractual arrangements between the merging firms short of merger. After all, inquiries into merger specificity entail comparison to a but-for world without the merger (which often differs from the status quo ante), so it is necessary to both characterize and analyze the hypothesized nonmerger scenario. As will be illustrated below, the analysis bears not only on whether the efficiencies would arise without a merger but also on whether some or all of the anticompetitive effects would result as well. Take the case of an exogenous doubling of economies of scale. If the alternative to allowing ten firms to pair off and merge is to prohibit the mergers and require internal expansion, this alternative path may likewise result in five larger firms with a similar reduction in competition. In the simplest case, efficiencies and anticompetitive effects would be the same whether or not the mergers were allowed. Elaboration below will introduce additional factors, some rendering internal expansion superior and others favoring merger because the alternative of internal expansion results in all of a merger's anticompetitive effects but only some of its efficiencies. The latter case illustrates the aforementioned possibility that anticompetitive effects may be less merger specific than are the efficiencies.

The examples just given suggest that there often will be a nexus between at least some of the efficiencies and anticompetitive effects, requiring an integrated assessment to that extent. An important reason that the two phenomena may be connected is the consideration of incentives. After all, the incentive alignment created by a merger can be efficient because of reductions in agency costs, but it also constitutes the central force that reduces competition. Moreover, echoing the preceding point, it may be that a hypothesized contractual alternative to a merger that generates the contemplated efficiencies would require a similar degree of incentive alignment that, in turn, would soften competition.

Two considerations, however, may favor contractual alternatives. First, there are typically diminishing returns with respect to controlling agency costs, whereas (under a total welfare standard) marginal distortion rises with the elevation of price. Hence, partial alignment may be socially optimal, although this outcome may require some regulation of the contractual alternatives, such as joint ventures, that may be difficult to implement. Second, there may be alternative ways to mitigate agency problems under contracts, such as when there is sufficient observability and verifiability to support contractual specifications, in which case the need for incentive alignment in order to achieve efficiencies may be reduced.

As a matter of theory and practice, it is necessary to consider the merger specificity of both efficiencies and anticompetitive effects. The discussion here suggests that focusing on the nexus between efficiencies and anticompetitive effects is a useful way to frame the analysis. The discussion to follow, as appropriate, takes this more integrated approach and thereby casts the analysis of horizontal merger efficiencies in a new light in some important applications.

B. Merger Specificity and the Theory of the Firm

Inquiries into the merger specificity of efficiencies (and of anticompetitive effects) address whether a proffered merger is necessary to achieve them, which entails comparisons to nonmerger alternatives. The contemplated alternatives, in turn, often involve contractual arrangements. One or both firms might outsource to a third party, one firm might license IP to the other, the firms might enter a joint venture, and so forth. In short, merger specificity is often centrally about the differences between what can be achieved inside a (merged) firm and what is possible via contracts involving the firms when they remain separate.

This distinction constitutes the core of the theory of the firm and related literatures on contract theory and organizational economics that have not penetrated the study of horizontal merger efficiencies.[3] This section makes this connection, emphasizes the challenges it poses, elaborates some strands of the relevant literatures, and closes by examining the relevance of vertical arrangements—the focus of much of this literature—to efficiencies that may be generated by horizontal mergers.[4] Resulting lessons are developed in the applications explored in section C.

Discussions of merger specificity ordinarily proceed as if there is some central difference between a firm and pertinent contractual alternatives but do not articulate what that difference is or how it matters. By contrast, literature on the theory of the firm, which began nearly a century ago and is associated with several Nobel Prizes, raises fundamental questions about the coherence of this distinction and offers some perspectives on how it might be understood.[5] Put simply: how does assembling various

---

3. Another pertinent field is the analysis of firm productivity (De Loecker and Syverson 2021).
4. Most of the analysis is directly applicable to vertical mergers yet has had little influence on merger analysis in that realm either.
5. Hart (2011, p. 102) states: "One problem any economist faces in analyzing the firm is one of definition. To pose a question that is often asked but rarely answered (at least satisfactorily)—what is a firm? Is a firm circumscribed by its legal status or by

"contracts" under an umbrella contract that may be called a "firm" change anything, much less solve subtle contracting problems involving the provision of incentives and the challenges of asymmetric information? Jensen and Meckling (1976) famously stated that a firm is a "legal fiction" that is nothing more than a "nexus for contracting relationships," and Alchian and Demsetz (1972) referred to the belief in commonly advanced differences between firms and market relationships as a "delusion."[6]

Coase (1937) launched the modern economic study of the theory of the firm by posing provocative questions. On one hand, why are firms necessary at all when, in principle, anything they do can be achieved by contract? Coase's answer pointed to transactions costs, but just what they consisted of and how bringing activities inside a firm avoided them without sacrificing the benefits of the market were not explained. On the other hand, if there are limits to contracts that are solved by bringing arrangements into a single firm, why (aside from regulatory constraints, notably, laws limiting horizontal mergers) doesn't the entire economy consist of one large firm, eliminating all incentive problems that interfere with profit maximization? Coase posited diminishing returns, but their source was likewise unclear, which could hardly be otherwise because Coase's firms were little more than black boxes. A related question was posed much later by Williamson (1985): Why, if there are some limitations on when intra-firm cooperation (somehow achieved) is privately efficient, could this not be overcome within a single firm? Specifically, why could it not decentralize its operations as it wished, mimicking the market whenever that was helpful, and then engage in selective intervention from the top of the internal hierarchy when, but only when, that was efficient?

---

its economic activities? This question is quite important if, for example, one wishes to understand the motives for mergers."

6. "The private corporation or firm is simply one form of *legal fiction which serves as a nexus for contracting relationships*. . . . Viewed this way, it makes little or no sense to try to distinguish those things which are 'inside' the firm (or any other organization) from those things that are 'outside' of it. There is in a very real sense only a multitude of complex relationships (i.e., contracts) between the legal fiction (the firm) and the owners of labor, material and capital inputs and the consumers of output" (Jensen and Meckling 1976, p. 311). "It is common to see the firm characterized by the power to settle issues by fiat, by authority, or by disciplinary action superior to that available in the conventional market. This is delusion" (Alchian and Demsetz 1972, p. 777). See also Masten (1988, p. 181): "the word *firm* is merely descriptive, a collective noun denoting a particular cluster of otherwise ordinary contractual relationships."

Before examining various answers that have been offered, two observations are noteworthy. First, academic work on horizontal mergers, as well as merger guidelines and court opinions, have made virtually no reference to any of this prominent literature that seems most relevant to the analysis of merger specificity. Conversely, these literatures have not attempted to say much about horizontal mergers and related efficiencies. These points are especially surprising regarding Williamson because he was a prominent player in both domains. Indeed, Williamson (1968) is the seminal article on the efficiency trade-off in horizontal mergers, and his work on the theory of the firm was partly motivated by his interest in antitrust policy, where he offered numerous applications (Williamson 1974, 1985).[7] Yet he never elaborated how this body of work applied to horizontal merger efficiencies, even when he revisited the subject (Williamson 1977) after publishing *Markets and Hierarchies* in 1975.[8] Nor do other scholars who write on the literature's applicability to antitrust elaborate implications for horizontal merger efficiencies (Joskow 1991; Klein and Lerner 2008).

Second, there is often a mismatch between the attributes that the literature associates with firms versus external contracts and how governance within firms and of contractual relationships actually operates. Specifically, firms are taken to employ hierarchical rather than decentralized decision-making, but in practice firms often are highly decentralized whereas some external contractual arrangements involve substantial hierarchy.

Regarding firms, it is familiar that many are significantly decentralized. A division or subsidiary may be run as an independent profit center, with compensation of the top manager determined accordingly. Separate units may engage in arms-length bargaining to determine transfer prices or may choose instead to deal with outsiders (Holmstrom and Tirole 1991).[9] In

---

7. Interestingly, Williamson (1968, p. 32, n. 12) referred specifically to the choice between contracting and bringing activities inside the firm.

8. Likewise, Williamson (1985, pp. 365–70) examines merger policy in its penultimate chapter, applauding the increasingly positive attitude toward efficiencies but failing to indicate how his body of work may aid in analyzing them.

9. Due to impurities in the transfer pricing process, some suggest that decentralized units may actually prefer to deal with third parties in the external marketplace rather than with other units of the same firm. Empirically, many vertically integrated enterprises rarely engage in internal shipments (that is, of physical products by contrast to intangible inputs) (Atalay, Hortaçsu, and Syverson 2014). However, when they do, the preference for internal trade seems to be high (Atalay, Hortaçsu, Li, and Syverson 2019).

other respects as well, separated parts of a firm may act differently on that account (Magelssen 2020). Wickelgren (2005) observes that, if decentralization is necessary to provide incentives to minimize costs, a horizontal merger of competitors may not generate the upward pricing pressure predicted by standard theory that presumes unified intra-firm decision-making.

From the other side, firms engaged in outsourcing sometimes impose a substantial hierarchy on their contractual relationships. For example, a firm that distributes through independently owned franchises may impose detailed restrictions on franchisee behavior, retain strong termination rights, and employ revenue or profit sharing to align incentives. In principle, managers of company-owned outlets may have more or less discretion than their franchisee peers and may be subject to similar incentive schemes (Lafontaine 1992; Mathewson and Winter 1985; Rubin 1978).

The domain of contractual hierarchy is, however, even broader. A firm may impose detailed restrictions on suppliers, embed its own employees in supplier firms, include hierarchical dispute resolution in the contract (rather than rely on courts), and align incentives in a variety of ways. Actual practice may involve something close to command regarding suppliers' product design, manufacturing processes, and even features of those suppliers' own supply chains (Stinchcombe 1990; Bernstein 2015).

We have seen that, in theory and in practice, the distinction between conducting an activity through contractual arrangements and locating the activity inside a firm may have little connection to what is usually imagined when inquiring into whether a proffered efficiency requires that the firms be able to merge rather than be left to enter alternative contractual relationships. And bear in mind: there is also the corollary point that these matters are relevant not only to efficiencies but also to anticompetitive effects. Consider, for example, whether a merger between two firms with significant geographic overlap at the retail level should receive an automatic pass because the merger is not regarded to be horizontal due to the fact that one merging party relies entirely on franchise arrangements with nominally independent firms that, accordingly, are not part of the merger (although the contractual relationships with those franchisees are).

Legal form—here, the distinction between contracts and firms—cannot guide our analysis; we need to examine the underlying substance. More concretely, it is necessary first to identify and understand the proffered efficiencies, then to consider and assess the extent to which identifiable contractual alternatives may be able to achieve many of the benefits, and finally to examine whether such nonmerger arrangements avoid the posited anticompetitive effects. The remainder of this section turns to the analysis of the first two components concerning the choice between merger and contract in achieving efficiencies, and the applications in section C will variously consider all of the pieces of the requisite analysis.

A variety of literatures are related to the theory of the firm, specifically concerning when and why it may be advantageous to bring groups of individuals, activities, and assets together in a single firm rather than to rely on contractual relationships between firms. These literatures vary in their degree of formal development, domain of application, and extent of empirical validation. And, as just noted, this body of work has not been employed in the analysis of efficiencies in horizontal mergers. What follows is a preliminary, selective sketch of some core ideas that will emerge in the applications that follow.[10]

Coase (1937) is most responsible for placing the subject on economists' map, although it was not much explored for decades thereafter. Later in the century, the study of organizations grew (March and Simon 1958; see also, e.g., Simon 1991), contributing to the emergence of organizational economics as a field of study (Gibbons and Roberts 2013). Some research emphasizes the employment relationship, a subject also extensively studied in labor economics, aspects of which are relevant to the current inquiry. Much focuses on employees' incentives, that is, the familiar moral hazard (principal-agent) problem. However, in a vacuum it is unclear how the available approaches differ when contracts are moved inside a firm. Consider, for example, the problematic distinction between independent contractors and employees.

Many subsequent branches of the literature focus on particular economic problems that the firm is sometimes considered to solve. One concerns the provision of high quality at low cost. An independent supplier would like to minimize effort while still selling its goods at the highest possible price, but it needs to convince buyers to purchase them. Buyers, in turn, may have limited information about quality. As a result, they may rely on reputation and repeat

---

10. The discussion here focuses on transaction cost economics (associated with Williamson) and property rights theory (associated with Hart and coauthors), but there are other branches as well (Gibbons 2005; Holmstrom 1999; Holmstrom and Roberts 1998).

dealings, hire their own inspectors, and so forth. But they may instead choose to produce the input internally, perhaps in a division devoted to that task. However, the manager and workers in that division present similar challenges. If the manager is given high-powered incentives linked to that division's performance and has substantial control over those workers, the division may operate much like an independent firm, with all the benefits and limitations that entails. Lower-powered incentives would lessen the motivation to cut quality but would also reduce effort overall, including to contain costs. The results would be akin to what transpires when procuring inputs from outsiders under cost-plus contracts. Relatedly, some techniques used to motivate and monitor workers inside the firm have contractual analogues.

A canonical setting addressed in modern work on the theory of the firm concerns the hold-up problem (Klein, Crawford, and Alchian 1978). A firm contemplating a relationship-specific investment appreciates that, once its investment is sunk, a counterparty may extract much of the ex post surplus. Anticipation of this outcome leads the firm to invest too little. An ex ante contract may solve this problem but can be fully effective only if complete contingent contracts are feasible, which in turn requires not only anticipating and documenting myriad possibilities but also achieving sufficient verifiability to enable enforcement. Ex post renegotiation, if effective (notably, in the absence of asymmetric information), addresses only ex post inefficiencies. It does not avoid the original hold-up problem, and its prospect may undermine the credibility of otherwise useful contractual commitments designed to address it.

In approaching such problems, Williamson (1975), seen as launching transaction cost economics, advanced as the central difference between contracts and firms the distinction between *Markets and Hierarchies*, the title of his book.[11] The marketplace is taken to entail one amalgam of attributes: high-powered incentives, specified obligations, and formal adjudication of disagreements through the legal system. By contrast, firms are taken to employ a different package of properties: low-powered incentives, discretionary authority, and their own informal systems of dispute resolution. These differences are regarded not as independent choices but rather as constituting complementary bundles. For example, one cannot give a manager high-powered

---

11. Also of particular relevance is Williamson (1985, ch. 6). See also Williamson (2002) as well as Simon (1991) and Holmstrom and Milgrom (1994).

incentives, say to incur up-front costs in order to secure a large future return, but leave to another administrator the discretion to take away the rewards when they materialize, which that administrator may well have an incentive to do.[12]

Williamson (1975) suggests that this distinctive cluster of features characterizing internal relations within a firm has a comparative advantage over the market (contracts) in some but not other settings, explaining why the former activities are efficiently brought within firms while the others are better left to the market with its high-powered incentives. For example, he suggests that more rapid adaptation is possible inside the firm.[13] More broadly, activities requiring a variety of subtle forms of coordination and interaction might best be conducted in such an environment.[14]

To suggest an analogy, individuals in a small village may be able to cooperate well due to myriad forms of informal social sanctions guided by rich, subtle information flows, norms, and overlapping relationships. Those who misbehave risk becoming outcasts, and separation from the village leaves

---

12. A primary motivation was to address Coase's question about why it would not be efficient for the economy to be one large firm. Williamson further pushed this point by raising the possibility of selective intervention. Combining these ideas, we can ask why otherwise separate firms cannot be operated as separate units in a single firm—each an independent profit center—thereby preserving incentives, while having a higher manager resolve conflicts, internalize inter-unit externalities, and so forth. Williamson (1985) emphasized that such a supreme manager, even if perfectly informed and motivated to maximize the firm's overall profits, would have incentives to act in ways that, being anticipated, would undermine the incentives of the unit managers.
13. The reasons for some of Williamson's conclusions are unclear. Although those with low-powered incentives may have less to lose by giving up their old ways, they also have less to gain from exerting the requisite effort. Indeed, many suggest that an important reason that major economic change often comes from new, disruptive firms rather than experienced, knowledgeable, and well-endowed incumbents is that large firms are less flexible and nimble than are small, independent, highly incentivized market actors.
14. Although this view is in accord with conventional wisdom, it is hardly obvious how the mechanisms operate and when they have the desired properties, a point reinforced by the example to follow in the text. Indeed, Hart (2009) and other work on "reference points" (including Hart and Moore 2008) suggest that frictions may be greatest when much is left fuzzy and open ended rather than fixed formally by contract because the former makes it more likely that one party will feel aggrieved by the other's actions and thus be induced to behave less cooperatively.

much behind, just as a long-term employee forced to leave a firm may lose both firm-specific human capital and, relatedly, an established internal reputation that may take significant time to reproduce elsewhere. Even basic knowledge of the employee's innate productivity may take a new employer significant time to learn, so starting afresh can cause a significant drop in one's wage. In part for that reason, activity inside firms generates its own hold-up problems. Indeed, it is familiar that small villages are also associated with exploitation and stultification, which is one of the reasons that, in modern societies, arms-length contracts and formal legal enforcement often prove to be superior. Williamson's point, however, was not that firms are generically or even usually superior, but rather that they are better than markets in handling an important subset of activities, which in turn define the efficient boundaries of the firm.

In light of the earlier analysis in this section, some puzzles remain. The foregoing depiction emphasizes repeated interaction and associated reputational effects, yet these phenomena are hardly distinctive to firms. They are more often discussed in otherwise decentralized marketplace settings with respect to contracting behavior, so it is unclear the extent to which the two supposedly distinct ways to organize activities differ in this regard. This angle is explored in Baker, Gibbons, and Murphy (2002), Garvey (1995), and Halonen (2002). Another problem, alluded to previously, is that the package of traits Williamson associates with firms is sometimes employed in outsourced contractual relationships and the amalgam he associates with contracts in the market is sometimes employed inside firms. Hence, even though it may often be important to match the right clusters of characteristics to pertinent types of activities, it is unclear the extent to which this informs the suitability of bringing those activities inside of firms rather than using contracts. Recall as well the corollary that the features necessary to achieve certain efficiencies may also generate anticompetitive effects, and this is so even when those features are embedded in contracts between distinct firms. This point serves as a reminder of the need to focus on substance rather than legal form when analyzing merger efficiencies, as well as contracts that may be scrutinized under other antitrust provisions.

Consider next the property rights theory of the firm advanced in Grossman and Hart (1986) and Hart and Moore (1990) and reflected on in Hart (2017). This theory focuses on ex ante investment incentives in determining who should own which assets.[15] Importantly, owners are understood as having the residual right to determine how their assets are deployed in situations that are left open in the pertinent contract—an important set of circumstances in light of the inevitable incompleteness of contracts. Suppose that there are two assets, A and B. The choice between separate and unified ownership involves a trade-off. On one hand, separate ownership in some settings heightens the incentive to develop each asset, maximizing stand-alone values. However, if there are benefits to coordination and associated relationship-specific investments, the hold-up problem suggests that the owner of asset A will not develop this asset in the manner that is most useful when combined with asset B—and conversely. Hence, joint ownership (merger) ex ante would be optimal when that incentive consideration was dominant.

Property rights theory, as in this example, focuses on the ownership of physical (or other nonhuman) assets. But, with some extension or formal departure from the theory and, in respects, combination with other theories, one can attempt to consider workers as well (Hart 2017). For example, suppose that there are two teams of workers, each of which has relationships that make it more effective than the stand-alone marginal products of the individual team members. Putting these two teams under a common boss may better coordinate their efforts but also partly undermine within-group cohesion and thus productivity.

A challenge in applying property rights theories and other theories of the firm is that it tends to be difficult to determine when unified ownership is optimal and, when it is, the size of the net efficiency gain from that arrangement compared to the most effective, albeit inferior, contractual alternative (Holmstrom 1999; Whinston 2003). Recall that we also wish to know the extent to which the contractual alternative likewise may result in some of the same anticompetitive effects as would arise under the proposed merger. After all, these literatures examine efficiency from the perspective of the firms in question (that is, they focus on firms' profits), implicitly setting aside externalities, here, negative ones in the guise of anticompetitive effects.

---

15. The theory abstracts from ex post contracting inefficiencies that may be important in understanding the internal workings of large firms (Hart 2011).

Before moving to applications, let us return to the question of why this body of work has not been drawn upon to analyze efficiencies in horizontal mergers. One reason may be that, on their face, these theories seem most relevant to vertical contracting and integration, not horizontal arrangements.[16] Motivating examples—like a power plant locating next to a coal mine or the Fisher Body case—and related models often involve supply or distribution relationships.[17] The property rights theory of the firm analyzes investments in assets that are complements; with substitutes, the theory suggests that combination is inefficient due to the diminution of incentives (Hart 1995).

Upon reflection, however, many horizontal merger synergies are vertical in nature or at least analogous, so many of the teachings are applicable after all. The concept of a vertical relationship is more of a metaphor (or a convention in creating blackboard or PowerPoint diagrams) than an analytical construct. Most synergies involve complementarities among assets (broadly construed), and it is familiar that complementarity and verticality have much in common.[18] For example, the problem of double marginalization most often associated with vertical contracting is understood to be an instance of contractual inefficiency with Cournot complements.

The applications in section C will show how most synergies associated with horizontal mergers involve the combination of complementary assets. For example, mergers that realize economies of scope typically involve the use of some capability, say A, of firm 1—which is already employed internally to enhance the performance of some other asset (or collection of assets) of type B—being extended to improve the performance of the B asset(s) of firm 2, which is deficient with respect to capability A. Perhaps firm 1 is distinctively skilled at marketing certain types of consumer goods that are also produced but marketed poorly by firm 2. Or firm 1 is skilled

---

16. This is also true of explanations relating to economies of scope, such as those involved with the transfer of intangibles across units of a firm (Atalay, Hortaçsu, and Syverson 2014).

17. Also of note, featured examples typically involve mining, manufacturing, and related activities, but these sectors collectively have long been a modest and shrinking share of developed economies. Today it would seem that IP and know-how are more often the locus of potential efficiencies and related contracting challenges.

18. Interestingly, the dictionary definition of synergy, the most commonly used term for merger-specific efficiencies, is close to economists' definition of complements, and common dictionary examples include vertical relationships in business.

at logistics, or working with suppliers, or using IT in sophisticated ways, or devising and deploying process innovations in manufacturing, relative to firm 2's proficiency in these domains. To foreshadow another of the applications to follow, it is usually thought that firms do not need to merge to achieve economies of scale made possible by new technology because they can instead grow internally. However, if these are not stick-figure firms but rather firms with employee teams, supplier and customer relationships, and so forth, the independently expanding firm may need to internally replicate those vertically related features at an additional cost, while the other, exiting firm may possess just these industry-specific, complementary assets, which would be wasted if they could not be transferred to the remaining firms that expand. In this case, the synergy from combining firms arises from the complementary, vertically related features rather than with respect to the core asset subject to scale economies.

Arguably, most types of efficiencies in horizontal mergers are vertical in character.[19] Complex contracts designed to coordinate economic activities that might better be conducted inside a single firm typically involve complementary activities and assets rather than identical ones. When horizontal mergers involve two firms that do not each consist solely of the same type of stand-alone asset, there will be vertical elements, and when those features are entangled with the purely horizontal ones, as they often are (which is why they are already conducted within at least one of the merging firms), there may be vertical efficiencies from horizontal integration.

C. Applications

1. Economies of Scale

Economies of scale are the most familiar type of merger efficiency and one not generally regarded as merger specific because scale economies are

---

19. A further implication, beyond the scope of this chapter, is that horizontal mergers accordingly may also involve some of the anticompetitive effects associated with vertical mergers, such as raising barriers to entry. Another key lesson challenges standard modern analysis of the potential anticompetitive effects and efficiencies associated with vertical mergers that focuses on raising rivals' costs and eliminating double marginalization. These analyses largely ignore the central teachings of the theory of the firm that were developed precisely to illuminate vertical integration.

thought to be achievable by internal growth (Williamson 1968; U.S. Merger Guidelines 1968; Farrell and Shapiro 2001). Under this view, merger-specific scale economies would only be those associated with any speed or rationalization differential. Why there might exist such a differential—or, indeed, why it might be positive rather than negative (perhaps internal growth would be more orderly than a merger)—is not obvious. Similar analysis can be applied to industry consolidation, such as when there is declining demand. Absent a merger, some assets will eventually exit the industry regardless; an efficiency in this setting will only be merger specific to the extent that the merger somehow achieves this inevitable transition more effectively.

The foregoing understanding may often lead to the right conclusion, but the underlying logic is incomplete and the concept of scale economies is underdeveloped. Let us begin with some terminology. Farrell and Shapiro (2001) usefully distinguish between the choice of a different quantity under a given production function and changes in the production function itself. If costs are lower when $2X$ is produced in a single plant than when X is produced in each of two (say, smaller) plants, there are what I will call pure economies of scale. Pipelines' capacity is related to the diameter squared, but construction cost is related to the diameter—a cost difference that may be greatly magnified if two smaller pipelines would each need to be buried separately. Importantly, such examples suppose that the plants or pipelines constitute the entirety of the firms in question, a point to which we will return shortly.

Independent firms, whether entrants or incumbents, ordinarily find it profitable to operate at an efficient scale even if no mergers are allowed. If new technology, say, doubles the optimal scale of new plants, then preexisting, independent, single-plant firms would either replace their old plants with new ones of the larger scale or exit (assuming constant demand). If all were that simple, it is not clear how firms pairing off and merging would either accelerate or retard that process. Nor is acceleration beneficial per se: it may well be optimal to continue existing plants' operation for some period if achieving the new scale economies entails fixed costs. Moreover, both independent firms and a merged entity would tend to do just that, so neither would be speedier in making the transition.

This familiar story, however, omits that anticompetitive effects would also tend to be generated—to the same degree and with the same speed—if the firms were not allowed to merge. Whether ten small firms pair off and merge or instead one of each pair exits while the other doubles in size, the market is left with five larger firms. Therefore, any anticompetitive effects from ending up with five firms rather than ten are not merger specific. In the simplest case, these contemplated mergers would be a matter of indifference, to the firms' owners and to consumers, because both costs and competitive interactions would be the same whether the mergers are permitted or instead the economies of scale are achieved through a mix of internal growth by some and exit by others.

Such mergers may nevertheless be undesirable on account of uncertainty and an implicit real option provided by the market when such mergers are disallowed. This idea may be related to the standard but usually fuzzy argument that internal growth is preferable to a merger because it is best if the firms compete for the market by remaining independent and fighting it out. Perhaps independent firms' decision-makers more intelligently adapt, or perhaps the most overly optimistic managers will reign over merged entities whereas survival of the fittest in a world with no mergers will entail more efficient selection. Or perhaps these pairings should be reversed as hubristic or empire-building managers of independent firms jump the gun, expand too early, and thereby induce better-managed firms to exit.

A more powerful reason to block such mergers may be grounded in the uncertainty that often shrouds the analysis of efficiencies because competition agencies usually know less than do firms' managers. Suppose that an agency believes that a merger would generate anticompetitive effects that are exceeded in expectation by large but uncertain scale economies. Allowing such a merger may nevertheless be a mistake, which we can see by examining the simple decision tree for this problem.

On one branch, if the economies are truly present and substantial, they will be achieved even if the merger is blocked. To be sure, the anticompetitive effects will also materialize. But, in the simple case described above, society is no worse off for blocking the merger even though the efficiencies exceed the anticompetitive effects. On the other branch, if the scale economies would not actually materialize, then blocking the merger matters and will enhance welfare. In this case, the anticompetitive effects would materialize only if the merger were allowed whereas the scale economies would not be achieved regardless. As long there is a nontrivial probability of the latter set of outcomes, blocking the merger is optimal. Accordingly, one should not naively compute the expected anticompetitive effects and expected efficiencies from the merger. Put another way, with some probability the anticompetitive effects are merger specific, but, under the stated assumption, the efficiencies never are. Market actors exercise the real option of expansion and exit, resulting in an increase in concentration, only when the efficiencies actually are present. Focusing on the nexus between anticompetitive effects and efficiencies helpfully recasts conventional wisdom about economies of scale.

Consider next how some of the theoretical work on firms and contracts contributes to our understanding of scale economies. A key limitation of the standard view and the discussion thus far is that pure economies of scale are a special, extreme case. Mergers rarely involve firms that constitute single plants (or pipelines) but rather multiple ones and/or clusters of related activities. Indeed, even a single plant typically involves myriad activities. Consider a hospital. Or a retail store that carries 10,000 SKUs. Even a firm with a single plant that performs a unitary function typically employs many types of workers (who must be hired, trained, and provided with benefits), needs to obtain all manner of supplies through sometimes complex arrangements, requires financing, engages in marketing and distribution, and establishes ways of doing business that motivate workers, comfort contracting partners, and reassure customers. Many proposed mergers that require substantial analysis by agencies involve entities that are vastly more complex than the stick-figure firms imagined in the foregoing analysis of pure economies of scale. Note in particular that the pertinent activities are complementary, say, to a firm's plant and, correspondingly, are often vertically related. Accordingly, even though the competitive threat is horizontal, the efficiencies may be primarily vertical.

Note first that there are efficiency-related reasons for these various functions to be undertaken in a single firm rather than each firm outsourcing every task and having each worker be an independent contractor.[20] This idea is advanced in some branches of the literature on the theory of the firm and is central to explaining why nontrivial firms exist in the first place and often demonstrate substantial marketplace superiority to their less

---

20. In light of the discussion in section B, the statement in the text should be taken as a shorthand. If the activities are not undertaken in a single firm, the set of contracts would resemble what is often associated with a single firm, so the contractual alternative would differ very little if at all.

complicated rivals. More important for present purposes, because of the myriad complementary assets and activities, economies of scale limited to a single plant or activity cannot usually be realized in isolation. The plant and the rest of the related activities are not modular but interdependent. As a consequence, mergers purportedly motivated by seemingly simple scale economies in a particular production function may not be so simple to analyze.

To see this, let us revisit the example of technological change that doubles the optimal scale of plants, while continuing to assume that demand remains constant. If some particular firm replaces its plant with one twice the scale and another firm exits, we should inquire into the fate of the complementary assets of the latter firm as well as how the former firm, once it has a new plant twice the size, will perform the many related functions at the now-larger scale. If all the complements can be obtained on spot markets with no frictions, we are back to the analysis of pure economies of scale. But here we are supposing the contrary. Workers may have specific skills, teams may have long-standing working relationships, and suppliers as well as customers may have long-term contracts and histories. There may be substantial going concern value associated with a firm that transcends its mere physical plant. Hart and Holmstrom (2010, p. 511) note: "It is remarkable how few practitioners, organizational consultants, or researchers studying organizations within disciplines other than economics (e.g., sociology and organizational behavior) ever talk about firms in terms of asset ownership. For most of them a firm is defined by the things it does and the knowledge and capabilities it possesses." Kellogg (2011) finds that the productivity of an oil production company and its drilling contractor increases with their experience in working together. It is even possible that the plant itself (the originally hypothesized locus of economies of scale) is organizationally inconsequential in that it could be rented on the spot market with little sacrifice in efficiency, unlike many of the complementary functions that are conducted inside the firm.

Continuing our story, if the remaining firm that doubles its scale also needs simultaneously to double (or at least substantially expand) everything else, there may be significant costs in doing so. Relatedly, if the exiting firm's assets leave the industry, this involves not merely scrapping its obsolete plant but also scattering into the wind the rest of what was associated with that plant, destroying the value entailed in that assemblage. Here, it may well be efficient for the expanding firm to buy, as a whole, the firm that otherwise would exit. Whether it literally merges (as that term might be defined under some jurisdiction's corporation law) or acquires most or all of the relevant assets intact (perhaps in a bankruptcy sale), including the assumption of contracts and assemblage of workers, the result may largely be the same and in any event generate the efficient outcome.[21]

In this instance, we may therefore have substantial merger-specific efficiencies. Moreover, this example may also be one in which the anticompetitive effects would not be merger specific. Prohibiting the merger or similar asset acquisition may sacrifice the aforementioned efficiencies associated with the complementary activities but not avoid the merger's anticompetitive effects if the same concentration would inevitably arise. The only difference may be that the surviving firms would have higher production costs in the resulting equilibrium because of the forgone efficiencies or the need to undertake additional expenditures to expand than if acquisitions were permitted. Although this too is a special case, its logical structure should be appreciated. Following section A, it emphasizes the relationship between the efficiencies and anticompetitive effects, as well as the question of how a merger versus a well-specified nonmerger alternative affects each of them.

Another lesson can be drawn from a modest variation on this example, which assumed for simplicity that symmetric firms were pairing off. Once the firms are asymmetric, as is typical, there is the further question of which (if any) incumbent firms should be permitted to acquire which no-longer-efficient (and perhaps smaller) firms. Consider a case in which there are no significant differences in the realized efficiencies for two potential acquirers of a particular target firm. The pairing generating smaller anticompetitive effects would be socially preferable, but, ceteris paribus, the more anticompetitive acquirer will be willing to offer the most for the target.

---

21. Furthermore, many analysts fail to realize that most merger regimes cover the bankruptcy sale of assets in the same manner as they cover the ordinary merger. Hence, if the latter is to be prohibited, the same analysis suggests that the former should be blocked as well. (In the United States, Section 7 of the 1914 Clayton Act only applied to acquisitions of stock, giving rise to what was referred to as the "asset acquisition loophole." A major motivation for the 1950 amendments, giving rise to a provision close to the current Section 7, was to plug this loophole by covering acquisitions of assets under precisely the same terms.) Many jurisdictions also have a failing-firm defense, although its application is greatly limited and its rationale is murky.

For a reviewing agency, the relevant and socially preferable alternative to allowing such a merger may not be the target's exit but rather allowing a merger with the less anticompetitive potential acquirer.[22] Accordingly, if that other merger were proposed, the resulting synergies might appropriately be deemed merger specific.

2. Economies of Scope

Another class of possible merger-specific efficiencies involves what are often called economies of scope (Panzar and Willig 1981; Teece 1980).[23] Potential merger synergies may arise when one firm has distinctive capabilities that could be valuable to another firm in the same industry. An acquirer may be particularly good at distribution, where the target is weak (or merely average); or good at marketing, managing supply chains, conducting and implementing process innovation, deploying other technology, or possessing know-how more broadly (Holmstrom and Roberts 1998). Note that, even though the anticompetitive threat of the merger is taken to be horizontal, we again have a case in which the economies in question have a complementary and possibly vertical relationship with the assets that create the anticompetitive threat. Consider when and why such efficiencies may be merger specific.

The most straightforward alternative to merger is the analogue to internal growth in the target firm. Perhaps that firm can just get its act together by hiring better employees, tightening its operations, and so forth, maybe with the aid of consultants. But if everything could so readily be done in a superlative manner, all retailers' supply chains would be as efficient as Walmart's, any tech firm could replicate Apple's products, any delivery firm could effectively compete with FedEx, and any coffee shop could compare favorably to Starbucks. There are often significant and sometimes huge differences in firms' capabilities that laggards and upstarts cannot readily erase. Learning by doing, which may be difficult for others to replicate fully, can contribute to such differences (Varian 2019).

---

22. Analogous considerations may arise with the failing-firm defense.
23. Relatedly, the resource-based view of the firm emphasizes identifying firms' particular strengths vis-à-vis their competitors (Collis and Montgomery 2005; Wernerfelt 1984). Such comparative advantages are suggestive of opportunities to exploit economies of scope through horizontal mergers.

Another alternative is for a target to outsource to a third party the task at which it is comparatively weak, but for related reasons that may often be inferior, particularly with more complex, industry-specific operations. In addition, contractual challenges addressed by the literature on the theory of the firm may limit the efficacy of this approach (as well as the next, as now elaborated; Panzar and Willig 1981).

The target might instead enter a contract with the prospective acquirer itself, in essence purchasing consulting services or other technology from it. The licensing of intellectual property, sometimes from competitors, is commonplace. But such arrangements face the usual agency problems with contracts as well as a distinctive one arising when contracting with competitors. As elaborated in the next subsection, the firm providing the services will suffer competitively the more effective is the assistance that it provides. On the other hand, the better contractual arrangements are in aligning incentives to avoid these problems, the more such arrangements may soften competition. An additional difficulty is that the firm supplying the consulting services or technology may be concerned that the other firm would thereby appropriate its skills, a prospect that may be difficult to limit contractually. Relatedly, asymmetric information, a particular problem with process innovation, may impede contracting because of the valuation difficulty that licensees face unless the licensor first divulges its secrets. As a consequence, the transfer of intangibles across units of a firm may be an important explanation for which activities are thus combined (Atalay, Hortaçsu, and Syverson 2014; Beneish et al. 2022).

Yet another alternative to merger is internal growth by the prospective acquirer. Instead of purchasing the target's assets in order to enhance their value, it could replicate those assets so as to expand on its own. If it is indeed more efficient, it would ultimately displace the target. Many firms such as Walmart have grown primarily through internal expansion rather than acquisition.[24] Forcing internal expansion by blocking such mergers

---

24. It is interesting to contemplate the heterogeneity in strategies across firms and industries. For example, Walmart may add much of its value through its headquarters' operations. Downstream, for retail, it has employed internal expansion and, notably, owns its stores (rather than selling thousands of SKUs to independent retailers or using a franchise model). These choices may reflect economies of scope, a need to control retailers (including to conduct A/B testing that requires common

has the advantage discussed with respect to scale economies of addressing a reviewing agency's uncertainty: the reduction in competition will tend to arise only when the efficiencies prove to be substantial. However, as we also saw with economies of scale, when there are important, complementary, industry- and firm-specific assets possessed by the target, this alternative to merger may be slower and result in significant losses from disbanding teams and dissolving other relationships that generated significant going concern value for the target. In addition, comparative advantage may run in both directions, such that the acquirer in our illustration may not be as good as the target at creating the target's assets. Indeed, targets may be acquired precisely because they possess important capabilities that the acquirer has been unable to replicate internally. Furthermore, to the extent that internal expansion is ultimately successful, it may entail anticompetitive effects similar to those associated with the proposed merger, in which case blocking the merger would sacrifice merger-specific efficiencies while the non-merger-specific anticompetitive effects would materialize anyhow.

When most of these reasons apply to a sufficient extent, the ability to achieve the economies of scope—while simultaneously avoiding most of the anticompetitive effects feared from the merger—may be significantly limited. For such efficiencies actually to arise, it must also be true that the merger itself would achieve these benefits, which has been taken for granted until now. That is, bringing the arrangement inside the firm has to solve the contracting problems to a sufficient degree for the economies to be realized. The literature on the theory of the firm reminds us that difficulties with contracting do not vanish, as if by magic, when activities are brought inside

---

formats or to prevent leakage of its expertise), and few industry-specific assets (which may otherwise have made acquisitions attractive). Upstream, where it may also have substantial specialized know-how, it generally contracts with independent suppliers, although when doing so its contractual relationships sometimes involve substantial governance (from Walmart to the suppliers) that may be directly concerned with the conduct of activities inside the supplier firms. This difference (particularly the failure to develop supply internally or to acquire suppliers) may reflect the heterogeneity of suppliers, economies of scope that are limited in domain, and suppliers optimally selling to (different types of) third parties. By contrast, large pharmaceutical firms often conduct innovation internally while also acquiring firms with promising innovations rather than contracting with them, which may be motivated by economies of scope in testing, regulatory approval, and marketing, but more heterogeneous abilities regarding initial innovation.

a single firm. It is also familiar that synergies that actually motivate mergers (many of which do not pose any anticompetitive threat) often do not materialize, whether because unified ownership cannot solve the underlying problems or because it creates others that were not adequately anticipated.

3. Sharing Assets between Competitors

Consider further the case in which proffered efficiencies involve the sharing of assets between the merging parties—perhaps each could use the other's plant to supply nearby customers—where the merger-specificity question is whether the gains could instead be achieved by contracts between the parties, who are competitors. Such arrangements raise anticompetitive concerns as well as a particular type of incentive problem that may be challenging for the parties to address, which in turn may suggest that efficiencies of this sort sometimes should be regarded as merger specific.

Suppose that we have a symmetric setting with ten firms. Each produces a different variety of a product in a single plant located in a different region. The technology is such that a plant can readily produce enough quantity of each variety for that region or of a single variety for the entire country, and it would be expensive to construct a second plant in a region. In the initial equilibrium, each variety is shipped to and consumed in every other region despite nontrivial transportation costs.[25] Should a merger between two (or more) of these firms be permitted?

Setting aside any alternatives to merger, we can compare the anticompetitive effects with the efficiencies resulting from saved transportation costs, assuming that the merged firms would produce their varieties at the plants nearest to that variety's consumers. Suppose further that the efficiency gain is sufficient to render the merger permissible (otherwise the merger should be blocked regardless). If, for example, a consumer welfare standard governs, this assumption entails that the marginal cost reduction from saved transportation costs is sufficient to result in prices that are the same or lower after the merger.

---

25. It is also interesting to consider an initial equilibrium in which transportation costs are prohibitively high, characterized by local monopolies of a single variety. Mergers would not sacrifice existing competition, but we could still ask whether contractual alternatives (among those that meet firms' rationality constraints) might be superior, particularly in light of potential competition from firms in other regions.

Our question now is whether this efficiency savings is merger specific, which sometimes seems to be taken for granted in existing discussions of analogous cases (U.S. Merger Guidelines 2010, p. 31). The relevant alternative is a contract between the proposed merger partners in which each agrees to produce the other's product in sufficient quantities at its own plant for sale locally. Such an arrangement saves the transportation costs without the firms having to merge. Nor is this possibility far-fetched: firms often license their patented technology to other firms in different regions (particularly different countries) for local production.[26]

Consider first the possible incentive problems that may accompany such a contractual arrangement. Each firm would naturally worry about the effort exerted by the other firm in producing its product (or performing ancillary activities, such as marketing and distribution). This is the standard agency problem, the severity of which would depend on the ability to monitor, to enforce contractual provisions (which may be unavoidably incomplete), to provide explicit financial incentives (on which more in a moment), and to rely on repeat business to generate incentives. We have a familiar outsourcing decision that is sometimes best made by keeping activities inside a single firm.

In contracting with a competitor, each firm faces the further problem that its contracting partner has an affirmative incentive to underperform. Reduced sales of the outsider's variety (say, due to poorer customer satisfaction with lower-quality output) redound in part to the benefit of the producer firm in selling its own variety. This enhanced agency problem may be potentially addressed in familiar ways, notably, with stronger contractual incentives, such as forms of profit sharing (including royalties and the allocation of regional price-setting authority).

Second, consider such arrangements' anticompetitive effects. Even without regard to the serious agency problems, the parties would wish to structure the incentives and decision-making in a manner that minimizes competition, internalizing the business-stealing externality between the contracting parties. If the operator of each plant, for example, charged the other firm not only its marginal cost per unit but also an increment

---

26. Another alternative—really a different industry structure—would entail vertical separation between the ownership of each of the varieties and of each of the plants, a configuration presenting its own agency challenges and competitive concerns.

reflecting the profit-maximizing price-cost margin on local sales (with the resulting surplus shared lump sum), then competitive pressure between the two firms would be averted, just as in a merger. If some sort of cross-production contract were to be permitted short of merger, therefore, a competition authority would need to scrutinize its terms—which may be challenging because it would involve regulation of interfirm pricing (and possibly more) and in any event may not be undertaken.[27]

Note further that the pricing arrangement that maximizes the firms' self-interest with regard to competition between them is also one that, as a first cut, may best address the agency problems. This should not be surprising because, regarding both agency concerns and competition, joint profit maximization entails shared interests: equal weight on a firm's own profits and those of its contracting partner. This, in turn, is just what a merger is ordinarily understood to produce. Hence, an unregulated contractual alternative may be equivalent to a merger regarding both efficiencies and anticompetitive effects. Neither would be merger specific, so the merger would be a matter of indifference.

There are further (now familiar) considerations as well. Incentives short of full internalization or other contractual provisions might solve much of the agency problems without generating most of the anticompetitive effect, in which case such a contractual alternative may be preferable, although

---

27. The regulation would naturally be associated, for example, with Section 1 of the Sherman Act or Article 101 of the TFEU. One might in principle suppose that each is applied to weigh anticompetitive effects and efficiencies in the same manner as would be done under the jurisdiction's merger regulation, although as a legal or practical matter this may not be so. For example, if the contractual alternative would be prohibited under a competition-protecting prophylactic rule, then the alternative is not in fact available, so the efficiencies might then be deemed merger specific and hence sufficient to justify the merger if they are sufficiently large. If assessed under a rule of reason, the permissibility of the contractual alternative may depend on the sorts of details addressed in the text, which would involve complex assessment and perhaps ongoing oversight. Interestingly, structural merger remedies—such as prohibition—are often favored over behavioral remedies—requiring ongoing oversight of the merged entity—precisely because of the difficulties of the latter. However, if prohibition is understood to be associated with the firms entering into a complex contractual arrangement that is quite similar to what might arise inside the merged firm, these oversight challenges would not thereby be avoided, that is, unless little if any oversight would be provided for the contractual alternative.

Efficiencies 107

ensuring that it is employed may require regulatory oversight. Also, just how is it that a merger avoids the agency problems in any event? That is, how is a firm able provide the right incentives for each plant manager (who requires incentives to minimize cost and maintain quality) and each variety manager (who requires incentives to innovate and to market the product), particularly if we are supposing—as would be necessary for the efficiencies to be merger specific—that this may be infeasible when attempted through contracts between separate entities?

We can see that the general analytical framework developed here significantly illuminates merger analysis with respect to the sharing of assets between competing firms that seek to combine into a single firm. However, as has been the case throughout, it will often be difficult for an agency (and even the firms themselves) to confidently assess the relevant factors.

Before leaving this application, it is useful to note that the structure of this problem is similar to that in some other antitrust settings, such as with the cross-licensing of patents. Under some parameters, we may have a natural monopoly. If variety is quite valuable, transportation costs are prohibitive, and the agency problems of contracting outside the firm are great, the best industry structure may be a single firm operating all the plants and controlling all the varieties. But if transportation costs are very low, intense competition may function well without contracts between competitors and with no horizontal mergers. The harder cases are those that fall somewhere in between.

D. Integrated Assessment of Efficiencies and Anticompetitive Effects

Merger analysis is to varying degrees characterized by a sequentially siloed approach: anticompetitive effects are considered first; if they are insubstantial, the merger is allowed, and if they are substantial, the analysis turns to efficiencies. It is usually said that most mergers are allowed without ever reaching the question of efficiencies, but when anticompetitive effects are established, efficiencies rarely if ever are found to be sufficient to permit the merger.[28] Taken at face value, efficiencies are infrequently analyzed and

---

28. Tellingly, the U.S. Merger Guidelines (2010, p. 30) relegate efficiencies to a late, modest section, and the key points are introduced in the following language of

virtually never decisive, even though their presumed widespread presence is the most plausible justification for insisting on substantial anticompetitive effects and ultimately allowing most horizontal mergers. As mentioned at the outset of this chapter, no plausible joint distribution of efficiencies and anticompetitive effects can rationalize this state of affairs.

This section explains why this formulation is conceptually and practically deficient—and it would appear that, at least within competition agencies, efficiencies often receive more attention.[29] Because academic literature, merger guidelines, and court opinions offer incomplete and misleading presentations of the proper approach, it is useful to sketch some of the key elements and then return to common depictions of existing practice.[30]

Merger decision-making involves a balancing of anticompetitive effects and efficiencies, although the particular formulation depends on whether the standard is consumer or total welfare. As section 2.A explains, it makes little sense in determining which way a balance tips to zoom in on one side of the scale (chosen a priori), with the other shielded from view. Whether at an early screening stage in an agency or at various subsequent points, one obviously should consider both sides. Importantly, if efficiencies in a given merger seem unlikely to be significant, the anticompetitive effects required to justify blocking the deal should be lower, and conversely if efficiencies seem likely to be large. In addition, at least in the United States, merging parties' initial proffers often emphasize the business case for the proposed merger and hence provide a starting point for the consideration of

---

skepticism: "The Agencies credit only those efficiencies . . ." "Efficiencies are difficult to verify and quantify . . ." "Efficiency claims will not be considered if . . ." The U.S. Merger Guidelines (2023) further downgrade the relevance of efficiencies and express similar skepticism.

29. U.S. courts purport to adopt this analytical rubric formally, although it is unclear the extent to which it affects practice. Having discussed the matter with economists and lawyers currently at the U.S. competition agencies, formerly having senior positions in them, and in private practice, I have heard a diversity of opinions, including confident yet opposite depictions by experienced individuals, suggesting to me that actual practice is often somewhere in between and perhaps varies greatly depending on the particular teams and nature of the case. See Kaplow (2021a) for further discussion. Deferring or never reaching the consideration of efficiencies is regarded to be more common in the European Union than in the United States.

30. The analysis in this section is developed in greater depth in Kaplow (2019, 2021a).

efficiencies, including the possibility of provisionally rejecting them when they are patently weak or seem to be pretextual.[31]

Even if all information fell into natural clumps that concerned only anticompetitive effects or only efficiencies (which they do not) and, moreover, could be analyzed in a vacuum (which they cannot), sequential siloing would make no sense. Optimal information collection proceeds sequentially, prioritizing information with the highest diagnosticity-to-cost ratio and adjusting such estimates about as-yet uncollected information as one proceeds. At any given point, the best next piece of information to collect could concern either anticompetitive effects or efficiencies, and alternation would be common. Diminishing returns with respect to either issue reinforce how unsound it would be to leave no stone unturned on anticompetitive effects before moving to efficiencies, or vice versa.

Furthermore, anticompetitive effects and efficiencies have many conceptual linkages. As explained in section 2.C, the merging parties' rationality constraint suggests that the sum of the effects on profits from the two sources needs to be positive, so any information influencing our estimate of one of the two necessarily shifts the conditional distribution of the other. Moreover, as explained there, we can consider an odds ratio formulation of Bayesian updating, wherein the odds ratio of one's priors is multiplied by the likelihood ratio to yield the odds ratio of the posteriors. The likelihood ratio is the probability of observing the pertinent set of additional information given the truth of one hypothesis—say, that anticompetitive effects motivate the merger—divided by the probability given the truth of the other—efficiencies. But it is impossible to compute a ratio without the denominator.[32] This is another way of saying that merger analysis involves triangulation, considering how incremental information bears on what is ultimately a single distribution of a proposed merger's expected effects.

There are also more specific connections between anticompetitive effects and efficiencies in merger analysis. Indeed, much of this chapter has addressed one of them: the nexus between the two, as it relates to the central

---

31. Agencies should insist on such proffers in any event, for this very reason, among others.

32. Hence, even a decision-maker who gives no weight to efficiencies, confining attention entirely to the existence of sufficient anticompetitive effects, must, as a matter of basic logic, integrate the analysis of efficiencies rather than ignoring them or back-loading their consideration.

question of merger specificity. Others emerge once the analysis of a merger becomes more concrete. For example, information on firms' cost functions is obviously relevant to both efficiencies and demand estimation, to understanding competitive interactions, and to other central determinants of anticompetitive effects (as well as to entry, considered in chapter 5).

We can also identify overlaps at a more granular level. Much information collection and analysis concerns basic understandings of an industry, which underlie analysis of both issues. Many pieces of information—from witness interviews and depositions to the merging parties' internal documents—will pertain to both. For example, documents may be examined to ascertain the parties' apparent motives in undertaking the merger, which in turn bear on the merger's likely effects. When such documents are ambiguous or their context is contested, it is necessary to bear in mind both anticompetitive effects and efficiencies. After all, an ambiguity can exist only if there are (at least) two interpretations, and it is incoherent to attempt to resolve an ambiguity with only one possibility in mind.

Taken together, these considerations render many statements of the place of efficiencies in merger analysis incoherent, impractical, and in certain respects unlikely to provide an accurate account of what agencies actually do. Nevertheless, it is often suggested that something akin to the sequentially siloed version of merger analysis does and should prevail.

In more recent parlance, this approach is sometimes expressed as involving the use of an "efficiency credit." This apparatus begins by recognizing that efficiencies are often present but, unfortunately, are difficult to scrutinize in a given case. Accordingly, in each proposed merger, it might be stipulated (credited) that an efficiency of some magnitude E^* will arise. As a consequence, anticompetitive effects must exceed E^* for a merger to be challenged. It so happens that such demonstrations are infrequent, explaining why so few mergers are challenged. Moreover, in those cases in which this hurdle is overcome, it happens to be rare for the parties to demonstrate actual efficiencies above E^*. The latter is true for two reasons: Because E^* has already been credited, only extraordinary efficiencies (above E^*) would suffice. And because efficiencies are difficult to assess, it is rare that such high efficiencies could convincingly be established even when they are present.

However descriptively accurate this formulation may be, it is highly problematic for all the reasons presented in this section. It is incoherent

Efficiencies

to assess anticompetitive effects in a vacuum, much evidence and analysis is directly relevant to both anticompetitive effects and efficiencies in any event, and it makes no sense in determining which way a scale tips to focus on one side while ignoring the other. And just assuming that the other side has a particular weight without even taking a peek does not eliminate the incoherence of the sequentially siloed approach.

This last point has particular relevance to the specification of the efficiency credit. Just how high is E^* in the first place?[33] Note that the rationale—that efficiencies are difficult to scrutinize in each case—suggests a one-size-fits-all credit, but such would obviously be much too high in some settings and far too low in others. The obvious alternative is to set the credit, at least crudely, case by case (or by industry, type of merger, and type of efficiency claimed). But then one is scrutinizing to some degree the efficiencies in the case under review. The real question, then, is not whether but how much to do so, in what order, and in what combination with the assessment of anticompetitive effects. At this point, one is analyzing efficiencies and anticompetitive effects as best one can.[34] Of course, if it is harder to obtain and analyze evidence on efficiencies than on anticompetitive effects (to the extent that the two are separable), optimal information collection, guided by consideration of the diagnosticity-to-cost ratio, will reflect that in any event.

Setting aside the level of generality with which the credit is set, it is also unclear how high E^* is taken to be. The foregoing depiction of the operation of the efficiency credit suggests that it is implicitly set quite high, for it is difficult to establish that anticompetitive effects are greater (despite the ubiquity of upward pricing pressure with horizontal mergers) and even harder to show that actual efficiencies ever exceed the credit. But why does that make sense? (For those who regard merger enforcement as having been

---

33. Some analysts posit, for example, 5% of price or sales revenue, but that is mostly for ease of exposition rather than as an empirically based optimal level.

34. A closely related point noted in section 2.A and elaborated in section 6.A concerns the difficulty of distinguishing prior probabilities (requiring case-specific analysis to determine which priors to employ) and their updating via likelihood ratios (requiring an understanding, from prior knowledge, of the likelihood of observing various signals conditional on different hypotheses). In a similar spirit, how often would it make sense to engage in substantial information collection and analysis concerning which prior to invoke, all the while eschewing consideration of evidence bearing on the likely efficiencies in the actual merger under analysis?

too weak in recent decades, might this be the culprit?[35]) Note that if E^* were set at the median of the distribution of efficiencies, it would be exceeded in half the cases, which is quite inconsistent with almost never finding this to be so. Why not set E^* much lower, while perhaps also easing the merging parties' burden of establishing greater efficiencies?

Furthermore, there is an anti-enforcement asymmetry under the efficiency credit as usually conceived: the merging parties are permitted to demonstrate that actual efficiencies exceed E^*, but the government is not allowed to show the opposite in order to lessen its burden on anticompetitive effects. As already noted, when proffered efficiencies seem feeble, anticompetitive effects are much more likely to be present and, perforce, are more likely to exceed efficiencies, so it makes sense to resolve uncertainty toward prohibition in such cases. One might plausibly choose to disallow this consideration of efficiencies only if E^* were set quite low—perhaps more like a de minimis threshold, due to fixed administrative costs of merger assessment—but that is quite different from what seems to be contemplated. Beyond that, an efficiency credit is not part of an optimal merger decision-making framework.

This section criticizes the tendency to delay—often indefinitely—the consideration of efficiencies in the analysis of proposed horizontal mergers. A partial explanation for this practice and an obstacle that needs to be overcome is that expertise at competition agencies involves a mismatch that has been accentuated by increasing specialization in modern economics. Staff economists are typically experts in industrial organization who are adept at modeling competition and performing demand analysis; those with that skill set may well find efficiencies to be inscrutable relative to anticompetitive effects. To some extent, however, this reflects agencies replenishing their staffs with ever-stronger analysts of already familiar subjects, whereas in the economy at large, firms' managers, venture capitalists, private equity partners, stock market analysts, and industry consultants draw on broader and often differing skill sets to assess investments, decide on mergers, and analyze all aspects of firms and industries. As chapter 7 elaborates, it would seem that additional research, more academic interconnection, broader agency hiring, and greater use of industry or context-specific expertise in merger review offer the most promise for enhancing the analysis of merger

---

35. Rose and Sallet (2020) advance this concern.

efficiencies—and of anticompetitive effects as well. An additional foundation for greater attention to efficiencies, of course, is greater development of the relevant analytic framework, which was the subject of sections A–C of this chapter.

E. Efficiencies and the Long Run

Reflecting a consumer welfare standard, many modern merger guidelines state that efficiencies can justify a proposed merger only if they would be sufficiently passed on to consumers so as to negate an otherwise anticompetitive tendency for the merger to raise price. As discussed in chapter 3, actual pass-through analysis, requiring an estimate of the curvature of demand, is not necessary in the basic case because it is sufficient to ask whether variable (marginal) cost savings are sufficient to offset upward pricing pressure from reduced competition, for then the net price effect is neutral or negative. Regardless, the focus is on savings in variable costs, with a concomitant focus on the short run. This approach, moreover, is taken despite the fact that many efficiencies (even those that lower marginal costs) do not ordinarily arise immediately. The motivation is that merger analysis is already difficult and, the further into the future one attempts to predict, the less reliable are the forecasts.

A fundamental shortcoming of this perspective—granting here the consumer welfare emphasis (which is examined in section 8.A)—is that optimal rules should aim to maximize long-run welfare, regardless of the standard. Even if the review of particular mergers requires the use of shortcuts and proxies, they should reflect likely long-run consequences, as best they can be determined over the range of cases.

Our understanding of an imperfectly competitive economy is grounded in equilibrium analysis, which familiarly refers to the long-run equilibrium that reflects not just price and quantity but also entry and exit (examined explicitly in chapter 5) as well as the consequences of investments that are of central importance to the functioning of firms and the economy as a whole. Moreover, there are no true (ex ante, risk-adjusted) profits in such an equilibrium in many standard models with imperfect competition (price equals long-run average cost), so there is no divergence between consumer and total welfare (producer surplus is zero) (Mankiw and Whinston

1986; Ericson and Pakes 1995).[36] Short-run profits associated with positive price-cost margins are quasi-rents that constitute recoveries on prior investments. Relatedly, the distinction between fixed and variable costs dissolves: all costs are variable in the long run. In addition, short-run analysis can be quite misleading, readily having the wrong sign: all investments by nature have negative value if a sufficiently short time frame is adopted.[37] Should an agency prohibit a merger if it thinks that the merged firms would redeploy some assets (raising prices in the activity partially abandoned) in order to innovate in a new area?[38]

Consideration of long-run effects is standard and powerful, guiding economic analysis in many domains. It is, of course, insufficient. Sometimes the long run is quite far off, so the transition path is important and, with a sufficient discount rate, the short run can dominate. Nevertheless, it is hardly clear that ignoring fixed cost savings and, relatedly, all manner of new investment provides a good estimate of the present value of effects on consumer welfare in most settings. Nor is it always easier to undertake short-run analysis, which requires disentangling fixed and variable costs—or, more precisely, estimating, say, over a few years the timing of various savings and disentangling which are variable along the adjustment path. Since the consequence of modestly different timing is all-or-nothing in nature (whether a savings counts or is ignored), some difficult assessments can

---

36. Ex ante heterogeneity among entrepreneurs allows those endowed with greater skill to earn more in expectation (which returns may be viewed as a type of labor income to those individuals), and the integer constraint can enable profits (unless they are dissipated in an ex ante rent-seeking game to obtain the opportunity to be one of the operating firms that earns positive profits).

37. Empirical analysis of merger efficiencies poses related challenges, as discussed in section 6.C. For example, most merger retrospectives examine price effects for only a couple years after a merger due to challenges of identification and data availability. Yet most efficiencies, when they do arise, are understood to be realized later than that, and the handful of retrospectives that indicate efficiency gains that may render the merger beneficial find that they materialize after the standard time frame used in most other studies (Ashenfelter, Hosken, and Weinberg 2014; Sheen 2014).

38. This question also casts doubt on the notion that so-called out-of-market efficiencies should be ignored. Even a single key employee leaving an established firm to launch a startup would, under this view, be regarded as reducing competition in an unjustified manner, and if that employee was joining an existing startup, such a move might even be deemed an anticompetitive merger.

be highly consequential under a short-run approach even when they have little effect on the value of the actual objective function. Nevertheless, it is impractical for competition agencies to conduct full, long-run analyses in routine merger cases. Hence, the main implication is that some sensitivity to this long-run perspective is appropriate in formulating protocols and proxies and should be attended to in particular cases in which long-run effects seem likely to be important. Considerations of ex ante and ex post entry, the subject of the next chapter, may often be within this scope, as are analyses of mergers' effects on innovation.

5 Entry

Entry and exit are central to the operation and welfare properties of a market economy. Entry occurs when prices otherwise generate excessive profits. Entry may enhance variety and innovation, and it also consumes additional resources. Because a horizontal merger reduces the number of firms and, when it is otherwise anticompetitive, increases price, postmerger entry can be consequential even if it is not immediate. Moving earlier in the timeline, the prospect of a buyout is an important form of exit for newer firms, and the expectation of buyout premiums induces premerger entry and investment. Hence, although entry has until recently received only modest attention in merger analysis, it warrants serious investigation.[1]

Section A examines ex post entry: that subsequently induced by a horizontal merger that would otherwise increase price. Conventional analysis, embodied in modern merger guidelines, adopts an ex post perspective on such ex post entry. Specifically, it asks whether postmerger entry would be likely, timely, and sufficient to deter or defeat a price increase (EU Merger Guidelines 2004; U.S. Merger Guidelines 2010,

---

1. This chapter draws on the more extensive treatment in Kaplow (2023b). See also Kaplow (2023a) for a general equilibrium analysis of competition policy with entry and exit that extends the analysis to a multisector setting. Although this chapter examines the role of ex post and ex ante entry in merger analysis, it does not examine how particular features of competitive interaction, cost functions, and other factors bear on anticompetitive effects and the nature of entry (ex post or ex ante) that actually would be induced by particular mergers. Aspects of that analysis relate to long-standing debates about the nature of "barriers" to entry (Schmalensee 1987; Tirole 1988). Many of those issues are reflected in the analysis that follows, but they are not the focus here.

2023).[2] Such analysis does not adequately recognize that, unless entry is unusually speedy, efficient, and possible without incurring fixed costs, it will not typically offset more than a portion of any price increase. Instead, the central reason that easier entry tends to favor permitting a horizontal merger is qualitatively different: because the prospect of postmerger entry reduces the ex post profitability of a merger aiming to increase price, easier entry shifts the proper inferences about the merger's likely anticompetitive effects and efficiencies due to the implications of the merging parties' rationality constraint. In addition, merger analysis usually ignores that any induced, ex post entry has direct welfare effects of its own. These effects can be advantageous or adverse, reflecting that entry decisions are distorted in imperfectly competitive markets. Indeed, ex post entry sometimes makes the overall welfare effect of a horizontal merger worse rather than better, contrary to the normal understanding in merger review.

Section B analyzes ex ante entry: that induced by the prospect of a subsequent buyout premium. In simple settings—with homogeneous goods, a dominant firm, and some other assumptions—the prospect of entry for buyout tends to be inefficient. In such cases, a tough merger policy may raise social welfare by discouraging inefficient entry. More broadly, entry and investment induced by subsequent buyout premiums may contribute to variety, innovation, and merger synergies. At the same time, acquisitions by dominant incumbents may extinguish disruptive threats posed by nascent entrants. A key challenge in the analysis of ex ante entry is that an agency reviewing a subsequent acquisition will naturally be inclined to take the target's existence and capabilities as given, whereas expectations about the permissibility of the merger regime influence ex ante investment incentives that determine whether the upstart would have emerged in the first instance. Both the magnitude and the channeling of such investment may be affected, making it difficult to determine the settings in which more stringent or lenient merger policy is optimal.

---

2. The U.S. Merger Guidelines (2023) are similar to prior guidelines in most respects, but they tack on a final sentence about whether merging parties' entry arguments are consistent with the merger's profitability.

A. Ex Post Entry

Suppose that a proposed horizontal merger would raise prices. Assume further that the price increase, were it to occur, would induce some postmerger entry.[3] That entry would have a number of effects: it would consume resources, possibly introduce further variety or innovation, and mitigate the price increase, thereby transferring some otherwise-arising producer surplus back into consumer surplus and reducing deadweight loss.

Each of these effects is consequential. Mitigation of the price increase—the traditional focus of entry analysis with regard to horizontal mergers—entails a reduction in deadweight loss as well as an increase in consumer surplus (from the no-entry benchmark), rendering the merger less unfavorable under a total or consumer welfare standard.[4] But that is not all. The prospect of a smaller increase in producer surplus reduces the profitability of the merger and thus, in light of the merging parties' rationality constraint, alters the appropriate inferences about predicted anticompetitive effects and efficiencies. Moreover, the effects of entry as such entail welfare consequences that are not second order due to the positive and negative externalities generated by entry when competition is imperfect.

To analyze these effects, start by considering the extent to which a merger would induce subsequent entry. Focusing on equilibrium entry behavior both before and after the merger, we need to identify the extent to which further entry would be profitable ex post when it was not ex ante (Werden

---

3. Following convention, entry is taken as a stand-in for broader postmerger reactions of both new firms and incumbents, including product repositioning. Firms' choices of which products to offer are endogenous premerger, the merging firms may have incentives to reposition their own offerings, and postmerger, nonmerging incumbents as well as new entrants make endogenous product choice decisions. Recent empirical work and simulation analysis have examined repositioning (generally without postmerger entry), suggesting in some cases that welfare losses may be greater and in others less than when product offerings are taken as fixed (Fan 2013; Fan and Yang 2020; Gandhi et al. 2008; Li et al. 2022; Mazzeo, Seim, and Varela 2018; Wollmann 2018).

4. The two standards are separately identified more often in this chapter than in others because some of the effects of entry differ as between the two. Nevertheless, much of this difference tends to diminish in the long run because, in the equilibrium of many models, price equals average cost and consumer surplus equals total surplus. On the choice of the welfare standard, see chapter 8.

and Froeb 1998).[5] Discrete entry in either setting will reduce price, so entry will occur only if the post-entry price is high enough to generate sufficient quasi-rents to cover fixed entry costs. In the premerger equilibrium, it may be that further entry at the prevailing price would have been unprofitable, but, more relevant, such entry would have been unprofitable at the price that would obtain with the additional firm in operation.

It is often helpful to consider the continuous case (with no integer constraint), in which event marginal entry premerger just breaks even.[6] If the merger would otherwise raise prices at all—taking into account direct anticompetitive effects as well as the extent to which they would be mitigated by any efficiencies—that will induce some entry (Kaplow 2023a). Furthermore, it would not induce enough entry to restore the pre-entry price because, if it did, the marginal entrant postmerger would then be unprofitable. (The marginal firm's sales would be lower than they would have been premerger, when less capacity was present, and hence its profits would be lower than their nonpositive level premerger.)

The discrete entry case will tend to be roughly similar, reflecting the simple point that the postmerger, pre-entry price is higher than the corresponding pre-entry price to begin with. Here, it may be helpful to think of an otherwise anticompetitive merger as raising the probability of entry or making it likely that entry would occur sooner in a growing market. Because entry predictions involve substantial uncertainty on many dimensions (about the magnitude of anticompetitive effects, firms' cost functions, demand, and features of entry itself), an assessment of the likelihood and expected effects of entry for the discrete case may be similar to those for the continuous case. For this reason, most of the exposition here will not distinguish these cases, instead referring simply to increased entry or tendencies for such to occur.

However, when the minimum viable scale is relatively large, there are important qualifications. A merger might increase prices substantially without

---

5. The analysis in the text, following convention, views entry decisions premerger as ones that ignore the possibility of the subsequent merger, which is unsatisfying. Section B considers entry induced by the prospect of a subsequent buyout and discusses the modest literature that takes a dynamic approach in which all entry, investment, and exit decisions are forward-looking.
6. Mankiw and Whinston (1986) examine the importance of the integer constraint in a homogeneous goods model.

inducing any entry. And it is also possible (setting aside ex ante profitability of the proposed merger) that prices will be lower as a consequence of an otherwise anticompetitive merger. Discrete entry may have been barely unprofitable premerger but become somewhat profitable postmerger, resulting in a lower yet still profitable price for the entrant. (The postmerger, post-entry price is above the premerger, post-entry price that would not have been high enough for premerger entry to have been profitable.)

A plausible working hypothesis is that, over a significant range of cases, the prospect of postmerger entry can be expected to mitigate but not nullify any net anticompetitive effect of a proposed merger. This conclusion is consistent with analysis and simulations by Caradonna, Miller, and Sheu (2023). Therefore, consideration of postmerger entry typically indicates that otherwise anticompetitive mergers tend remain so, although to a lesser degree.[7]

Consider next the more complete welfare consequences of such entry that does occur. The teachings crystalized by Mankiw and Whinston (1986) (drawing on, among others, Spence 1976 and Dixit and Stiglitz 1977) about the inefficiency of entry decisions under imperfect competition have been largely ignored in analyzing antitrust policy, including with regard to horizontal mergers (Whinston 2007 being an exception). Discussion will again focus on the case of continuous entry and exit, following Kaplow's (2023a) extension of Mankiw and Whinston (1986) to marginal changes in the strength of competition regulation (although not analyzing mergers as such).

With homogeneous goods, we have (only) a business-stealing externality. Each sale by the marginal entrant is taken from an incumbent that sells at a price in excess of marginal cost. Hence, the entrant's gains are offset by incumbents' losses, so, with identical cost functions, these are precisely

---

7. Analysis of how much entry may be induced and how much it may reduce any price elevation that otherwise would occur may differ qualitatively when assessing coordinated effects. The extent to which entry would disrupt merger-induced coordination will depend in part on the manner in which the merger facilitates coordination in the first place. Perhaps the merger reduces asymmetry (or, relatedly, involves acquisition of a maverick firm), in which event entry by a new, perhaps asymmetric firm may have an offsetting influence on the effectiveness of coordination. Note as well that entry may be more attractive when the entrant expects to be able to participate in coordination, but in that event entry may be socially wasteful (as developed below) while not reducing the postmerger price. By contrast, an entrant that expects to undermine coordination, restoring price to the premerger level, would tend to find entry unprofitable.

offsetting. Furthermore, the marginal entrant's gains just equal its fixed entry costs, so what were previously profits of incumbent firms are converted into resource costs expended by the entrant. Therefore, total welfare falls. Note further that, in long-run equilibrium, price equals average cost, so all costs (including fixed entry costs) are borne by consumers.

Reflecting on this case, we have that entry is already socially excessive premerger and that the effect of a merger that otherwise raises price is to induce yet additional entry, exacerbating inefficiency. As in Kaplow (2023a), entry resulting from higher prices may well reduce total welfare by more than if such entry did not occur (for example, if it were barred by regulation or discouraged by an entry fee). That is, even though entry mitigates price increases—the traditional reason that consideration of entry is regarded to favor more lenient merger policy—it actually results in lower total welfare in this case.[8] It is possible that merger-induced entry could be the largest social cost of a horizontal merger, a result at odds with conventional wisdom that easier entry favors more permissible treatment of a merger.

Mankiw and Whinston (1986) also elaborate a second, positive externality from entry. When products are differentiated, more variety is valuable; moreover, some of that value is not captured by firms because of the inability to engage in perfect price discrimination. Entry increases inframarginal consumer surplus, which constitutes the positive externality that a new entrant generates. Similar analysis applies whenever entry generates positive spillovers, such as through innovation or other learning that entrants cannot fully appropriate. Note that this externality will often accrue directly to consumers, not to other firms (which, as before, suffer from business-stealing).

In such cases, we have both a positive and a negative externality from entry. If the value of variety is small, welfare effects are close to those in the homogeneous goods case. At some point, variety or other spillovers are sufficiently valuable to just offset the negative, business-stealing externality.

---

8. This effect also creates an additional channel by which it matters whether efficiencies involve variable or fixed costs and how much cost savings are passed through to consumers. The more efficiencies would be passed through, the smaller would be the direct price increase caused by the merger and thus the magnitude of the (here, inefficient) entry thereby induced. This welfare effect reverses in the next case, when postmerger entry is independently beneficial.

This will be so when, at the premerger equilibrium, a social planner would have been indifferent to inducing slightly more or less entry. Beyond that, further entry raises total welfare. Taken together, there will be settings in which ex post entry is not quite as detrimental as in the homogeneous goods case (with no spillovers), the special case in which entry is on-balance neutral, and others in which entry itself will generate net benefits that accordingly would tend to offset a merger's net (conventionally defined) anticompetitive effects, after allowing for entry.[9]

Until now, we have followed convention and merger guidelines in taking what may be regarded as an ex post perspective on ex post entry. Let us now return to the merging parties' rationality constraint (elaborated in section 2.C) to consider the implications of the foregoing for making inferences about a merger's direct anticompetitive effects and efficiencies (Stigler 1950; Willig 1991; Werden and Froeb 1998; Whinston 2007). Merging parties are assumed to care only about their own profits—ignoring not only consumer welfare but also entrants' profits as well as any externalities on other firms from the merger itself (which ordinarily are positive) or externalities from the entry it induces (which are negative).[10]

In this regard, the more entry a merger would induce, ceteris paribus, the less profitable the merger will be. It is important, however, to be precise about what is being taken as given and what perspective is being adopted. If one took an ex post perspective like we adopted previously, then the knowledge that entry in fact occurs would often be a signal that the merger should have been prohibited. After all, postmerger entry occurs only when the net

---

9. Note that methods used to predict the price effects of mergers—often assuming the absence of subsequent entry—involve estimating features of consumers' preferences that bear on how much variety is valued.

10. The analysis here, like that in the most of this book, makes the conventional assumption that merging parties are motivated purely by profit maximization and that the only ways that mergers affect their profits are through anticompetitive effects and efficiencies. As discussed in section 2.C, however, it is possible that agency problems (leading, for example, to empire-building motivations) or behavioral considerations (such as optimism bias) affect decision-making. Mergers can also be profitable because of stock market misvaluations and tax savings. Incorporating such additional considerations (which, if the sole motivation, may imply that there are no price effects or efficiencies) may be important but would complicate the exposition without qualitatively changing the forces examined here.

effect (before such entry) is to increase price. Moreover, as explained, the entry typically does not fully defeat the price increase and, in many cases, the entry as such reduces overall welfare.

But here we are explicitly taking an ex ante perspective on the *prospect* of ex post entry. As the merging parties contemplate a particular merger, they will have a distribution as to its possible anticompetitive effects and efficiencies. Let us conceive of this as the distribution under the hypothetical assumption that entry would not occur. Each point in that distribution would be associated with some level of profitability. The firms would merge if and only if expected profitability was sufficiently high in light of transaction costs (and the value of relevant outside options). Introducing the consideration of postmerger entry to varying degrees (or raising the likelihood thereof relative to their priors) reduces expected profitability in states in which the merging parties' anticipated postmerger prices would have risen. That is the channel by which easier entry implies reduced profitability.[11]

Now take the reviewing agency's perspective. It will have its own priors regarding the distribution of possible anticompetitive effects and efficiencies of any given proposed merger. Reasoning from the merging parties' rationality constraint, the agency will form a conditional distribution of these effects, recognizing that it will not see merger proposals that are insufficiently profitable. Consideration of entry (or, again, an upward revision to priors regarding the ease of entry) calls for further revision of this conditional distribution. Because the merging parties' profits are lower in states that otherwise would have had price increases, this revised distribution places relatively greater weight on mergers that would increase efficiency relative to those that would involve significant anticompetitive effects.

A complete analysis is even more subtle. It is not as though an agency receives a simple signal on the ease of entry that exists in a vacuum. Instead, all three considerations—anticompetitive effects, efficiencies, and the ease of entry—are influenced by myriad factors, many of which affect

---

11. A further implication of this logic is that efficient mergers whose direct effect is to *lower* postmerger prices are rendered *more* profitable by highly responsive entry because that also tends to be associated with greater exit when prices fall. This point reinforces the argument for a more permissive approach to mergers via inferences from the rationality constraint when entry is easier.

more than one of them. For example, firms' cost functions may be directly relevant to both efficiencies and the ease of entry (and also competitive interactions), perhaps with negative interdependence: low levels of scale economies may imply easier entry but smaller efficiencies, and vice versa (Farrell and Shapiro 2001).[12]

Even so, the broader lesson stands: a central implication of the ease of entry regards not (only) the welfare effects of a merger with given (sans entry) anticompetitive effects but also and importantly the proper predictions of both anticompetitive effects and efficiencies that would be generated by a proposed merger. Taking the extreme case in which entry would be swift and involve few sunk costs, the inference is that the merger is likely to raise welfare due to efficiencies, with the result that the entry would not actually occur postmerger because prices would not rise and may even fall. In this case, ease of entry may be associated with less, not more, actual postmerger entry.

As a final note, most of the foregoing analysis contrasts sharply with that in merger guidelines (EU Merger Guidelines 2004; U.S. Merger Guidelines 2010, 2023). In the example just offered, the ease of entry favors permitting the merger not because such entry will deter or defeat most of the price increase—the criterion in merger guidelines—but instead because we infer that the merger would be unlikely to cause the price increase in the first place. Also, even from an ex post perspective on ex post entry, merger guidelines' formulations are misconceived. In most standard models of oligopoly, limit pricing does not arise, so the prospect of entry does not deter price increases. And, as explained earlier, when entry is induced, it does not ordinarily defeat price increases but only mitigates them.

---

12. Interestingly, the entry sections of the EU and U.S. Merger Guidelines precede the efficiencies sections and make no reference to them (and the efficiencies discussions do not reference entry), whereas the analysis here suggests that a core reason that entry analysis is relevant is that it bears on inferences about efficiencies (and, through that channel, inferences about anticompetitive effects as well). The present analysis accordingly reinforces the arguments in chapter 2 and section 4.D against siloed analysis of anticompetitive effects and efficiencies. Moreover, viewed practically, sometimes it may be easiest to determine that rapid, substantial entry would be triggered by even a modest price increase, in which case considering entry early in the process would be more expeditious than postponing it until after a substantial consideration of likely anticompetitive effects, viewed in a vacuum.

Relatedly, the traditional focus on the timeliness, likelihood, and sufficiency of entry is only loosely connected to what matters. Collapsing these multidimensional factors to a single scale, the expected impact of entry seems to be understood in this ex post sense—how much of a price increase would in fact be offset—rather than considering as well the possibly more important question of entry's expected impact on the merging parties' profits, which is most relevant for inferences. The two are related, but they are not the same. For example, a moderate degree of entry that would offset only half of a price increase might still be sufficient to turn the merging parties' expected profits from positive to negative, that is, unless efficiencies motivated the merger.[13] However, it is not surprising that guidelines would employ the wrong metrics in light of the fact that entry does not seem to be considered for this other, more appropriate purpose. Likewise, these factors are not what we need to know to assess the welfare impacts of merger-induced entry as such, in light of the externalities associated with entry decisions under imperfect competition. The expected degree of entry tells us nothing about whether entry was already excessive or insufficient (and by how much); that is, the ease of entry itself is uninformative about entry's externalities.

B. Ex Ante Entry

Section A focuses on entry that would be induced following a merger because of the merger's direct effect of raising prices, which makes postmerger entry more profitable than it had been premerger. This section shifts attention to the qualitatively different question of how a prospective entrant may be encouraged by the possibility of its subsequently being acquired by an incumbent offering a buyout premium. It is important to take this ex ante inducement into account when determining the overall welfare effects of policies regarding the permissibility of mergers, particularly those in rapidly evolving sectors in which new entry, investment, and innovation are particularly important. Indeed, this may be the major welfare effect of the stringency of merger policy in this domain.

---

13. An important reason that ex post entry may not fully offset price increases is delay, relating to the emphasis on timeliness. Merger retrospectives, which tend to employ short time frames due to data limitations and to help with identification, would not capture effects of entry that some research suggests takes a few years to materialize (Hilke and Nelson 1993; Geroski 1995).

The ex ante inducement of entry by the prospect of a subsequent acquisition has been largely neglected in merger analysis until recently, although the phenomenon has long been appreciated in some of the relevant economics literature. Viewed broadly, mergers are part of the dynamic ecosystem that includes entry, investment, competitive interaction, and exit (Ericson and Pakes 1995). The permissibility of a merger regime can have ex ante effects on entry and on investment more broadly, which have important implications for both competition and efficiencies.[14] Hence, the usual focus on a prospective merger's subsequent competitive effects—which takes for granted the merging parties' existence and capabilities—omits an important dimension that is central to the economy's functioning. This section sketches some of the pathways, all of which present areas for further research.[15]

One of the few developed lines of work begins with Rasmusen (1988), who analyzes entry for buyout in a homogeneous goods industry.[16] In the second stage of the model, a dominant incumbent firm will buy out an entrant in order to extinguish its competition. In the first stage, a prospective entrant anticipates this outcome. As a consequence, there exists a range of parameters and sets of assumptions—regarding cost functions, demand, bargaining, and competitive interaction post-entry—for which entry will be profitable.

Rasmusen (1988) emphasizes that this domain includes settings in which entry would not have been profitable were it not for the subsequent buyout. If post-entry competition would be sufficiently intense, the entrant

---

14. The exposition here largely follows custom in referring only to investment by prospective entrants, although the logic applies to existing firms that may, for example, invest in capabilities whose value lies primarily in use by another firm that would subsequently acquire it.

15. The need of some entrants' owners to cash out is set to the side, in part because private equity markets may render mergers unnecessary to accomplish this. Nevertheless, incumbents in the entrant's sector may suffer less from asymmetric information than do private equity buyers, in which event allowing acquisitions by incumbents could enhance ex ante investment incentives for this reason as well. Furthermore, if entrants' value lies largely in synergies from combination with incumbents, private equity buyers will not pay as much and their purchases will not create those synergies (that is, if they cannot be achieved without a merger, such as by licensing intellectual property).

16. A version of this argument was previously developed in the context of determining whether combinations of competing patents should be permitted—which could induce wasteful expenditures devoted to inventing around patents without benefitting consumers (Kaplow 1984).

would not expect to earn enough quasi-rents to recover its fixed cost of entry. However, once the entrant is present, it would be profitable for it to remain if the price would be sufficiently high to cover variable costs. Having sunk the entry costs, it is thus credible that the new firm will continue to operate. Hence, the incumbent would wish to buy it out. Finally, if the bargaining between the entrant and incumbent is such that the buyout premium would be high enough, the prospect of buyout would then motivate entry at stage one that otherwise would not have occurred.

In this model, entry arises solely due to the anticipation of the buyout premium. This entry is socially inefficient because the fixed costs of entry are wasted (recall that the model involves homogeneous goods). Therefore, prohibiting such mergers would raise welfare. Interestingly, prohibition would also raise the dominant firm's profits. The incumbent would like to be able to commit to not buying out the entrant so that the entry would never happen in the first place, but that commitment would not be credible. Legal prohibition solves its problem.

As Rasmusen (1988) discusses, there are limitations to this analysis. First, if instead of a dominant incumbent firm we have multiple incumbent firms, the free-rider problem may render acquisition of such entrants by any one of them unprofitable. Second, depending on the number of prospective entrants and the frequency of their arrival, it may be that even a dominant incumbent firm would not buy entrants out, knowing that the cost incurred purchases only brief protection from competition. Interestingly, these possibilities in a sense substitute for the commitment that an incumbent wishes it could make on its own, for the result is that the prospective entrants no longer enter. As mentioned, these considerations are material only when parameters are in the range that such entry would be unprofitable without the prospect of buyout yet profitable because anticipated buyout premiums tip the balance.

Subsequently, this idea has been developed in more sophisticated models and simulation analyses. This work extends that of Ericson and Pakes (1995) and other dynamic models that make firms' entry, investment, and exit endogenous by incorporating mergers as well. Gowrisankaran (1999) initiated this approach, which was subsequently refined by Mermelstein et al. (2020), who modeled mergers in a more neutral fashion regarding investment decisions and production functions. In featured simulations, a tough merger rule tends to be optimal precisely because it discourages inefficient entry for buyout. Even mergers that under a static analysis raise total welfare (even if not consumer welfare) are often best prohibited because of their effect of encouraging inefficient entry.[17] Easier entry can therefore favor a tougher merger policy.

As these investigations make clear, the conclusions are limited in important ways. Relevant parameters and the nature of competitive interaction must be such that entry is unprofitable without buyout but becomes profitable if buyout is permitted. Moreover, results are sensitive to whether there is only one dominant incumbent and to the timing of prospective entry decisions. Relatedly, for reasons of tractability as well as concerns about how best to model multiparty bargaining, these analyses limit the total number of firms and specify particular time sequences of entry, investment, production, and bargaining.

Another important limitation is that such analysis has been conducted in models with homogeneous goods, where entry tends to be socially excessive, a point emphasized in section A in the context of ex post entry. Hence, except for their short-run competitive force and their investment in capacity that an acquirer may put to use, entrants contribute nothing. If instead entrants created new varieties or engaged in other innovation that the acquiring firm found profitable to continue or otherwise benefited from, the social calculus would be different. In such cases, entrants contribute value that they do not fully capture, so entry may—without the additional inducement from the prospect of buyout—be socially insufficient. Moreover, inframarginal surplus is not captured by either firm. Some innovation also generates spillovers that, if partially captured by the dominant firm via the acquisition, would boost the buyout premium and thereby confer some of that benefit on the entrant, which would induce investment of that type.[18]

---

17. Note how this dynamic analysis (with repetition) blends the present section's analysis of ex ante entry with section A's analysis of ex post entry, which entry tends to be excessive in this homogeneous goods setting. Nevertheless, permitting mergers here may induce subsequent entry not only or primarily because prices rise but instead because mergers make subsequent buyouts more likely.
18. In many settings, such ex ante investment is insufficient both because of spillovers that the acquirer would not capture and thus pay for and also because the entrant will generally get only a portion of the surplus it generates (the entrant's prior investments having been sunk at the time of the acquisition). A reservation

Until this point, the analysis largely has taken as given the nature of the investment that a prospective entrant might make, focused on the case in which a buyout premium is necessary to induce that investment, and then noted the welfare implications of permitting or prohibiting buyouts by a dominant incumbent firm. The conclusions largely follow our general understanding of when equilibrium entry tends to be socially excessive or insufficient. Yet we have seen that this analysis covers only some of the cases, and we need to explore in particular how prospective entrants or existing firms choose among different channels of investment, notably, when their choices may affect whether a subsequent buyout will occur (if permitted) and the magnitude of any buyout premium.

Return to the homogeneous goods setting and assume further that a subsequent merger between an incumbent and the entrant would generate no synergies. In that case, prohibiting such a merger seems efficient. We have seen this outcome for the case in which the prospect of such prohibition discourages ex ante entry. Suppose instead that entry would nevertheless be profitable and hence arise. Then we may have the problem of socially excessive entry, but permitting buyouts would only exacerbate the problem. Moreover, allowing a merger would extinguish the competition that the entrant provided (the only part of the analysis usually considered).

Next, modify the analysis to allow for merger synergies. Section 4.C's exploration of economies of scale and economies of scope emphasizes the importance of complementarities. An extreme but quite common case of the latter is where the entrant is not independently viable, perhaps because it engages only in research, and contracting problems would make it difficult for it to capture much of the value that it generates. More broadly, an entrant—like any other firm that is more established—may be better at some tasks and worse at others. In that case, we have the familiar trade-off between merger efficiencies and anticompetitive effects, to the extent that the synergies cannot be achieved through nonmerger alternatives such as

---

regarding innovation is that some settings, such as those involving patent races, involve excessive entry and levels of investment in innovation (Dasgupta and Stiglitz 1980; Loury 1979). This tendency will be greater when a high share of benefits is appropriable by the winner of the race, whereas the scenario envisioned in the text contemplates significant spillovers, such as to other firms (possibly including competitors).

broad licensing of an industry.[19] Furthermore, entrants in particular often have only one or a few capabilities, particularly in settings in which successful operation is a complex undertaking.

The difference here is that we are not taking the entrant or an existing target firm's existence as given. We need to account for the ex ante incentives to undertake the investments that generate the subsequent assets or functionalities that give rise to merger synergies. Put another way, in comparing the outcomes when a proposed merger is allowed to the best outcomes that the merging firms could achieve independently, all the analysis in chapter 4 takes as given those firms' current capabilities. A more complete, dynamic analysis recognizes that many capabilities and, relatedly, many potential merger synergies are the products of ex ante investment decisions by both prospective entrants and incumbent firms.

Hence, it is insufficient to ask whether a contemplated degree of merger stringency might forfeit merger-specific efficiencies that, let us suppose, are not large enough to outweigh anticompetitive effects under the prevailing welfare standard. We also wish to understand forgone efficiencies from discouraging investment as well as gains or losses in efficiency from altering the direction of ex ante investment. Relatedly, we cannot take for granted the greater competition that would prevail if a merger were prohibited if a stringent regime might have discouraged the target firm from entering in the first place or from investing as much in becoming as viable a competitor. A growing literature has begun to model how the permissibility of subsequent acquisitions affects incumbents' and entrants' incentives for innovation, including the course such innovation may take (Callander and

---

19. Another ex ante effect of the prospect of a subsequent acquisition—however appealing to the target—is that it may make pre-acquisition counterparties more reluctant to make relationship-specific investments in dealing with the entrant when the value of those investments might be stranded by an acquisition, which in turn makes entry less attractive. By contrast, Kamepalli, Rajan, and Zingales (2022) analyze reluctance due to a lack of necessity, where customers anticipate that they will soon realize the benefits an entrant offers without having to switch away from the incumbent who is expected to acquire and incorporate the entrant and thus itself provide the entrant's enhanced functionality. One can also imagine the opposite effect in their setting, wherein counterparties are more willing to associate with a new entrant due to the prospect of a subsequent buyout and resulting incorporation into the incumbent.

Matouschek 2022; Gilbert and Katz 2022; Katz 2021; Motta and Peitz 2021; Letina, Schmutzler, and Seibel 2023; Wickelgren 2021).[20]

Taken together, we have a diversity of possible scenarios wherein the effect of a more restrictive merger regime on welfare via its influence on ex ante entry can be beneficial or detrimental. When an entrant brings nothing to the market except additional competition—cases with homogeneous goods and no synergies—prohibition tends to be beneficial, indeed all the more so if it discourages excessive entry. When entrants do bring other value, a more permissive regime might be desirable both because mergers themselves may generate synergies, as explored in chapter 4, and because buyout premiums encourage ex ante investments that may otherwise be insufficiently incentivized due to spillovers. Combining these two points, differential stringency between these two settings can channel ex ante investment in more productive directions. It is important to further explore dynamic models that incorporate more of these features and provide better guidance on the determinants of when ex ante investment is best encouraged versus when its loss is likely to be desirable or at least not very problematic.[21] It is also necessary to explore empirically, to the extent feasible, how acquisitions influence ex ante activity.[22]

Competition agencies and tribunals face a daunting task when attempting to assess a proposed merger raising these issues. Determination of the

---

20. Gilbert and Katz (2022) emphasize two potentially opposing incentives: Entrants that expect to be acquired have an incentive to innovate in ways that would add value to the incumbent's operations because that raises the buyout premium. On the other hand, entrants wish to maximize their negative stand-alone impact on incumbents' profits, which also raises the buyout premium. Additional work on mergers, entry, and innovation includes Cabral (2021); Gautier and Lamesch (2021); Gilbert (2020); Jin, Leccese, and Wagman (2023); Katz and Shelanski (2007b); Phillips and Zhdanov (forthcoming); and Shapiro (2012).
21. A further consideration, one not unique to nascent entrants, is that efficient mergers involving even pure complements may make subsequent entry into the incumbent's core business more difficult because such subsequent entrants may find it difficult to replicate the additional capabilities and, because of the merger, may be unable to contract for them at all or on terms that are as good as those available if the earlier merger had not been allowed and thus the firm producing the new complement had remained independent.
22. Prado and Bauer (2022) find that big tech acquisitions have tended to raise subsequent VC funding in the short run, although there are challenges to identification and the data does not enable disaggregation across types of investment.

effects of any given treatment—particularly, the anticipation thereof—on the dynamic evolution of an industry or the economy is infeasible. Even roughly categorizing a given merger can be difficult because the analysis depends on the frontier of ex ante investment possibilities and assessments of the future role of an entrant's offerings: Are they really complements? Might they evolve into substitutes? These considerations, of course, are in addition to the factors analyzed in chapters 3 and 4 concerning ex post effects on competition and efficiencies.

A further obstacle often arises naturally or strategically when acquisitions of nascent firms must be assessed at very early stages in the firms' existence. Many such firms may have no revenue or even any readily identifiable product or capability. Or, if they appear to have one, that may not be what the acquirer sees as the primary source of value. Instead, the entrant's contribution may lie in its existing teams of human capital (without regard to the value of projects in the works) or instead in its future potential. Perhaps that potential is quite abstract: the target's talent may be great yet lack any fruitful direction. Perhaps the target may be onto some path that might address an important gap in the acquirer's operations. Or perhaps the target is a nascent disruptive force that the acquirer is keen to extinguish (Cunningham, Ederer, and Ma 2021).

An acquirer may be particularly inclined to purchase such targets early on, before others (including the target itself) fully realize their value, so that it can obtain the assets at attractive prices. Likewise, early acquisitions are more appealing if they make it particularly difficult for a competition agency to recognize the dangers, let alone to demonstrate that risk under a given legal standard. For that reason, it may sometimes be prudent or simply unavoidable to allow the acquisition, leaving open the possibility of challenging it later. As elaborated in section 7.C, however, this approach can be difficult to implement because it may require unscrambling the eggs, and the merged firm's anticipation of that prospect itself creates perverse incentives, including to excessively integrate operations to make subsequent separation unappealing, or to underinvest in developing the target's capabilities for fear that ex post success will, with hindsight, be viewed as inhering in the target itself. Moreover, if the acquirer intends in essence to snuff out the competitive threat rather than to develop it—redeploying the talent to unrelated projects—the agency may never discover the problem or be in any position to provide an effective remedy even if it subsequently did.

This strategy of acquiring nascent entrants quite early is not without costs to incumbents. The earlier the stage of an acquisition, the greater may be the degree of asymmetric information. Most upstarts are worthless, but it is challenging even for industry insiders to know which are which. It is common lore that premier venture capitalists often took a pass on many of the most successful startups, and it is also well known that many firms they initially sponsor and continue to fund, given their detailed inside knowledge, ultimately fail. Furthermore, if a large incumbent was making a habit of acquiring everything in sight at very early stages, that would induce substantial entry for buyout by pretenders, the prospect of which would induce the incumbent to hold off in many cases.

The fundamental concern with incumbent firms undertaking anticompetitive acquisitions of all sorts is familiar: extinguishing competition raises total firm profits (consumer losses are externalized). Moreover, the most anticompetitive acquirer will make the highest bid, ceteris paribus, because total industry profits rise the most and that acquirer tends to reap the greatest share of any boost. This point, noted previously with regard to merger specificity, is relevant here as well. When there are multiple incumbent firms, such as in the pharmaceutical industry, it may be competitively preferable to require that a biotech startup be acquired by a firm other than the one or few that already specialize in its line of research. Such an alternative acquirer may possess the requisite complementary skills and offer a buyout premium without sacrificing competition. On the other hand, perhaps it is the incumbents that are active in competing lines of research that have the most important complementary skills, such as in conducting further research and making intelligent feasibility assessments along the way. Moreover, these potential acquirers may suffer much less from information asymmetries in evaluating the target and hence they may offer larger buyout premiums that more fully reflect the value that the target has created. In addition, some complementary innovations, such as process innovations that might be difficult to license, may generate greater synergies when applied to the more extensive operations of a dominant firm that can make better use of the improved methods. Hence, limiting what may be the most anticompetitive acquirers from purchasing an entrant may significantly reduce buyout premiums, thereby diminishing ex ante incentives, and also reduce ex post synergies.[23] As a final complication, recall that, the more homogeneous the goods—the more the entrant has a "me-too" drug rather than a genuine innovation in this example—the more ex ante incentives may be excessive, so reductions in such investments due to the prospect of a tough merger regime tend to be efficient.

---

23. Sometimes greater synergies will be associated with a smaller acquirer that most lacks the skills the entrant offers, but the dominant firm may nevertheless bid more, in part because it profits from the smaller competitor's continued weakness. Prohibiting acquisition by the dominant firm would enhance both competition and efficiencies, although it would reduce the buyout premium and thus ex ante incentives. Note that removing some firms from the bidding not only eliminates their higher bids but may also enable the smaller acquirer to make the acquisition even more cheaply because of the reduction in bidding competition. That may arise even when the smaller acquirer's bid would have been the highest, because the restrictive merger regime removes other incumbents from the bidding contest.

6 Priors, Predictions, and Presumptions

This chapter addresses the difficulty of analyzing anticompetitive effects, efficiencies, and entry in the review of proposed mergers because of information limitations and the inherent challenges of prediction. To sharpen the discussion that follows, section A addresses the relationship between Bayesian priors and the processing of information in the case at hand that is undertaken to update those priors. Section B considers the so-called structural presumption, a shortcut that has superficial appeal given the challenges but is incapable of assisting decision-making and, in practice, actually degrades it.

Section C, the bulk of this chapter, examines the strengths and limitations of different types of evidence that can illuminate merger review: industry studies, merger retrospectives, merger simulations, stock market event studies, and industry expertise that may be drawn on in an investigation. Some of these are primarily useful in formulating priors while others focus more on updating. Given the qualifications associated with most of these information sources in many merger settings, it is particularly important to triangulate among all that are available.

A. Overview

A helpful heuristic for understanding the prediction of a proposed merger's effects is the odds ratio version of Bayes' rule that was discussed in section 2.A. This formulation takes a decision analytic rather than mechanism design perspective and simplifies further by focusing on the likelihoods of two competing hypotheses—that a proffered merger is anticompetitive or procompetitive—thereby abstracting from the magnitudes of these effects and the fact that competing forces are often present. The ratio of the posterior probability of the anticompetitive explanation to that of the procompetitive explanation equals the ratio of their prior probabilities times the likelihood ratio.

This simple statement helps identify the challenges of predicting a proposed merger's effects. On one hand, the strength of the signal embodied in the evidence pertaining to a particular merger is often weak, which is to say that the likelihood ratio associated with the signal is often near one. When that is true, the ratio of the posterior probabilities will be close to the ratio of the priors, so the priors will often be decisive or at least carry a great deal of weight.[1]

On the other hand, our prior probabilities are not that informative about proposed mergers for many reasons. We know little about past mergers' actual effects relative to the hypothetical world in which they were blocked. We do not observe counterfactual outcomes of the mergers that were in fact blocked. Many proposed mergers are distinctive in important ways that make it difficult to select appropriate priors. And merger proposals are a selected sample, a point we will set to the side for a moment. When priors are fairly flat, our posteriors are determined primarily by the signal, which is to say, the likelihood ratio.

Combining these two observations sharpens the predicament facing competition agencies and reviewing courts. It also motivates the search for simple proxies and shortcuts. Unfortunately, the structural presumption fails, as explained in section B, and that analysis highlights the difficulty of attempting to circumvent or ignore the underlying problem. Hence, even as significant progress is made on the analysis of anticompetitive effects, efficiencies, and entry, it is ultimately necessary to make headway on the empirical front, the subject of section C, and also to improve institutional capacity, discussed in chapter 7.

Before commencing these explorations, it is helpful to reflect further on the distinction between priors and likelihood ratios—a distinction that proves to be elusive, both conceptually and practically. Although not in itself a problem, it is worth some reflection. Regarding priors, there is the

---

1. If this were the only problem, one might describe placing emphasis on one's priors as the use of "presumptions." This approach, however, is qualitatively different from the structural presumption addressed in section B that instead uses the information-destroying practice of market definition, which is not grounded in priors, to trigger an obscure presumption of another form.

familiar challenge of choosing the right ones for the situation at hand. Are we interested in priors about all mergers? All horizontal mergers? All mergers in a specified industry? But how defined? All of a particular type? Perhaps distinguishing manufacturing and retail, or services for businesses and for final consumers? Or between mergers of adjacent and geographically remote hospitals, or those involving medical facilities that provide certain clusters of services? And so forth. Inevitably, one seeks to apply the most appropriate priors, which can be determined only by undertaking some analysis of the merger at hand. Yet such analysis might be regarded as in the province of extracting and analyzing the signal and thus as an input to the likelihood ratio.

Regarding the likelihood ratio itself, the numerator and the denominator are each the probability of observing the signal conditional on the associated hypothesis. But where do those conditional probability functions come from? Abstract analyses generally take them as given. For purposes of practical application, however, these functions have to be articulated using prior knowledge rather than the facts of the case. Indeed, how best to analyze price and quantity data and how to interpret internal documents in a given merger draws primarily on general economic learning and understanding of an industry, that is, preexisting knowledge.

Taking these points together suggests that different types of prior information and understanding indeed constitute much of what is being deployed when examining a particular merger. Of course, the actual signal—whether data, documents, views of industry players, or otherwise—is quite important as well. But determining what sorts of information to collect and how then to process that information depends on preexisting learning. Those understandings, in turn, reflect economic theory and empirical evidence, employed in a symbiotic manner. Prior knowledge helps us select the appropriate model, and our understanding of models helps us organize and integrate prior evidence and the information in the case at hand. As the field of industrial organization economics has developed over the past half-century, much more has been learned. Nevertheless, we have also become increasingly aware of how much we do not know and the extent to which much of our understanding is provisional, sometimes built on conjectures that lack strong foundations or on formulations motivated in significant part by tractability rather than an established close fit with reality.

Bayes' rule also reminds us that, even in this oversimplified presentation, inferences regarding our competing hypotheses—whether the merger is anticompetitive or efficient—are interdependent. In the language of section 2.A, one cannot have a likelihood ratio without a denominator. In the odds ratio formulation, priors and posteriors are also ratios. Information that raises the likelihood of one hypothesis tends to reduce that of the other. The resulting need to keep all explanations in mind when examining the signal was emphasized in chapters 4 and 5 on efficiencies and entry, where we repeatedly saw this principle in action.

Reinforcing this interdependence is the centrality of the merging parties' rationality constraint. Taking a proposed merger to be profitable (or subject to other behavioral explanations) means that the mergers we see are selected samples of the underlying population of possible mergers. Anticipating some of the discussion of stock market event studies in subsection C.4, we can immediately see, for example, that making inferences about conventionally understood efficiencies should differ between horizontal mergers and unrelated acquisitions, for in the former set the possibility that mergers are profitable because they enhance market power is of central importance whereas in the latter set that possibility is often remote.

When one recalls as well that competition regulators care greatly about magnitudes and not just probabilities, additional avenues of inquiry are highlighted. Much commentary, some formal rules and protocols, and the language in many court opinions unfortunately focuses solely on probabilities (or purports to do so on the surface). For example, the applicable standard of proof in the United States seems to consider only probabilities. This problem can also generate confusion about ancillary inquiries. For example, regarding the structural presumption considered next, much attention is placed on whether anticompetitive effects can be presumed, typically without regard to their imagined magnitude. Section 3.A posed the question: When the postmerger HHI is 3000 and the ΔHHI is 300, is the presumed price effect 18%, 1.8%, or 0.18%? When no quantification is even hinted at, it is difficult to know what should be deemed to constitute a sufficient rebuttal of such a presumption, whether regarding anticompetitive effects themselves or possible efficiencies that might offset upward pricing pressure. More broadly, because decisions whether to allow or block mergers involve uncertainty and there often are competing considerations, it is clear that magnitudes and not just likelihoods are central. To the extent that empirical evidence is available, of course, we usually are given insight into both.

B. Structural Presumption

Because predicting the effects of mergers is difficult, it is natural to consider whether there might be some fairly simple proxies, shortcuts, or rules of thumb that can guide the way. This desire may be strongest at the beginning and end of the merger review process. Early on, when agencies must screen large numbers of merger proposals to identify the modest fraction that warrants more careful review, information and time are limited. At the conclusion, when a challenged merger comes to court, generalist judges must assess battles of experts and other evidence about complex industries, where it is difficult even for specialists to make confident predictions about the consequences of a proposed transaction.

Hence, one can see the allure of the structural presumption, under which anticompetitive effects are presumed to arise when certain market share thresholds are exceeded. In *Philadelphia Bank*, the 1963 U.S. Supreme Court case most associated with the structural presumption, the Court referred to the merged firm "controlling an undue percentage share of the relevant market, and [the merger] result[ing] in a significant increase in the concentration of firms." Modern merger guidelines likewise focus on the increase in concentration but, instead of the merged firm's postmerger share, refer to postmerger concentration as a whole (although the U.S. Merger Guidelines 2023 add a second structural presumption based on the merged firm's postmerger share). These concentration levels and changes in concentration are measured by the postmerger HHI and ΔHHI, each calculated naively from premerger shares in a market defined by the HMT or otherwise.[2]

---

2. The U.S. Merger Guidelines (2010) state thresholds for low, middle, and high ranges, indicating that no further inquiry is usually necessary in the low range, whereas "[m]ergers that cause a significant increase in concentration and result in highly concentrated markets are presumed to be likely to enhance market power, but this presumption can be rebutted by persuasive evidence showing that the merger is unlikely to enhance market power." The EU Merger Guidelines (2004) use a similar methodology to state similar ranges and to suggest a safe harbor at the low end, but they do not deem there to be a presumption of anticompetitive effects at the high end.

Chapter 3 presented a systematic critique of the market definition paradigm, emphasizing its circularity and how it generates inferior predictions using the same information set. The approach was seen to conflict with extant economic analysis and generate misleading results when applied in each of the standard merger settings—sometimes greatly so. This section applies some of these insights specifically to the structural presumption.[3]

The structural presumption rests on market definition. One cannot measure market shares except by reference to some market. *Philadelphia Bank* and subsequent cases require that concentration be measured in the "relevant" market, and modern merger guidelines examine HHIs and ΔHHIs in HMT-defined markets or in markets defined more loosely. As a consequence, in light of market definitions' deep infirmities, the structural presumption cannot possibly accomplish what it seeks to do. In many quite different settings, like medical diagnosis, proxy indicators can be useful: an elevated blood count may be correlated with the presence of some disease. But as chapter 3 develops at length, market definition's flaws are not merely rough edges, some sort of measurement error, or a failure to include all potentially relevant factors. Instead, they involve fundamental logical infirmities that render the process useless, producing outputs that are never better and are generically worse, often much worse, than the inputs employed.

Some leading commentary that defends the structural presumption or seeks to provide empirical support fails even to mention market definition.[4] This point is startling in light of the structural presumption's obvious dependence on market definition and the dubious standing of market definition among industrial organization economists and antitrust practitioners more broadly. It is also familiar that market definition disputes typically dominate horizontal merger cases and often appear to decide their outcomes.

Let us directly examine the implications of chapter 3's analysis for the essence of the structural presumption. Motivated by the difficulties of

---

3. For further elaboration, references to the literature, and discussion of legal aspects, see Kaplow (2022).
4. Kwoka (2017), Kwoka and Gu (2015), Sullivan (2016). Also notable are contemporary legislative proposals in the European Union and United States that would reinforce the structural presumption for mergers or extend similar presumptions to other domains, again often without even mentioning market definition.

Priors, Predictions, and Presumptions   143

actually predicting anticompetitive effects, the structural presumption constitutes an apparatus under which anticompetitive effects are to be *presumed* rather than proved when the presumption is successfully triggered. This core capability, however, has to be a myth because it is impossible.

One way to see the problem is to reflect on figure 3.1, reproduced as figure 6.1 for convenience. Section 3.A elaborated how this figure illustrates both the circularity of the market definition paradigm and the inevitable loss of information. These points can be seen even more clearly with respect to the structural presumption by adding some further labels, shown in figure 6.2. (Figures 6.1 and 6.2 appear stacked on the following page for easier comparison.)

The effects that are purportedly presumed toward the right of the diagram—the label indicating where the structural presumption is operative—had to have already been proved in some sense at the left, where market definition is undertaken. The entire point of the structural presumption is precisely that it involves a *presumption* that Shares High → Price ↑ High, *without the government having to prove anticompetitive effects*. Yet the structural presumption can be triggered only if the party challenging the merger wins on market definition, and *that decision requires proof of anticompetitive effects*. (Nevertheless, as explained in section 3.A, the effects presumed at the right generally differ, for the worse, from those proved at the left.[5])

Furthermore, recall from section 3.A that this core logic applies without regard to the stage in a proceeding or how much information one has in hand. When a competition agency engages in preliminary screening, it will need to form a guesstimate of anticompetitive effects. It is

---

5. As a strictly logical matter, the structural presumption's internal incoherence can be avoided if the information inputs to market definition, or the analysis leading to market definition, are not about anticompetitive effects but instead address something else. This logical escape hardly commends itself if we are concerned in fact with anticompetitive effects, and such are indeed what statements of the structural presumption purport to be about. *Philadelphia Bank*'s famous pronouncement is quite explicit about this, as are modern merger guidelines. (Interestingly, the U.S. Merger Guidelines 2023 eschew most explicit statements of competitive effects—except for a notable mention in the introduction—but all of the proffered approaches to market definition draw on the same sorts of considerations as before.) Moreover, such matters are obviously the focus of intense litigation about market definition, including battles of experts, even if anticompetitive effects are examined indirectly and often obscured in the process due to application of the market definition paradigm.

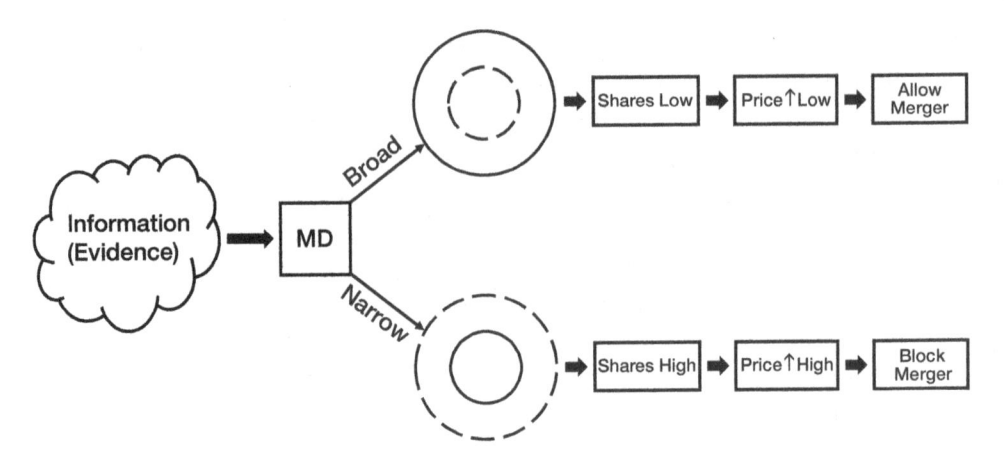

Figure 6.1
Market definition.

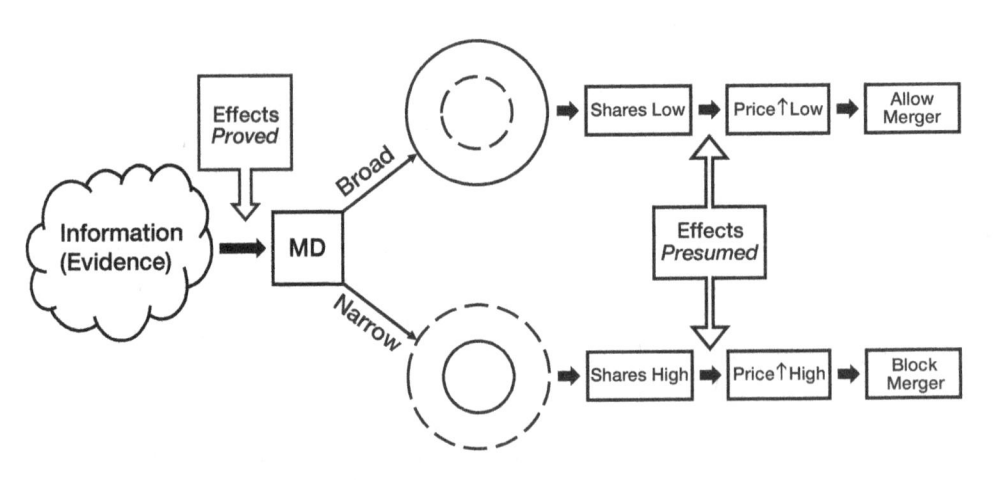

Figure 6.2
Market definition and anticompetitive effects.

not able to presume them without regard to the proper analysis of what limited information is available. To invoke a structural presumption, the agency staff would still have to begin by defining the market, using whatever they know. But using that information to define a market and then indulge in presumptions cannot create something out of nothing. Worse, as previously discussed, some of the scarce information is destroyed in the process, so the result can only be inferior to what it would be if one eschewed the structural presumption and, indeed, the entire market definition process.[6]

Might the structural presumption be partially rescued, as a crude indicator, by the simple intuition that greater concentration and larger increases in concentration are associated with greater price effects? And what of various studies that might be interpreted to give some analytical or empirical support to the structural presumption? Unfortunately, in light of the aforementioned logical infirmities, the structural presumption cannot perform even this limited role. This conclusion is reinforced by section 3.B's analysis of the actual implications of the economics literature on merger analysis in every setting, including recent research that might have seemed to provide some support for merger guidelines' use of HHIs and ΔHHIs.

To begin, we know from the demise of the structure-conduct-performance paradigm that higher concentration does not carry the implications that many accepted in the 1960s, the time of *Philadelphia Bank* and the first U.S. Merger Guidelines. The simple reason is that there is no such thing as higher concentration, ceteris paribus: market shares are endogenous and hence can differ only if underlying parameters differ as well. Moreover, those differences can readily be material to the analysis and in some settings indicate effects of the opposite sign.

Nevertheless, a merger itself may be taken as a causal force that can affect prices (even though endogenous forces generate merger proposals). Indeed, in many models of unilateral effects, all mergers that generate no efficiencies create some upward pricing pressure. Neither a structural presumption

---

6. Sometimes a structural presumption might seem useful because market definition is obvious. However, this can (correctly) be so only when anticompetitive effects themselves are obvious. One might instead imagine that a one-way negative presumption is possible: perhaps if the HHI and ΔHHI are not very high even with a narrow market definition, the merger should not be scrutinized further. If anticompetitive effects are fairly obviously low, that is a sensible outcome. However, if elasticities are sufficiently low, nontrivial anticompetitive effects can still arise even when market shares are fairly low. Stepping back, it makes sense, as a first pass at the screening stage, to consider the most appropriate (even if highly simplified) formulas for anticompetitive effects, such as those discussed in section 3.B, plugging in plausible parameter guesstimates, to see whether anticompetitive effects seem sufficiently likely. That back-of-the-envelope approach, however, employs neither market definition nor any structural presumption, affirmative or negative.

nor market definition machinery is required for that minimal result. The question remains: how much upward pricing pressure?

Section 3.B makes clear that market definition and hence any structural presumption cannot help in generating an answer, and going down that path only confounds the analysis. Moreover, even when one sticks with narrow markets—which contradicts the structural presumption's insistence that market shares be considered only in the relevant market, after the market definition process—the associated market share information is not close to constituting a sufficient statistic. Most obviously, some demand elasticity measure is important, and it can influence the predictions enormously.

Recall Nocke and Whinston's (2022) simulations for simple versions of the Cournot case, discussed in subsection 3.B.1. They examine elasticities of demand in the homogeneous goods market that range in magnitude from 1.0 to 2.5, corresponding to hypothetical monopolists able to raise prices from infinity to ~67%, respectively (in the case of an unconcentrated premerger market). Taking one of their table entries, which uses an elasticity of 1.0 and an assumed marginal cost reduction of 5%, the ΔHHI that makes the merger consumer-welfare neutral is ~45. However, if one instead inserts an elasticity of 10.0 into their formula (suggesting that a hypothetical monopolist of an otherwise unconcentrated narrow market could raise prices by approximately 10% rather than infinity), the critical ΔHHI is instead ~4500 (because ΔHHI enters their formula with a square root)—out of a theoretical maximum ΔHHI of 5000. Hence, if one was defining structural presumption thresholds on the strong assumptions that all mergers were Cournot mergers and that the special case generating their simple formula was correct, what critical value of the ΔHHI would one select? Under the HMT, the pertinent elasticity can span an even wider range than that used in these illustrations. Knowing only that a higher ΔHHI generates more upward pricing pressure in this particular model does not allow us to answer the ultimate question within two orders of magnitude, even leaving aside any ceteris paribus assumptions that, due to the endogeneity of market shares, cannot hold.

In setting thresholds for a structural presumption, we would also have to consider, among other possibilities, mergers involving differentiated products with Bertrand competition, contemplating as well different demand systems and more—even if we confine attention to demand systems under which substitution is proportional to equilibrium market shares. Nocke and

Whinston (2022) offer simulations for a demand system calibrated to Miller and Weinberg's (2017) empirical analysis of the beer industry, which in that paper's underlying empirical estimation featured a demand elasticity with a magnitude of ~0.6 (implying that a hypothetical monopolist would generate infinite upward pricing pressure). If one seeks market share thresholds so that a structural presumption applies to all industries—even if one sticks to narrow markets that pass the HMT—we again cannot generate a workable answer.

The literature that aims to determine the effects of horizontal mergers based on limited information draws on extant economic analysis to derive, under strong but indicative assumptions, formulas that can use a few basic inputs to generate predictions of price effects. These methods can aid agency screening and are useful as starting points, before embarking on more refined analyses. The structural presumption and its requisite market definition exercise, by contrast, are an unhelpful distraction that cannot aid these efforts, difficult as they may be, and can only generate confusion and additional prediction error.

Nor does empirical research validate or calibrate the structural presumption, an obviously impossible feat in light of the foregoing analysis. Some researchers use HHIs, ΔHHIs, or other concentration measures as independent variables in regressions undertaken to predict which mergers the competition agencies actually challenge or, more relevant here, to predict price effects (such as those suggested by merger retrospectives, examined further in subsection C.2; Kwoka and Gu 2015). Again, market definition (remarkably) goes unmentioned, but it is lurking, now in a qualitatively different manner. The market share measures used as independent variables must, of course, come from *some* market, even if the researchers do not tell us which ones or how the underlying market definition was chosen for each observation. As best one can tell, the implicit market definitions were chosen by some analyst, perhaps in a competition agency, *after* investigating the merger at hand.[7]

The problem is that the resulting independent variable is not independent, but in a manner different from and more problematic than familiar

---

7. In some of the literature discussed in section C, market definitions may in essence be drawn from government (e.g., census) or other data sources that do not delineate relevant markets in the antitrust sense.

endogeneity concerns. A competition agency seeking to challenge a merger in court or to extract concessions in a negotiation presumably believes that the merger is likely to be anticompetitive. Hence, when stating a market definition in such cases, it will present a narrow one so that market shares are high. Likewise, if analysis of a merger leaves the agency unconcerned about anticompetitive effects, one would expect the agency's documentation of that merger to indicate a broad market with low shares, to avoid raising questions about why it was permitting a highly concentrating merger. Assuming that those in the agency have some ability to predict mergers' effects and some tendency to choose underlying market definitions that are harmonious with their predictions rather than contradictory to them, any regression relating such market share measures to any outcome (dependent) variable cannot validate a structural presumption. Instead, a reverse-engineered market definition is generating reverse-engineered independent variables that were chosen precisely because they were thought to correlate with the dependent variable. All that the reported regressions tell us is that those doing the underlying work have some capacity to predict outcomes. When that outcome is, as in some papers, whether the agency in fact challenged the merger, we learn that the agency can predict itself (indeed, after it has made its decision). And when the dependent variable is the change in price, we learn that agency analysts can predict competitive effects using whatever means they employ to analyze mergers, which analysis generated the "independent" market share variables.[8]

---

8. Another important limitation will emerge in subsection C.2's discussion of merger retrospectives. As is familiar, they are performed (even before considering publication bias or problems of multiple hypothesis testing) on mergers that generate both interest and data, which disproportionately tend to be those that agencies challenge or were inclined to think may well have anticompetitive effects. Aside from any resulting biases regarding the core outcomes, one should also consider the implications of this selection for the use of such results in agency screening. Knowing that some group of independent variables may predict price effects (with associated regression weights) on a sample selected because of likely anticompetitive effects may not be very informative regarding how well those variables predict price effects in the much larger, unscreened set of all merger proposals—many of which would have been screened out in the past (during the time period of the mergers on which retrospectives were performed) precisely because the available information indicated the absence of price effects. To make this point more concrete, if it can be shown that price increases were caused by two-thirds of mergers that were permitted after a

C. Priors and Predictions

Because priors and predictions are interrelated in the manner described in section A, the presentation here does not sharply distinguish between them in much of the discussion. That said, most of the evidence assessed here concerns priors or the updating function that indicates how likely the evidence is given one or another merger explanation. For example, the industry studies examined in subsection 1 may indicate the likelihood that a hospital merger with certain attributes will raise prices. That might be viewed as a case-specific prior or as providing a mapping of case-specific facts to a likelihood.

The analysis is organized by methodology, although even in this respect there is overlap. For example, merger retrospectives—involving studies of particular consummated mergers—are examined in subsection 2, yet some of the industry studies in subsection 1 are properly regarded as retrospectives involving larger samples within a given industry. Likewise, the predictive accuracy of merger simulations, the subject of subsection 3, is often assessed by comparison with the results of merger retrospectives of some sort. The stock market event studies examined in subsection 4 could be used to cross-check any of the other sources of evidence (when there is sufficient public company data), although that has not been done systematically. Finally, subsection 5 discusses how industry expertise, extracted from the merging firms or provided by others, offers one of the most important independent sources of information and also provides context for assessing the usefulness of these other methods when analyzing a particular merger.

1. Industry Studies

The richest potential information base may be prior studies of the industry in which a proposed merger takes place. Occasionally, there may be analyses of numerous prior mergers, such as with hospitals. More often, there may be research undertaken for unrelated purposes that sheds light on demand, costs, and the nature of competitive interaction in an industry.

---

second request if they had some concentration measures above posited thresholds, it does not follow that, among mergers that were thought not to merit a second request, anywhere near two-thirds of them would cause a price increase if the same concentration measures were above those same thresholds.

And sometimes, particularly with new products or technologies, there may be little in this domain to guide prediction.

Let us begin with what may be the most favorable case, hospital mergers, where there have been large numbers that have been subject to extensive examination (Gaynor and Town 2012). These studies mostly find that, on average, prices increase.[9] A straightforward approach runs regressions that have some measure of the change in price as the dependent variable and a variety of independent variables. To predict the price effect of a proposed merger, one could insert pertinent values of the independent variables and use the coefficient estimates from past mergers. Some of these variables may be traits of the merging hospitals themselves, such as the type of care they offer and their distance from each other, taking the case of a simple merger of two hospitals rather than a merger involving hospital systems.

Of particular interest in light of merger guidelines and the structural presumption are independent variables constituting functions of market shares, whether each hospital's individual share, their combined share, the ΔHHI or postmerger HHI (naively computed), or otherwise. Regressions in the literature often include such variables, which immediately raises the question of how they address market definition. First note what is not done: there is no attempt to apply the HMT or various courts' informal rubrics to define the market for each merger; hence, these studies do not at all address how market shares in such "relevant markets" predict price increases. That would be impractical if not impossible, and it would lead to less reliable predictions even if it could be done.[10]

---

9. Some literature focuses on quality and does not clearly identify effects (Gaynor, Ho, and Town 2015). Craig, Grennan, and Swanson (2021) focus on purchasing power and find some evidence of target cost savings involving physician preference items. Other work examines how mergers of hospitals or insurers affect bargaining power between firms operating at different levels in the market (Gowrisankaran, Nevo, and Town 2015). Schmitt (2017) finds cost reductions only in out-of-market acquisitions, a result contrary to expectations (because the potential for in-market efficiencies seems strictly greater) that might be explained by selection (out-of-market mergers are undertaken only when there are efficiencies, whereas in-market mergers may be motivated by market power).

10. If one wishes to use a prior regression study (of the sort described in the text to follow) in order to predict the price effects of a proposed merger, the appropriate market for that purpose is emphatically not the HMT market or any other so-called relevant antitrust market. Instead, it is whatever "market" was used in the regression

Instead, studies typically use off-the-shelf "markets" from some standard data source or, particularly for geographic markets, simply stipulate (and perform sensitivity analysis on) market size, measured in miles or driving time. For example, an independent variable might be the ΔHHI in a market with a twenty-five mile or a thirty-minute radius from some center point or in some predefined metropolitan or hospital service area. Ultimately, the preferred specification may be selected using neither standard market definition, nor theory, nor some other a priori indication, but instead is based simply on whatever choice generates the best prediction (Dafny 2009; Garmon 2017).

It may also be true that the best fit would not use much or any market share information as such but instead some other indicator. For example, one might assess the competitive constraint imposed by nonmerging hospitals based on some formula reflecting their distance in geographic or product space rather than their market share when examining all hospitals inside some boundary. For assessing scale economies, patient volume is probably more relevant than market share in any market. But even these suggestions regarding how much one might appropriately deviate from using anything like market shares do not go far enough. Garmon (2017) finds that measures of willingness to pay and of upward pricing pressure predict mergers' price effects better than does the best of a variety of ΔHHI measures, even his own weighted service area measure that departs from traditional geographic market definition. And none of the tested methods perform well for mergers that appear to produce variable cost savings, which should not be surprising since none of them are designed to do so.

Reflecting on this somewhat atheoretical (and nonlegal) approach, we can see that it overcomes some of the key challenges. Obviously, it avoids the need to define markets in the manner depicted in competition law. Also, it implicitly (if only partially) embraces the endogeneity concerns with the structure-conduct-performance paradigm. Such a regression is agnostic

---

equation being employed to make the prediction. The converse is also true: if an industry merger regression of this sort indicates, for example, that ΔHHIs above some level predict price increases, it does not follow that those ΔHHIs can be used to calibrate a structural presumption (in that industry or more broadly) if such a presumption is to be applied, as under current law and guidelines, only in relevant antitrust markets that are defined differently and perhaps much more broadly or narrowly than those that underlie the particular regression estimates.

regarding where the market shares come from. It aims to predict changes in price from the actual mergers that endogenously occurred, in stark contrast to predicting price levels from concentration levels (Gaynor and Town 2012). Another benefit is that predicting a merger's effects ordinarily requires knowledge of demand, costs, and the nature of competitive interactions, whereas a regression estimated using a significant number of similar prior mergers employs a reduced form that implicitly captures the interactive effects of all these factors.

There are still important limitations. One is that observed mergers are still a selected sample, and they may have been selected differently during periods with more lax versus more rigorous enforcement. And even if the enforcement environment is constant, attributing causation still requires the strong and difficult-to-test assumption that firms choosing to merge do not differ from the comparators that do not (Dafny 2009).[11] In addition, past mergers may have occurred when there were different competitive conditions (government payment rules, degrees of competition among health insurance companies) and different technologies (expensive medical equipment subject to economies of scale). It may be possible to address some of these concerns, but not entirely.

Even with these and other important qualifications, however, a regression using large numbers of previous hospital mergers may well provide the best prediction—or at least a very significant piece of information—about the likely effects of a currently proposed hospital merger. This point is particularly powerful in light of the limitations of other methods. Also, anticipating subsection 3's consideration of merger simulations, it would be helpful to assess their reliability not only against single-merger retrospectives but also in light of regressions involving large numbers of mergers, although such attempts may be limited by the ability to obtain sufficient data on the underlying individual mergers to perform the simulations.[12]

---

11. Dafny (2009) focuses on effects on rivals' prices and uses rivals' co-location with other hospitals as an instrument for mergers, the strong identification assumption being that cost, demand, or other determinants of preexisting location close to other hospitals influence price growth only by affecting whether a subsequent merger occurs.
12. As suggested below, however, if agencies routinely kept such data on proposed mergers that were permitted, and likewise reported results of preferred and other simulations, subsequent retrospective analysis would be facilitated.

However much studies of past hospital mergers may facilitate prediction of the effects of proposed hospital mergers, this evidence provides little basis for predicting merger effects in other sectors. In addition to the usual caveats—even differences in just the demand elasticity in otherwise identical models can yield widely different predictions—many aspects of the hospital industry are idiosyncratic, including distinctive payment intermediaries (individuals obtain insurance from employers who contract with insurers who in turn bargain with hospitals), the importance of large government payors, and the regulation of entry. Although some other industries' mergers have received some attention, few have as many roughly similar mergers or have been subject to as much analysis as have hospital mergers.[13]

Another industry with many fairly similar past mergers is airlines. Kim and Singal (1993) examined mergers in the late 1980s, none of which were challenged. They compare routes influenced differentially by mergers and focus as well on rivals' prices. They find some evidence of efficiencies but overall higher prices. It is unclear the extent to which the price increases reflect unilateral or coordinated effects, although it may not be important to know the source of price increases in deciding whether to block a merger. A larger practical limitation is that the U.S. airlines industry and those in many other jurisdictions are now substantially more consolidated, so future mergers (or joint ventures) are likely to differ from those previously studied. Anticompetitive effects of subsequent airline mergers may well be greater, and efficiencies associated with scale and scope smaller, although possible efficiencies may now have a different character than they did decades ago.

In some industries, natural experiments that do not involve mergers may provide insight into competitive conditions and the likely impact of a merger. A familiar instance is the 1997 case in which a court blocked

---

13. There have also been a large number of mergers of kidney dialysis centers, where the evidence suggests reductions in quality (prices are substantially regulated by Medicare), although these effects may be explained by the transfer of management practices to acquired facilities rather than reduced competition (Eliason et al. 2020; Wollmann 2021). There are also a number of earlier studies of banking mergers (Pautler 2003) that present evidence of both increases in market power and of efficiencies, as well as recent work on some consumer goods (Bhattacharya, Illanes, and Stillerman 2023) that covers mostly small mergers and finds quite heterogeneous effects, with higher prices more common than lower prices.

the proposed merger of Staples and Office Depot. That dispute, like many, turned on market definition: whether office supply superstores constituted a relevant market. In reaching its decision on this question and on the merger overall, the court appears to have been influenced by the government's evidence suggesting that prices were higher in local geographic markets with fewer superstores and that prices tended to fall when another superstore entered the market. As is familiar, however, drawing conclusions from such evidence is problematic given the endogeneity of concentration and entry.

Regarding concentration, lower costs may both attract more firms and themselves result in lower prices, whereas higher demand may attract more firms but itself lead to higher prices. The effects of costs and competition in determining prices need to be disentangled (Bresnahan and Reiss 1991). Manuszak and Moul (2008) analyze more recent and complete data than that available to the litigants, employing a correction for the endogeneity of market structure, and find that a second and third superstore competitor each significantly reduce price.

Events involving entry are somewhat different. Like mergers, they have their own causal impact on prices. As discussed in section 5.A, in almost all settings entry will reduce prices. Exceptions tend to involve limiting cases: perfect competition with constant marginal cost and no fixed costs, and perfect cartels whose success and ideal price are unaffected by entry. Of course, mergers likewise generate upward pricing pressure in a broad range of settings, and it may be possible to look at past entry events to help illuminate the magnitude of this effect in a proffered merger.

Many of these issues were contested in the aforementioned *Staples* merger case, but it is difficult to ascertain from the court's opinion whether these rebuttals were mostly ignored, misunderstood, or found to be unpersuasive.[14] One interpretation is that the impact of superstore concentration and entry on price helped to convince the judge that superstores were a relevant market, at which point the extremely high concentration levels and increase in concentration carried the day. Regardless of the specific insights that may be gleaned from this particular case, we can see that in some instances there

---

14. For discussions by FTC economists, see Ashenfelter et al. (2006), Baker (1999), and Dalkir and Warren-Boulton (2004).

may be natural experiments in an industry from which cautious inferences may be drawn. Given that other sources of information bearing on a proposed mergers' effects are themselves usually subject to serious limitations, these experiments can sometimes assist the triangulation process.

Many proposed mergers are in industries for which there is no significant information base involving either prior mergers or natural experiments that enable strong inferences about a proffered merger's likely effects. Nevertheless—and even when some such evidence does exist—prior study of the industry without regard to mergers may be highly informative. Because such work involves a large portion of industrial organization research, little will be said here. Most familiar is work on demand estimation in the style of Berry, Levinsohn, and Pakes (1995), which is the basis for merger simulations in industries with differentiated products.[15] For example, Nevo (2000) presents such simulations (elaborated in subsection 3), drawing on the methods subsequently published in Nevo (2001). Whether as a direct input to merger simulation or otherwise, prior industry studies will often provide the best academic source of information for merger assessment. As discussed in subsection 5, such work complements what may be learned from industry experts as part of a merger investigation.

2. Merger Retrospectives

Merger retrospectives are generally understood to refer to studies of the effects of a single merger or a few past mergers in a particular industry. These may be contrasted with the research just examined, which retrospectively studies larger numbers of mergers in a single industry, wherein the observations in a regression typically involve different mergers in that industry rather than different price observations related to a single merger. There is some overlap; the distinction is used here only for expositional convenience.

A merger retrospective can be seen as a case study, where deep analysis may yield rich insights even if causation, precision, and external validity are uncertain. In recent decades, a number of retrospectives, along with analyses that seek to draw inferences from collections of these studies, have attempted to make further headway.

---

15. Technical challenges are explored in Dubé, Fox, and Su (2012) and Knittel and Metaxoglou (2014). Conlon and Gortmaker (2020) offer methods to help surmount these obstacles.

Identification often poses a powerful challenge. Consider a standard difference-in-differences design wherein the change in prices charged by the merging firms postmerger is compared to the change in prices charged by a comparator firm (or group of firms, such as with the use of a synthetic control). Fundamentally, we have what might be called an $n=1$ problem that is related to the increasingly recognized need (which was not well appreciated when many of these retrospectives were conducted) to cluster standard errors appropriately (Bertrand, Duflo, and Mullainathan 2004; Donald and Lang 2007). Take an idealized setting with no noise or other form of measurement error, which is as if we had a perfect measure of price, before and after, for the merging firms and the comparator. In that case, we in a sense have four data points that we are using to estimate the intercept and three additional coefficients: those on the postmerger dummy, the merging firms' dummy, and the interaction term. With no degrees of freedom, no conclusion can be drawn.

Put more intuitively, the identifying assumptions in this type of difference-in-differences framework are that there exist no factors that affected just the merging firms or just the comparator, either before or after the merger. Some or all these assumptions may fail to hold, in part because the decision to merge is itself endogenous. They often cannot be verified independently, so inferences are treacherous.

There are additional, partly related concerns. Consider the challenge of choosing the comparator firm(s) (Nevo and Whinston 2010). To minimize the likelihood that the comparator is influenced by the merger itself or the forces that endogenously led to the merger proposal, one would like the comparator to be in an unrelated environment, but the more that is true, the more likely it is subject to distinctive shocks before or after the time of the merger. Hence, in order to maximize the similarities in order to address this identification problem, we would like the comparator to be as similar as possible, but in many settings this will mean that it may be affected by the merger.[16] Splitting the difference might help, but it also may result in substantial problems of both types.

---

16. Ashenfelter and Hosken (2010) use private label products as their control and nonmerging firms' branded products for robustness checks. Both may underestimate mergers' price effects because one would expect the prices of these control products to rise as a consequence of an anticompetitive merger, albeit to a lesser degree.

Sometimes, substantial insight may be gained when a merger spans heterogeneous, partly independent settings. With an airline merger, we can compare price changes on routes with competitive overlap to ones without overlap. And with a merger of hospital chains rather than of single hospitals, analogous comparisons are possible. Some retrospectives are able to take advantage of additional features of the merging firms. For example, they may produce two products with similar technologies and inputs that are sold under very different competitive conditions, so a price increase for the product subject to little competition, relative to that subject to intense competition, may more plausibly be identified as an anticompetitive effect of the merger (Ashenfelter, Hosken, and Weinberg 2013). Clearly, some judgment is involved, and what can be learned will vary substantially across retrospectives.

Another difficulty concerns the length of the event window. Shorter periods, often a few years, are preferred to reduce concerns about confounding shocks in the before and after periods (and they may also be required due to limits of data availability).[17] But some merger effects take longer to materialize. Retrospectives that find merger efficiencies tend to see them emerging a couple years out, turning initial price increases into price decreases or mitigating a significant portion of the initial price increase (Ashenfelter, Hosken, and Weinberg 2014; Focarelli and Panetta 2003). Sheen (2014) obtains similar results in a large sample of consumer product mergers. Entry and product repositioning may likewise take time. Indeed, so may some anticompetitive effects, particularly those involving capacity reductions. As noted in subsection 3.B.1, Berry and Pakes's (1993) simulations in a Cournot setting show that many mergers will not immediately affect price because of the continued utilization of preexisting capacity, whereas prices eventually rise over time as postmerger investment falls.

Finally, there are more mundane but potentially important issues. Because so many specification choices must be made (and some, like the

---

17. A related (but avoidable) problem is that most retrospectives pool postmerger years rather than separately identifying price effects year by year. Mariuzzo and Ormosi (2019) examine the minority of retrospectives that report each year separately and find that those mergers had significant price increases in the first year but small, statistically insignificant price declines (relative to premerger prices) in the second year.

choice of comparator, may be made with some awareness of how prices actually changed), there are familiar concerns with multiple hypothesis testing. The choice of which mergers to study may likewise be made with some knowledge of the mergers' effects, along with salience that may be related to competition agencies' expressed concerns, and we also have familiar concerns about publication bias.[18]

For these reasons and others, Carlton (2009) has proposed that competition agencies record specific contemporaneous predictions—and how one might test those predictions afterward (analogous to the preregistration of protocols and hypotheses to test)—which would permit not only more credible but also more refined assessments of the agencies' methods. For example, if different merger simulations were run and certain specifications were preferred for particular reasons, one might learn more about agencies' choices among methods and not just their bottom line from subsequent merger retrospectives. This suggestion is elaborated in subsection 3.

Even with these substantial limitations, some merger retrospectives may serve as valuable case studies for particular merger proposals. Expanding an agency's field of view to encompass even a single prior merger of a similar type can significantly enhance analysis, particularly in the early stages when information and time are scarce. By contrast, the actual results of a retrospective often provide limited direct indication of the effects of a subsequently proposed merger in light of the often significant differences between substantial mergers even within a single industry (Nevo and Whinston 2010). Subsection 1's discussion of past versus future airline mergers illustrates this point.

Separate from providing insight into a particular proposed merger in a specific industry, Kwoka (2014) and others suggest that the overall findings from dozens of retrospectives, which suggest that a majority of the studied mergers raised prices, imply that merger enforcement has been too lenient, at least over the earlier time periods when most of the mergers subject to retrospectives occurred. That insight can be useful in calibrating overall stringency, including perhaps by suggesting the need for additional agency

---

18. For example, Ashenfelter and Hosken (2010) consciously selected five mergers that seemed most likely to be problematic. Additional limitations of difference-in-differences analysis in antitrust settings are discussed in Simpson and Schmidt (2008).

resources to the extent that agencies' challenge rates are significantly constrained by their capacity. However, even this modest conclusion has generated significant differences of opinion, in part for the aforementioned reasons but also because retrospectives have tended to cluster in a handful of industries and various idiosyncratic limitations apply to some particular investigations (Ashenfelter, Hosken, and Weinberg 2014; Hunter, Leonard, and Olley 2008; Kwoka 2014, 2019; Vita and Osinski 2018; Werden 2015). Asker and Nocke (2021) catalog merger retrospectives published in leading journals from 2000 to 2020 and conclude that it is difficult to reach firm conclusions: price changes vary widely, outcome variables differ across studies, and few examine effects on price, entry, investment, or innovation over longer time periods.

Nevertheless, it appears that several particular retrospectives are quite informative even if they fall short of directly providing confident predictions of the effects of a proposed merger in a similar setting. Moreover, the fact that many find that approved mergers resulted in notable price increases suggests that merger regulation may have been too cautious in the past.

3. Merger Simulations

Merger simulations have come to be the leading formal means by which industrial organization economists predict the effects of horizontal mergers (Baker and Bresnahan 1985; Nevo 2000). Using the now-familiar methods noted in subsection 1, this methodology begins by using instrumental variables to estimate a structural model of demand using additional assumptions about the supply side, including Bertrand-Nash behavior. A merger is then simulated using the estimated parameters, typically assuming that nothing changes except that the firms' products come under common ownership—and perhaps the merged firms' marginal costs are taken to fall by some stipulated amount (Angrist and Pischke 2010; Nevo and Whinston 2010).

In academic work, the data is that available to the econometrician. When merger simulations are undertaken by competition agencies in the course of merger review, they may have access to more precise data, although that may be limited in various ways. As suggested in subsection 1, in this setting some of a simulation model's calibrations could be drawn from prior studies of the industry, particularly when performing the analysis at an early screening stage.

It is well understood that both the estimation and simulation aspects of these efforts depend on a number of assumptions that themselves are often untested (Berry and Reiss 2007; Angrist and Pischke 2010; Nevo and Whinston 2010; Conlon and Gortmaker 2020). These include the functional form of demand and of firms' cost functions and the nature of competitive interaction, supplemented by standard assumptions on the instruments employed in the estimation. Assumptions regarding the supply side have received relatively less attention. In addition, there needs to be more exploration of how best to think about the appropriate confidence intervals or bounds resulting from such simulations in light of the fact that they should reflect not only estimation error but also model error, the latter relating both to the model as such and what is and is not assumed to change as a consequence of the simulated merger.

In addition, it is familiar that these techniques primarily enable the estimation of unilateral price effects in mergers of firms offering differentiated products.[19] Importantly, they do not address coordinated effects. As suggested by the discussion in subsection 3.B.3, however, this approach does enable estimation of how much prices would increase if a merger were successful in enabling coordination. It may also help to address some factors bearing on the ease of coordination, such as by estimating how much a merger would affect Nash reversion payoffs in the punishment phase of a supergame.

A natural way to assess the reliability of merger simulations would be to compare their predictions to the actual price effects of consummated mergers. Efforts to do so have proved to be challenging. At a high level, one must choose which of many simulation predictions should be compared to which of many possible estimates of the actual price effects of a completed merger. Hence, whenever it is stated that a merger simulation over-, under-, or accurately predicts the effects of an actual merger, the statement is conditional on structural choices of the functional form for demand, the validity of the instruments, and also the selection of comparator firms for the merged entity, time periods for assessing price effects, and more.

---

19. Merger simulations can also take other forms, such as when bargaining models are estimated and then used to simulate a merger's effects.

Because there are important judgment calls with each and many possible combinations of the two, it is inherently difficult for a researcher performing an ex post analysis to determine the reliability of merger simulation and to credibly convey findings to a broader audience. If there were large numbers of such comparisons—perhaps a hundred actual mergers, each with predictions and outcomes, undertaken with common methodologies—we would have usual problems with noise but may be able to draw more confident conclusions. Instead, there have been only a handful of such comparisons, undertaken using a variety of approaches (typically chosen after the fact), so generalizations are difficult.

Weinberg and Hosken (2013) and Weinberg (2011) together examine three mergers of branded consumer products, the mergers having been chosen because they seem to fit well the target domain of merger simulation methods. One simulation modestly underestimated the price increase, another estimated a large price increase when there was none, and the third found a price increase with the lower bound of the confidence interval above the price increase predicted by the simulation. Even with the benefit of hindsight, it was difficult to explain the reasons for the mismatches.[20]

These and most other assessments of merger simulations mentioned next pay less attention to the actual price effects of the mergers under examination, by comparison to the effort devoted to the simulations themselves. The aforementioned two articles use private label products as comparators, although their prices may have been affected by the mergers under examination. Some of the articles noted below use more informal observational means of determining the actual effects of the merger. This raises the possibility that the discrepancies between predictions and actual price effects are difficult to reconcile not because of weaknesses of the merger simulations but because the mergers' price effects are mismeasured. But it is also possible that the actual discrepancies were larger or even of different signs, so

---

20. Some of the particulars are alarming, including signs of intermediate estimates that seem difficult to understand; in one case, a standard method yielded estimates that seemed two orders of magnitude too high. The authors were able to find some combinations of model and estimation technique that generated simulation results close to estimated price effects, but this does not illuminate how to make appropriate merger simulation choices ex ante.

perhaps the gaps between predictions and reality are even more concerning than they at first appear.

Peters (2006) assesses the predictive power of merger simulations of five airline mergers in the 1980s. He finds that, even using postmerger information, it is difficult to reconcile the merger simulations with actual price effects. He suggests as a primary explanation that some of the mergers changed firms' conduct in a manner that resulted in more effective price coordination, which is outside the scope of standard merger simulation. Many of his more detailed findings are also of interest, including that certain demand assumptions overpredicted price increases in some mergers but underpredicted them in others and that the requisite conduct adjustments needed to reconcile results even with a single demand system seem to differ in sign across the mergers. The study also highlights the need in some settings to rely on questionable assumptions about instruments, here that airlines' decisions about airport presence, flight frequency, and network structure are exogenous.

These efforts have been supplemented by analyses of other mergers (Nevo 2000; Björnerstedt and Verboven 2016). For example, Miller and Weinberg (2017) use merger simulation to predict the price effects of a beer merger and find that these predictions (undertaken after the fact) underestimate the price effects they attribute to the merger. Their preferred explanation takes both the predictions and the estimates of observed price effects to be correct on their own terms, suggesting that the discrepancy should be attributed to the merger's creation of coordinated effects.

Taken together, research to date that compares the predictions of merger simulations to actual price effects does not yet enable us to gauge the reliability of the standard approach or to suggest best practices regarding the design of merger simulations in different contexts. Given the state of the literature and the inherent challenges involved in the exercise, it appears that an elaborated version of Carlton's (2009) previously discussed suggestion is in order. To begin, it would be helpful if competition agencies documented in some detail their analysis of proffered mergers that plausibly would result in nontrivial anticompetitive effects. This requires more than point estimates of the prices of the merged parties' products and nonmerging firms' products after the merger. For example, one would want to know the methods employed, data used, and why one or another specification was ultimately preferred. Moreover, agencies should record the other sources of information employed in the triangulation process, such as what could be gleaned from the merging parties' internal documents, interviews with competitors, and opinions of others knowledgeable about the industry—and how the agencies assessed that information.

Moreover, this documentation would ideally be supplemented by a sketch of a plausible research plan for subsequently determining a merger's actual effects on prices. Due to the many ways of choosing comparator firms and other aspects of merger retrospectives, subsequent assessments would be more credible if many of these choices were outlined in advance. The combination of the two would maximize the potential to learn which methods of merger prediction—including through the use of merger simulation—are most effective. Independently, the retrospectives themselves would add to our knowledge base, and they would contribute even more value through this form of preregistration of research design. As a final note, which is taken up in chapter 7, these considerations reinforce the value of using independent expertise in the adjudication of pending mergers.

Despite its limitations and uncertainties, merger simulation has significant value. First, its power has to be compared to alternative means of prediction, which have their own weaknesses. Second, different methods of prediction are complementary. For example, merger simulation can be used to assess whether basic understandings of an industry and various other sources of predictions are mutually consistent. To the extent that they are not, merger simulation can identify paths of inquiry that might help reconcile conflicting information and inferences, such as by providing bounds on what one would have to believe about certain parameters to reach a particular conclusion about a proposed merger. Indeed, at its core merger simulation can be understood as combining all available information about a merger to draw inferences about the merger's effects. Making such determinations in a disciplined manner should improve the quality of decision-making even if we remain unsure, for example, about the estimated diversion ratio between the merging firms' products.

4. Stock Market Event Studies

A rather different source of information about the effects of horizontal mergers comes from stock market event studies, which are sometimes supplemented by post-acquisition studies of firm performance derived from merged firms' financial statements. Although much less granular than industry studies, retrospectives, and simulations, and often quite noisy, this type of evidence may help in the formulation of broad priors about the effects of horizontal mergers. It generally cannot provide information about a proposed merger because announcement effects—which are all an agency would have initially—entangle too many types of information, some unrelated to the effects of the merger as such.[21] Given the many limitations of the other methods, this research—and extensions thereof with greater involvement of industrial organization economists—may provide incremental illumination. At best, however, these event studies are limited to public acquirers, and, as we will see, they are subject to their own substantial qualifications.

The first significant obstacle in this research program is the determination of which mergers are horizontal. Because these investigations use broad samples of mergers and data sources constructed for other purposes—mostly the study of corporate (including managerial) behavior and the efficiency of financial markets—researchers must determine the relationship between the acquirer and target through other means. Most commonly, this is done with broad industry codes that are quite coarse, although newer methods are also being employed.[22]

Not only does this approach introduce significant noise, reducing statistical power (an important point because many findings in this literature are imprecisely estimated nulls), but it often confounds horizontal and vertical mergers. Many methods of determining the relatedness of the merging parties have this problem. Hence, a study might conclude that related-firm acquisitions as a whole improve efficiency rather than contribute to market power (using methods discussed below), but that would be consistent with a large portion of the sample involving vertical mergers that have this feature and a minority of the sample involving horizontal mergers, many of which generate little efficiency gain but augment market

---

21. Nevertheless, an agency might examine the stock market reaction to its own actions, such as second requests. But if the market knew an agency would use such reactions in making its decisions, inferences would be confounded.

22. Kahle and Walkling (1996) document very large discrepancies between CRSP and Compustat regarding which mergers are horizontal. Fan and Lang (2000) take a different approach that constructs input-output measures to identify vertical relationships between merging firms. Hoberg and Phillips (2010, 2016) develop text-based analysis of public firms' filings with the SEC.

power.²³ Some studies emphasize results from mergers that are challenged by agencies, which substantially alleviates this problem. This aspect of the subject could be further illuminated by more cross-fertilization between industrial organization and financial economists.

The next challenge is to distinguish between market power and efficiency explanations for mergers by using stock prices or other performance measures, because these mainly indicate whether the merger is profitable rather than the source of any anticipated profits. (There is also a significant literature that assesses whether managerial and behavioral explanations rather than profit maximization drive mergers, finding significant evidence for the former.²⁴) The standard approach is to focus on the stock price reaction of the merging firms' rivals: efficient mergers that reduce price tend to

---

23. This possibility is reinforced by selection: vertical mergers typically need efficiencies to be profitable, whereas horizontal mergers that enhance market power can be profitable even without efficiencies—indeed, even when diseconomies are present.

24. Some of this literature includes market power as a synergy because the alternative explanations under consideration are that CEOs are overly optimistic or seek to enhance their pay or build their empires (Harford 1999; Datta, Iskandar-Datta, and Raman 2001; Harford, Humphery-Jenner, and Powell 2012). Malmendier and Tate (2008) find significant evidence that CEO overoptimism drives acquisitions. Some of the finance literature addresses whether market misvaluations may explain mergers. For example, Shleifer and Vishny (2003) suggest that acquirers will be inclined to use their own overpriced stock to make acquisitions, in which case negative announcement returns or subsequent low returns may reflect adjusted valuations rather than non profit-maximizing decisions. Rhodes-Kropf and Viswanathan (2004), Savor and Lu (2009), and Fu, Lin, and Officer (2013) investigate additional aspects of this hypothesis. Importantly for present purposes, however, most literature exploring non-neoclassical merger motives does not separately examine horizontal mergers, which would have limited sample size and raised significant challenges of categorization that are explored earlier in the text. It is an open question whether optimism bias, for example, may be attenuated in horizontal acquisitions because information about the target is better, and if bias remains it is unclear whether a CEO is more likely to be overly optimistic about achieving efficiencies or enhancing market power. Malmendier, Moretti, and Peters (2018) find evidence that acquirers of unrelated targets fare worse than acquirers of related targets. Morck, Shleifer, and Vishny (1990) find evidence of managers undertaking mergers in order to obtain private benefits. Considering another hypothesis, acquirers may be better able to identify market undervaluation of a target firm when that firm is in the same or a related industry than when its operations are unrelated to those of the acquirer.

hurt rivals whereas mergers that raise market power and hence price tend to benefit rivals (Eckbo 1983; Stillman 1983).[25] Sometimes supplemental tests are used to examine effects on the merging firms' customers (who benefit from efficient mergers but lose from those that enhance market power) and suppliers (which also permits assessments of whether horizontal mergers contribute to monopsony power). These methods are valuable but raise the additional challenges of identifying these rivals, customers, and suppliers. Focusing on mergers challenged by competition agencies helps when the agencies have made public the requisite information.

For each of these groups of related firms, and often for one or both of the merging firms, there is the further difficulty that often only a modest fraction of a firm's activity is related in the specified manner. Hence, any stock price reactions in the hypothesized channels are likely to be small and often swamped by other information associated with merger announcements (McAfee and Williams 1988). For this reason, some analysts examine the effects on more narrowly defined rivals (those with more focused businesses) or on rivals as a whole (Fee and Thomas 2004).

A central challenge in all such studies is the need to disentangle information about the effects of the merger as such from other information revealed to the market, particularly from merger announcements. Even large samples may be of little help, for example, if merger announcements tend to signal improved or diminished opportunities for rivals to be acquired, rising or falling prospects in the industry, or prior overvaluation of acquirers or undervaluation of targets. Keeping in mind that mergers are endogenous and that any announcement effects arise only when the merger proposal was not fully anticipated, there is every reason to believe that the market may be learning more than just the likelihood that the particular merger will ultimately occur. The solution advanced by Eckbo and Wier (1985) and followed in some subsequent work is to focus on the market's reaction to merger challenges, successful decisions to block mergers, and merging

---

25. Stiebale and Szücs (2022) employ a complementary approach (to mergers in the EU) that uses accounting data to estimate changes in rivals' markups. They find higher postmerger rival markups, suggesting anticompetitive effects. Yet surprisingly, these changes, which presumably are due to price increases by the merging parties, rise over time and only become significant years after the mergers occur.

parties being permitted to proceed with their merger when a challenge is dropped or overturned in court. Although still subject to qualifications (notably, that these events affect how subsequent mergers in the industry are likely to be treated by the competition regime), they do provide cleaner tests, and the outcomes noted below often differ from what one may have inferred from initial announcements.

All inferences from stock market price reactions, particularly in short event windows, presume that those driving stock prices—notably, analysts—have genuine and fairly rapid insight into mergers' effects. Here it is worth noting that they have complementary information to that usually available to industrial organization economists or competition agencies, and their incentives are strong even if sometimes misaligned (because they are in large part predicting others' short-run reactions rather than long-run effects). Here, large sample sizes are particularly helpful, although they permit only fairly broad characterizations of mergers' effects. Some research has questioned the ability of announcement returns to predict subsequent performance (Ben-David, Bhattacharya, and Jacobsen 2022). In this respect, results focusing on subsequent challenges and other post-announcement events are more likely to be probative, in part because analysts by that point will have spent more effort assessing the likely effects of the previously proposed merger.

Having explored a variety of important obstacles, consider now some of the findings that employ the methods that have been suggested to offer the most plausible means of inference. Fee and Thomas (2004) examine announcement-related stock price reactions and postmerger changes in operating performance of rivals, customers, and suppliers in a large sample of horizontal mergers in the 1980s and 1990s. They find some evidence of improved productive efficiency and enhanced buying power and little that is consistent with increased market power. Shahrur (2005) undertakes a complementary investigation, which employs a different method to identify rivals, suppliers, and customers, and obtains roughly similar results while identifying some differences and refinements regarding buying power. Some of the evidence suggests countervailing power, which is to say that buyer power is enhanced particularly when upstream suppliers are concentrated. See also Bhattacharyya and Nain (2011). The survey by Betton, Eckbo, and Thorburn (2008) emphasizes results on challenged mergers from Eckbo (1983) and Fee and Thomas (2004), finding that rivals experience positive returns when mergers are challenged. This survey also points to results on gains to customers that are inconsistent with a market power explanation. Other studies are less sanguine about mergers generating efficiencies (Röller, Stennek, and Verboven 2006).

One must be cautious, however, in drawing conclusions from average results in large samples. Even when analysis is confined to horizontal acquisitions, there remains the problem that averages can be quite misleading a guide to merger review. They may provide us with priors for these mergers as a whole, but it is also important to know the distribution of the outcomes. Horizontal mergers may collectively benefit customers because many generate efficiencies while only a minority are anticompetitive.[26] But most competition agencies are not contemplating whether to challenge all horizontal mergers.

It would be helpful to know what portion of these mergers—even supposing that on average they are benign—may nevertheless be anticompetitive and to what degree. This presents a challenging inference problem, particularly in light of how noisy this evidence is and all of the obstacles to interpretation. Nevertheless, further work that tries to determine the fraction of these mergers that may be anticompetitive would be useful. Even supposing, as seems likely, that some nontrivial portion is anticompetitive, competition agencies would still need to determine which mergers make up that portion. Nevertheless, knowing whether that fraction is tiny, small, or fairly large would be quite helpful. Perhaps this task is infeasible given data limitations and challenges to identification, but some effort at the intersection of industrial organization and financial economics could provide further illumination. In light of the significant difficulties of drawing inferences from other sources of evidence, it is important not to overlook even lines of research that offer only modest prospects for enlightenment.

---

26. If this body of evidence or future refinements do support the claim that horizontal mergers as a whole benefit consumers, that in itself would helpfully inform priors about efficiencies, which many merger analysts find to be dubious. That said, there remains the important point about selection and the merging firms' rationality constraint: for a proposed merger to be profitable, it is sufficient for it to generate just efficiencies or just anticompetitive effects, and the larger are the latter, the lower need be the former (including the possibility of no efficiencies and the presence of diseconomies).

5. Industry Expertise

We generally suppose that firms understand the demand for their products, cost functions, and competitive conditions better than do outside observers, be they econometricians or competition agencies. We make inferences from firms' rationality constraints. Specifically, in demand estimation, we ordinarily suppose that the firms themselves know their marginal cost and marginal revenue.

Accordingly, an important source of evidence in merger review consists of firms' internal documents, particularly those produced in the ordinary course of business, many of which may not pertain to contemplated mergers. In addition to constituting a useful information base in itself, such evidence is also complementary to other sources for formulating priors and predictions. Internal evidence can help guide the analysis of broader industry characteristics, and the latter information can help place internal documents in context. This documentary evidence can be further supplemented by questioning pertinent employees of the merging firms.

Many who have spent time at competition agencies view internal evidence as valuable, but with familiar caveats. Obviously, presentations to a board deciding whether to approve a merger may be lawyered, in the sense of being crafted to smooth the path to approval by the reviewing agency. Another, often opposite concern is with so-called hot documents, often brief passages (in modern times, in emails and chats) whose interpretation may be subject to dispute and whose generation may raise questions regarding the actual knowledge, authority, and motivation of the author.[27]

---

27. It is not always appreciated how complex the internal workings of organizations can be, which can pose significant challenges when attempting to extract a "firm's" understanding of important phenomena. Internal emails and other documents may reflect firm politics, bureaucratic infighting, disagreements, statements by disgruntled employees who may have strong views that are largely ignored, and cryptic indications from key decision-makers who do not clearly articulate their actual thinking lest they upset those who disagree. One suspects that these concerns are greater for hot documents (and for "cold" ones that might appear to rule out anticompetitive motivations) than for raw data, analyses thereof, decisions regarding the reconfiguration of production and distribution, and other matters that may better reveal operational understandings that guide concrete decisions rather than stated opinions of particular individuals that may or may not command agreement or generate action.

On the other hand, it is difficult to successfully operate a complex business with little internal understanding of costs, demand, and competitive conditions. Moreover, in the course of business, much relevant data will be collected and interpreted, leaving significant written traces. These points apply not only to competitive effects but also to efficiencies and, relatedly, to entry and product repositioning. The nature of economies of scale and scope and realms of plausible synergies should be appreciated inside the merging firms. An important qualification here is that some merger-specific synergies—particularly if they are specific to a particular merger and not one of many possible horizontal mergers that might have been contemplated—are more likely to be explored in connection with the acquirer's exploration of the merger under review, raising questions about whether the written record produced is sincere or crafted to ease merger clearance. These observations seem particularly apt to acquisitions of small, distinctive upstarts.

Industry expertise does not, however, reside only in the merging firms. Agencies often contact large, sophisticated buyers who understand competitive conditions and have an incentive to provide credible input to the investigation because their self-interest tends to align with consumer welfare. This alignment can be imperfect: for example, a merger may raise their prices somewhat but disadvantage their competitors even more due to differences in product mixes, production technology, and geography (Heyer 2007). And their knowledge of the merging firms' technology—both existing cost functions and potential merger synergies—is likely to be thinner than their understanding of demand and competitive conditions.

More broadly, agencies can seek the advice of other industry experts, including consultants, analysts, financiers, retired executives, and so forth. As with all sources of industry expertise, even limited knowledge can be highly illuminating, particularly with respect to mergers of a type that the agency rarely sees. Qualitative insights may not dictate ultimate decisions but can illuminate paths of investigation and help put assembled information in context. These benefits suggest one of the points in the next chapter on institutions: agencies' teams of economists and lawyers should be supplemented more extensively by complementary expertise regarding particular industries, offering perspectives reflecting business insights about competition, technology, marketing, and more.

7 Institutions

The preceding chapters focus on how best to analyze proposed mergers in order to decide whether they should be permitted or blocked. However, a merger regime can only be as good as the institutions that administer it. Section A considers enhancements to competition agencies' skill sets through greater expertise regarding business operations and organization as well as knowledge of particular industries. Section B briefly discusses how U.S. courts could better adjudicate merger challenges by drawing more directly on expertise of all types to help structure litigation in a manner that would better engage with battling experts, business witnesses, and other evidence. Section C examines whether greater use of ex post merger review may be valuable given the difficulty of predicting mergers' effects, particularly for acquisitions of nascent entrants in rapidly changing industries. Finally, section D comments on the division of regulatory labor between competition agencies and other government entities.

A. Agency Expertise

The prediction of proposed mergers' future effects is understood to be a challenging enterprise but one that is necessary to undertake in order to preserve competition while avoiding undue suppression of potential synergies. Over the past half-century, industrial organization research has improved techniques, particularly regarding prospective unilateral anticompetitive effects in differentiated products industries. On the other hand, beginning with the demise of the structure-conduct-performance paradigm, we also have come to better appreciate the limits of our knowledge.

The analysis in the preceding chapters reinforces this perspective and exposes additional obstacles along several dimensions. Regarding unilateral effects with differentiated products, it is necessary to estimate—or guesstimate using triangulation from a range of sources—not only diversion ratios but also the merging firms' margins. Analysis of coordinated effects is particularly challenging. The correct theoretical underpinnings of efficiencies and entry (both ex post and ex ante) are still being developed, and it is clear that many practical applications will be difficult, particularly under the time and resource constraints of merger review.

This section aims to elaborate some of these ideas with a particular focus on the types of expertise that are required and how agencies might broaden their skill sets to enhance their ability to scrutinize aspects of proposed mergers that have not often been carefully assessed in the past. Specifically, the suggestion is that business expertise of various types, particularly in sectors where the agencies have less experience, would usefully complement existing strengths in mainstream areas of industrial organization economics. Moreover, such expertise is quite valuable from the outset, at the early screening stage, and throughout investigations conducted by economists and lawyers, not just after a challenge has been launched, when the agencies employ experts to conduct analyses to bolster their case in court.

To begin, consider the greatest strength of current merger analysis: the prediction of unilateral price effects in mergers involving differentiated products. With sufficient data, valid instruments, and functional form assumptions, we can determine both diversion ratios and margins and thereby conduct merger simulations. Even so, better understanding of an industry—which academic researchers may take years to develop whereas agencies have only months—provides useful guidance. Much more often, particularly in the relevant time frame and given limitations on the data that agencies can obtain, it will be impossible to undertake such estimation nearly as well, if at all. Agencies can sometimes consult large, sophisticated buyers to request their insights on substitution, but they will not be as able to illuminate sellers' margins. The merging firms' accounting and other internal information can be examined for this purpose, but it is often difficult to extract the relevant measure of marginal cost even to a good approximation. For example, it is challenging to determine what portion of selling, general, and administrative expenses (SG&A) are marginal costs, and of which products.[1]

---

1. This has proved controversial even on an aggregate basis, as reflected in attempts to measure markups in the economy as a whole (De Loecker, Eeckhout, and Unger 2020; Traina 2018).

By contrast, as developed below, individuals with industry experience may be able to offer significant illumination even if not precision.

The prediction of coordinated effects is far more difficult. One can attempt to calibrate models indicating whether price elevation can be sustained as an equilibrium of a supergame. But that requires knowledge of many features that, again, are difficult to extract even over a period of years of academic study. There are familiar factors regarding the plausibility of coordination, many of which are soft and also difficult to combine. Is it likely that some coordinated price elevation is already taking place? How easy is it for the firms to detect deviations, whether presently or postmerger? How long does detection and a punishment response take to implement? Which firms are most likely to cheat, preventing coordination premerger or posing the greatest constraint postmerger? Data available to an agency is woefully insufficient to enable detailed analysis of these and other questions. Nor is it straightforward for agency economists or lawyers to extract answers from the merging firms' documents or when taking depositions of key employees. Given this low baseline, industry expertise would be quite helpful in addressing such questions.

Chapter 4 analyzes efficiencies, which receive much less attention in agencies' merger reviews due in part to difficulties of assessment. The analysis there suggests that the challenges are even greater than appreciated. Merger specificity can be understood only by reference to literature on the theory of the firm and in organizational economics, supplemented by a better empirical understanding of internal firm practices as well as complex contracting arrangements, such as those used in many manufacturing supply chains.[2] One of the reasons that verifiability often proves to be an obstacle to assessing efficiencies is that agency economists do not have a good understanding of true synergies and, relatedly, what corroborating or contradictory internal evidence we should expect to find or how to best interpret it.[3]

---

2. As discussed in chapter 4, another challenge is that alternatives to merger that involve contracts between competitors often require substantial supervision that itself is even more difficult when agencies lack the relevant expertise. A lack of relevant expertise likewise inhibits the effectiveness of behavioral remedies and, often overlooked, of structural remedies, such as in determining who should be permitted to purchase spun off assets.

3. These obstacles are by no means the only reasons. Often the merging parties' proffers are quite thin, suggesting that actual efficiencies are likely to be negligible. There is

Efficiency assessments could be improved by supplementing agencies' skill sets in two ways. In terms of general skills, expertise lies in organizational economics, management practices, operations, contracting, and other fields typically associated with business schools and consulting firms that advise on operations and restructuring. These competencies would usefully complement industrial organization economists' training in modeling and structural estimation.

In order to assess efficiencies in particular merger investigations, however, expertise specific to the industry is likely to be essential. To some degree, breadth may be possible; for example, retailing, logistics, aspects of manufacturing and related supply chains, and the use of business IT have significant common elements across applications. At a minimum, such experts could help guide investigations, identify situations where their experience may not extend, and work better with industry-specific experts, as well as process information from key employees in firms, such as when the merging parties bring them to the agencies or when their depositions are taken. Individuals with both general business skills and industry-specific expertise will better know the right questions to ask and have a better sense of what constitutes plausible answers.

Chapter 5's assessment of ex post and ex ante entry raises additional questions that could better be illuminated with similar assistance. Determining the prospects for ex post entry and, importantly, how that feeds back on the expected profitability of a proposed merger is essential to making proper inferences from the merging firms' rationality constraint. These matters are again more in the domain of industry expertise than part of the modern industrial organization economics toolkit.

Ex ante considerations are substantially more difficult and often would require even more focused industry expertise. Of particular note is the long-neglected but recently emphasized concern about incumbents' acquisitions of nascent entrants, particularly in rapidly evolving technology sectors. Even determination of whether targets' perhaps not-yet-existent products

---

some risk, however, of being caught in a self-confirming cycle. Teams working with the merging firms likewise do not understand these matters very well, and they also anticipate that agencies would be unlikely to give significant attention to synergies even if more substantial presentations were made. This state of affairs is also unconducive to learning through experience.

are substitutes or complements to those of the incumbent, at present or in the likely near-term evolution of an industry, can pose an almost impossible challenge for agencies. Agencies also cannot readily discern whether the target is distinctive or soon to be joined by other firms earlier in the pipeline, or whether established firms operating in adjacent spheres are likely to expand into the seemingly sparse domain now inhabited only by the target and a few others.

By contrast, venture capitalists and private equity firms make these assessments for a living when choosing investments, performing interim assessments, offering advice, and serving on boards. Recently exited entrepreneurs, some industry analysts, and consultants likewise are in the business of understanding and predicting such things. Despite significant limitations, such individuals probably have a significant comparative advantage over those at competition agencies who assess these mergers. Perhaps agencies could employ a few such individuals with these experiences and skills or at least have some on call, to be quickly engaged when important investigations in those sectors commence.

Competition agencies obviously now draw on industry expertise in several ways. In some sectors, such as hospital mergers in the United States, there have been so many investigations and challenges that in-house expertise is undoubtedly substantial. But many proposed mergers are in areas where agencies have little experience. Another important obstacle concerns inherent limits on agencies' ability to learn even in industries where there have been a number of prior merger proposals. Learning requires feedback. In the absence of retrospectives, which themselves pose the challenges discussed in subsection 6.C.2, those making predictions rarely discover whether they proved accurate and are not in a good position to diagnose the cause of any errors. Simply put, trial-and-error learning presumes that one observes the errors so that one can improve. This point is even more powerful regarding such topics as coordinated effects, efficiencies, and entry (both ex post and ex ante). Little analysis is usually attempted, so there are few concrete hypotheses that can even in principle be rejected if inconsistent with the subsequent evidence, and that evidence, in turn, is not collected and receives attention in only a handful of the existing merger retrospectives.

Agencies can also draw on industry expertise during particular investigations. Often sophisticated buyers are contacted, but their input is usually limited to substitution, particularly information about the magnitude of diversion ratios. Lawyers and economists at agencies examine the merging parties' documents, the most reliable being those generated in the ordinary course of business. They may also hear presentations from the merging firms' executives or, as an investigation proceeds, take depositions. However, when the agency staff making these inquires has little industry-specific knowledge and generally is not expert about many of the issues being explored, particularly on the cost side, there are significant limits to how much can be learned. Experience teaches that there are many important questions that outsiders may not think to ask, some seemingly plausible explanations that are in fact dubious, and important subtleties that are hard to distinguish from pretextual defenses but sometimes go to the core of what a transaction is really about. Agencies cannot be very effective when they have little ability to scrutinize firms' decision-making.

Serious industry expertise is most often employed once a case is headed to litigation, at which point an expert report may be required. Although important, this use of industry expertise is too late to guide initial screening decisions or investigations. Mistakes of permitting anticompetitive mergers cannot be corrected. And even for challenged mergers that are indeed anticompetitive, important lines of inquiry may have been forgone by not having collected the necessary evidence during the investigation.

Competition agencies have continued to improve, but mainly on those tasks with which they are most familiar and that are in the domains of their existing expertise. There may also be a tendency for self-replication, as they seek to hire individuals who are well trained to do what the agencies already do. Relatedly, many state that important subjects like efficiencies are inscrutable and thus are best left mainly toward the end of the investigation or omitted altogether. These attitudes and practices may reflect not only inherent difficulties but also that the requisite analysis is outside agencies' training and comfort zone.[4] For example, as discussed in section 4.D, agencies appear to impute a high "efficiency credit," perhaps implicitly

---

4. Scherer (1991) offers a colorful depiction of this state of affairs. This phenomenon also relates to Schmalensee's (2012) suggestion that modern industrial organization economists tend, for understandable reasons, to look where the light is, although the present argument adds that there is also a tendency to look only where analysts are able to perceive the benefits of illumination given their training.

motivated by the practice rendering it unnecessary to have to undertake serious efficiency inquiries in most investigations. Yet, as explained, it is better to analyze efficiencies in tandem with anticompetitive effects, right from the beginning, including as screening decisions are being made. If agencies had greater capacity to scrutinize efficiencies, in house or rapidly on call, they would be less likely to allow some mergers with anticompetitive effects because they would sometimes have greater confidence that efficiencies were at most minimal, and they would be more likely to credit serious efficiencies if they could better determine when they were likely to be real.

Similarly, agencies would be more likely to challenge mergers creating risks of coordinated effects if those effects could better be assessed, and agencies would be more able to sort mergers regarding their effects on ex post and ex ante entry if those effects could be identified and understood. Even matters more at the heart of current agency analysis could be assessed more accurately if agencies benefited from greater industry expertise.

B. Litigation Reform

Greater agency expertise can facilitate the analysis of a wide range of pertinent considerations. Nevertheless, for those mergers that are challenged, there are additional limits on the quality of ultimate decision-making due to courts' even more limited institutional capacity. Particularly in the United States where judges make initial decisions whether to block mergers—rather than being confined to the review of agencies' decisions, as in most jurisdictions—this constraint poses a serious obstacle. Even intelligent, conscientious judges typically have no training in any of the skills required to analyze mergers, no prior knowledge of the industry, no expert staffing to support their work, little business experience, and only modest ability to adjudicate battles of experts and ascertain the credibility of business witnesses. These limitations, in turn, can feed back perversely on agencies, who thereby have diminished incentives to undertake relevant but subtle analyses and stronger motivations to emphasize so-called hot documents and rely on ill-devised shortcuts like the structural presumption. Merging parties' proffers of evidence will likewise be shaped by their appreciation of the tribunal's capacity to process different types of information.

Nevertheless, it seems feasible to enhance judicial decision-making within the confines of current procedural rules if judges were to make better use of economic and industry expertise.[5] The most obvious change would be for judges to regularly employ court-appointed experts, which is permitted under current rules but rarely done (Sidak 2013). Even excessive deference to a court's own experts might be superior to judges' attempts to adjudicate often incomprehensible battles between the parties' experts. This point is reinforced when recognizing the incentives of parties' experts as well as the ability of some merging firms to greatly outspend the agencies in litigation.

Expert input could also contribute in other important ways. Court-appointed experts might not just, or even primarily, present their own analyses but rather comment critically on those presented by each side. Such efforts may, in anticipation, generate more rigorous initial presentations by the parties. In addition, parties' experts may moderate their positions as well as omit misleading claims that are currently presented to distract the opposition and confuse the judge, but would instead undermine their credibility in the presence of a court-appointed expert.

These benefits suggest another, broader use of economic and industry experts in connection with modifications to the conduct of merger litigation that may have even greater promise to improve decision-making. A judge might appoint an expert magistrate or other sort of expert assistant to better structure litigation from the outset. Such an expert might help narrow the issues early on, meet with the parties' experts to agree on or otherwise precommit to paths of investigation (a soft version of preregistration), organize information transfers, and plan the conduct of litigation. Such techniques are occasionally employed in some jurisdictions.

This broader set of tasks enables many opportunities for improvement. It makes little sense for the government to present its entire case, followed often with significant delay by defense witnesses who will present their disagreements, with yet further time elapsing before the government's reply. Instead, trials may more usefully be organized to a substantial degree by topic, with relevant witnesses and documents presented together. Some jurisdictions have opposing experts testify side by side, allowing them to

---

5. The present discussion focuses on U.S. trial courts making initial decisions whether to block mergers. More modest adjustments might be helpful to reviewing courts as well. Moreover, if the suggested reforms were employed, more coherent records and initial judicial opinions would be produced, which itself should assist appellate review.

question and respond to each other. All these possibilities could be organized and conducted better with expert assistance. The court's expert could act as a referee and participate in exchanges between the parties' experts. Issues could also be further narrowed along the way, with earlier testimony influencing the attention given to other subjects that are best deferred. Likewise, many framing questions, themselves raising factual disputes, might best be examined up front, where both parties' presentations are considered more fully than in traditional pretrial conferences and opening arguments, and with more resolution or at least refinement through constructive interaction and subsequent iteration.

The foregoing suggestions should be taken as a proposal for greater experimentation (ABA Antitrust Section 2017). They would move adjudication closer to how a sophisticated organization with a free hand would design a decision-making process. Competition agencies might take the lead in such a venture. To avoid the concern that the competition agency was proposing some stratagem for self-interested reasons in a particular case, the agency might embark on a process drawing on a range of participants—including judges, lawyers who regularly represent merging parties, and others—to develop a proposal that the agencies would commit to offer and follow, if the judge agreed, going forward for some period of time.

Such a path may well improve the quality of merger decision-making. It also may lead to improvements regarding the use of court-appointed experts, although still within the confines of more traditional litigation. Another large potential gain is that, if agency lawyers, economists, and testifying experts as well as merging parties' defense teams knew in advance that litigation would be conducted in this manner, many weak lines of argument that have only superficial appeal might be eschewed, and more moderate and subtle positions might be developed from the outset. There is an endogenous and symbiotic relationship between merger investigations and case preparation up front and how adjudication will be conducted at the end of the process.

There are also even broader potential gains. Firms would be more likely to propose socially beneficial mergers and avoid advancing anticompetitive ones. Merger guidelines could focus more on correct and refined analysis of competitive effects, efficiencies, and entry if it was contemplated that a more sophisticated assessment would be undertaken in those cases that went to court. The entire ecosystem of merger review might usefully evolve in good directions if both agencies' and reviewing courts' institutional capacities were enhanced.

Perhaps most important, a central reason that courts are used to make initial decisions in cases brought by agencies or to review agency decisions is not just to correct occasional errors made by conscientious agencies that are ordinarily presumed to have greater expertise than the courts. Court involvement is insisted upon in order to deter and correct other types of misbehavior, ranging from modest overreach due to the understandable zealousness of those assigned the task of preserving competition to more serious abuse, such as when individuals or firms are targeted for improper reasons. Courts can better determine whether agencies' actions are on the merits or reflect abuse when judges can better process agencies' analyses and the merging parties' rebuttals.

C. Ex Post Merger Review

At best, prediction of proposed mergers' future effects is a difficult enterprise subject to significant uncertainty. Hence, there is some appeal to supplementing ex ante merger clearance decisions with ex post merger review. That is, we may sometimes benefit from adopting a wait-and-see approach wherein a consummated merger would later be divested if it in fact turned out to be sufficiently anticompetitive. This possibility is only occasionally employed by competition agencies and has received little attention in the literature (Ottaviani and Wickelgren 2011).[6]

---

6. Another regulatory strategy that is often used in other settings is the imposition of ex post fines or damages that internalize the social costs, here, of an anticompetitive merger, rather than either blocking it ex ante or requiring divestiture ex post. Although fines and damages play a central role in competition regimes' deterrence of price fixing, they are rarely employed with mergers (even though damages actions are permitted in the United States) and have not been analyzed in this setting. The challenge discussed below regarding the limits of information even in hindsight would be a major consideration. This point is accentuated with damages because the truncation of negative values creates potentially significant biases. To see this point, suppose that a moderately efficient merger sometimes looks very efficient and sometimes quite anticompetitive ex post (with an unbiased mean). The latter error would generate a high damages award whereas the former error would not generate an offsetting (negative) damages payment, so this efficient merger would be deterred by the prospect of noisily measured (even if unbiased) damages determinations.

The present preclearance regime employed in much of the world initially emerged in the United States a half-century ago because of the perceived failure of ex post review. Although the government had been successful in most merger challenges since the 1950 amendments to the Clayton Act, many regarded these as pyrrhic victories because of the difficulty of unscrambling the eggs years after a merger had been consummated (Elzinga 1969). This led to 1976 legislation that requires merging parties to file information with the competition agencies and that provides the agencies time to review proposed mergers before they may go into effect.[7] Since then, most government merger challenges in much of the developed world have focused on whether to enjoin proposed, not-yet-consummated mergers.

Abstracting from a number of complexities, the optimal regime can be understood to have a few basic features.[8] The ex post challenge criterion would take into account the quality of the newly available information, the costs and efficacy of divestiture, and, supposing that the agency has the ability to commit to a standard, the interim effects on merged firms' incentives to behave competitively and to integrate their operations. In addition, the more aggressive is ex post review, the more lenient should be ex ante review because permitting a borderline merger up front preserves some prospect of reversing it later, with only modest costs due to interim anticompetitive effects. The option value of the overall regime is rising in the degree of uncertainty ex ante. For example, if an agency knows for certain that a proposed merger is modestly anticompetitive, the merger should be blocked, whereas another merger with a lower expected social value might optimally be permitted if the uncertainty is large, including a significant possibility that the merger will turn out to be beneficial.

Let us now consider more carefully some of the predicates of this formulation. First and foremost, the central motivation for supplementation with ex post review is that better information will become available after

---

7. This raises the question of the appropriate filing threshold and the concern that small anticompetitive mergers are too freely allowed because they are rarely reviewed (Wollmann 2019, 2021).
8. As in much of this book, incentives to propose mergers and even earlier incentives to enter and make investments (some of which is considered in section 5.B on ex ante entry) are abstracted from here. In addition, for simplicity the exposition compares a combined regime to a pure ex ante regime even though, as mentioned, there is some ex post review currently.

a merger has been consummated. Although this is undoubtedly true, the analysis in subsection 6.C.2 of merger retrospectives suggests that the magnitude of this informational gain may often be modest. An agency undertaking ex post review is in a sense conducting a merger retrospective. It may have some advantages over academic researchers in this task because of its greater access to the merged firm's information. The agency nevertheless faces substantial obstacles.

Ex ante, the agency had to predict two counterfactual worlds and compare them. Ex post, it only has to predict one, the world in which the merger had been blocked. That task will be difficult for familiar reasons. The greatest challenge is in choosing comparator firms for conducting a difference-in-differences analysis, even if informally. As explained previously, there may not exist firms that are both largely unaffected by the merger and sufficiently similar to the merged firm so as not to have been subject to different shocks. In addition, there is the challenge regarding the time frame. It needs to be sufficiently short to make identification credible, but it also needs to be sufficiently long for efficiencies to be realized and for other adjustments such as product repositioning to have occurred.

It is also necessary to take into account the merged firm's interim incentives to the extent that they may influence the ex post review, which will pose a greater problem when the agency cannot commit to a standard. The merged firm may undertake a more cautious competitive strategy early on, moderating price increases, postponing the shuttering of capacity, and so forth. Some of these effects may be favorable. Even if they obfuscate ex post review (which is their purpose) and may ultimately let an anticompetitive merger survive, they may raise social welfare for some period of time. On the other hand, some of these interim acts may also postpone the realization of efficiencies. Retiring inefficient capacity sooner, as production is shifted to newer plants, may be one of the merger's benefits, but the merged firm may resist doing so because its capacity retirements may be perceived by an agency as evidence that the merger is anticompetitive.

A second set of interim incentives concerns the degree to which the merged firm integrates its operations. On one hand, it may postpone integration because of the probability of subsequent divestiture, which would be made more expensive if greater integration had occurred. The merged firm would expect to bear that additional cost. On the other hand, and perhaps the greater problem, the merged firm may excessively scramble the eggs so as to render subsequent divestiture infeasible or so costly that the competition agency would not then order it. Such actions may also be designed to obscure what would otherwise have been the trajectory of the target's assets and activities. One may therefore lose much of the informational benefit of hindsight and incur additional efficiency costs as well.[9]

As mentioned, a central motivation for creating the ex ante clearance system was precisely that ex post merger challenges often came too late, when operations had been consolidated, teams disbanded, and parallel systems eliminated, all of which rendered divestiture ineffective or impossible. It is unclear the extent to which those experiences reflected strategic behavior by merged firms or simply that sufficient time had elapsed that the natural course of integration undermined the ability to reverse the process. Indeed, if such integration was the point of the merger, one would expect it to be far along years later, even without supplemental strategic behavior. The possibilities span a substantial range. If two hospitals merge but subsequently continue to operate largely separately (perhaps integrating only procurement or some headquarters operations), divestiture may well be feasible. By contrast, if a tech giant intimately integrates an acquired firm's software product and engineers into its overall system, the target's product may no longer have an independent existence and the supporting team that understood its inner workings and future potential may have long ceased to exist.

In light of these considerations, some of the settings in which a wait-and-see approach may have the most appeal may also be ones in which ex post review is particularly difficult and otherwise problematic. As discussed in section 5.B, it is quite hard for an agency to assess the competitive effects,

---

9. These points raise many subtleties. For the merged firm, it may be playing a game of chicken, deciding how much to incur costs of excessive scrambling in order to induce the agency not to order divestiture, recognizing that if these strategic efforts fall short, the firm will be divested nonetheless and then must incur additional unscrambling costs. The agency, as noted, faces a commitment problem: the more it can commit to a tough ex post standard, including ordering ex post inefficient divestitures, the more merged firms are discouraged from excessive scrambling. However, divestiture costs that would be generated by appropriate interim integration are real social costs of divestiture that should factor into an optimal ex post assessment even with commitment. But it would be difficult for an agency to differentiate between these channels and thus for an unavoidably fuzzy standard to be implemented so as to generate the requisite beliefs by merging firms in the interim.

potential synergies, or competitive landscape in terms of other prospective entrants when the acquired firm is a nascent player in a new, rapidly evolving sector. However, in just such instances, it may be extremely difficult years later to identify comparator firms (all the more so if the acquiring firm is particularly distinctive), to control for numerous shocks, and to subsequently divest a target whose product at the time of the acquisition may not yet have been identifiable.

This may not be true in all settings, however. Coordinated effects are also particularly difficult to predict, even in fairly stable settings. Coordination as such may also be hard to detect postmerger, but the coordinated effects—higher prices—may be possible to observe subsequently. An implication of these contrasting examples is that the argument for greater leniency ex ante because of the possibility of divestiture ex post has its greatest force in settings in which ex ante uncertainty is particularly high but, in addition, ex post resolution of that uncertainty is reasonably likely.

Given these challenges to ex post review, it is understandable that agencies have only occasionally undertaken it. That said, the subject has not been extensively studied. Moreover, we must keep in mind the core motivation for its consideration: ex ante review is itself quite difficult, even more than is widely appreciated in light of the analysis in the preceding chapters.

D. Competition Agencies' Domain

Considerations of expertise and specialization importantly determine the appropriate domain or jurisdiction of competition agencies. In complex organizations in both the private sector and government, there are usually significant divisions of responsibility. When considering the objectives of consumer or total welfare in chapter 8, for example, it will typically be assumed that competition agencies should and do limit their inquiries to matters most related to the preservation of competition in some sense. For example, a merger that does not raise prices or reduce quality, but instead does the opposite, would not ordinarily be blocked because greater output of better products may be bad for the environment and thereby reduce overall welfare. The reason for this and many other limitations on what competition agencies appropriately consider relates to the optimal matching of instruments to problems and the benefits of specialization. In principle, there could be a single agency of government that controlled all policy levers and aimed to maximize social welfare on all fronts, ranging from competition and the environment to infrastructure, national security, and macroeconomic stability. But that is not generally optimal. Instead, we have many agencies that pursue the same broad objective, perhaps total social welfare, but each may maximize that objective only within its assigned domain and only through the use of the instruments under its control.

The subject of the optimal assignment of tasks and tools to different entities is a complex one that should take into account the degree to which broader problems are modular in the sense that they can decomposed into largely distinct analyses that can be conducted largely independently, even though their outputs may feed each other or be channeled to a higher-level decision process. Relatedly, specialization, incentives, and accountability can often be enhanced by narrowing and sharpening responsibilities. For these reasons and others, there is substantial similarity across jurisdictions in competition agencies' domains; for example, none focus on national security, provision of social insurance, or infrastructure. As well, sometimes their jurisdiction over conventional competition issues is assigned to another, more specialized agency that focuses on a particular sector of the economy, such as an industry regulatory body. These considerations will also be important in chapter 8's discussion of competition agencies' proper objectives, for it typically does not make sense for an agency to give significant weight to an objective that is outside its expertise and is best addressed by instruments that are not under its control.

Within these broad contours, however, there is significant variation across jurisdictions on important matters, and it is hardly obvious whether certain more closely related tasks should be combined or separated. Some competition agencies, for example, also have jurisdiction over consumer protection, but others do not. And even those that do—for example, the U.S. Federal Trade Commission—largely separate consumer protection and competition regulation within the agency. Many aspects of international trade, including state aid, are related to competition policy, and thus certain aspects are sometimes combined, but these and others also connect to the conduct of foreign policy, which is usually conducted separately.[10]

---

10. Other realms that usually are kept separate but have important overlap are the protection of intellectual property, which involves trade-offs like many considered

Even within competition policy as conventionally understood, there is often separation and specialization within agencies. Merger review may be distinct from the investigation of price-fixing. Or investigations may be divided by sector so that lawyers, economists, and other experts can specialize, drawing on different skills and accumulating more focused experience. These important dimensions of the design of competition regimes, including merger review, have received little attention in the literature, which mostly takes the state of affairs in a jurisdiction as given.

---

in competition regulation, and industry-specific regulation, such as that done by public utility commissions. The interaction of optimal patent policy and competition regulation of the exercise of patent rights is itself the subject of significant literature, some of which emphasizes interdependencies. See, for example, Kaplow (1984), Chang (1995), and Farrell and Shapiro (2008). Much labor regulation, including occupational licensing and the operation of labor unions, also has significant overlaps with competition policy but, again, is usually conducted separately.

8 Objectives

This chapter explores the question of the appropriate objectives and focus of a competition regime as a matter of optimal policy, with some attention to matters of institutional design that are the subject of chapter 7. It does not address particular jurisdictions' treaties, legislation, regulations, or court decisions that may dictate objectives or otherwise constrain competition agencies, courts, or other actors.

Section A considers the choice between consumer and total welfare standards—the contrast of objectives most discussed in the literature on competition policy—and suggests that the optimal matching of instruments to policies may be the most important consideration. Section B examines an important and intertwined choice that has received less attention: whether to focus on short- or long-run outcomes of merger decisions and merger policy as a whole. Long-run welfare ultimately matters more, and consumer and total welfare prescriptions tend to converge in the long run. Section C analyzes the almost entirely neglected matter of whether to adhere to the single-sector partial equilibrium approach used in most industrial organization research, as is currently done in scholarship on competition policy and in agency practice, or to consider as well multisector general equilibrium effects of competition policy that may substantially amend or upset conventional enforcement protocols and priorities. Section D takes up the possibility that competition rules should aim to protect competition as a process rather than directly seek to obtain good outcomes, whether for consumers or for society more broadly. Finally, section E briefly discusses some other objectives that have been advanced as appropriate goals of competition regulation, including of horizontal mergers.

A. Consumer versus Total Welfare

Total welfare is the objective that most economists ordinarily embrace and that had been advanced in most writing by economists on competition policy until the last decade or two (Williamson 1968; Katz and Shelanski 2007b). It is also the objective that has typically been invoked and often followed in other areas of regulation, such as that directed at safety or the environment. More recently, consumer welfare has been increasingly favored in the competition domain, often on distributive grounds reflecting that, on average, the distributive incidence of supracompetitive prices hits lower in the income distribution than that of anticompetitive profits, which are heavily skewed toward the top.[1] Even though not addressed in most competition legislation, modern merger guidelines in many jurisdictions, including the United States and European Union, embrace a consumer welfare standard (whereas Canada, for example, embraces a total welfare standard). This choice is often implicit in requirements that merger efficiencies be credited only to the extent that they are passed on to consumers rather than being stated explicitly.[2]

---

1. For competing views, see Farrell and Katz (2006), Heyer (2006), Kaplow (2012b), Pittman (2007), and Salop (2010). The rise of a consumer welfare standard in U.S. case law, notably, in the Supreme Court, reflects an interesting path dependence and some confusion. Bork (1978) advanced consumer welfare but actually meant total welfare; the view being attacked was one that sacrificed both consumer and total welfare to the protection of small producers. But as his misnamed term became adopted (notably, by the U.S. Supreme Court in 1979)—and no doubt because of the appeal of the consumer welfare standard to less sophisticated audiences and subsequent increasing concerns about economic inequality—embrace of the consumer welfare standard in the literal sense has become increasingly common. Regarding mergers specifically, 1960s U.S. Supreme Court cases like *Brown Shoe* and *Clorox* suggested that efficiencies boosted the case for blocking mergers because lower prices and better products would make it more difficult for small, independent producers to operate. The Supreme Court has not decided a substantive merger case since the mid-1970s, but other subsequent Supreme Court antitrust decisions and lower court merger decisions have increasingly embraced the view that efficiencies are favored by the antitrust laws and have emphatically rejected the objective of protection of less efficient rivals. Rather broadly, activities that lead to better products and lower (but nonpredatory) prices are taken to be hallmarks of competition rather than its antithesis.
2. Kaplow (2012b) discusses how merger guidelines giving significant weight to the postmerger HHI level—which section 3.B explains to be largely irrelevant to a

Objectives

As a preliminary clarifying note, the notion of consumer welfare is not generally taken to refer solely to the welfare of final consumers but rather to the welfare of those on the other side of the market from the firm or firms whose behavior is being challenged. The analogue to consumers would be sellers, including workers supplying labor, in the case of a proposed horizontal merger that is believed to increase monopsony power.[3] Hence, consumer welfare might better be viewed as total welfare minus the producer surplus of the parties under scrutiny.

Both institutional considerations and the principle that instruments should be appropriately matched to targets favor a total welfare approach. Competition agencies, like environmental protection agencies, occupational health and safety agencies, and many others, do not have expertise in income distribution, do not in fact typically analyze distributive effects, do not state social welfare functions or offer preferred estimates of labor supply elasticities in their published or internal rules, and do not seek to coordinate their regulatory efforts with the activities of the income tax and transfer system, including social insurance.[4]

---

merger's likely price effects—might be rationalized as a proxy for the level of market power, which is to say, the degree of supracompetitive pricing aside from the merger's effects. (This point is further elaborated in note 23 in section C, below.) That, in turn, is relevant under a total welfare standard for the familiar reason that the contribution of a given price increase to deadweight loss rises with the magnitude of the preexisting price elevation. By contrast, consumer surplus is largely unaffected by that magnitude. (Actually, the fall in consumer surplus per unit of price elevation is smaller when the base price is higher because the base quantity is therefore lower.)

3. See, for example, Werden (2007) and Hemphill and Rose (2018). Note also the familiar point that, in basic models, greater monopsony power pushes down not only input prices (such as wages) but also quantity; hence, monopsony power tends to enhance merged firms' profits but does not reduce their marginal costs, properly understood, and instead raises output prices, a conclusion that follows in any event from the reduction in input quantities.

4. Interestingly, if some of these other agencies did seek to advance income redistribution (taking as given the income tax and transfer system), many would be led to impose less stringent regulation than what would be dictated by conventional, unweighted cost-benefit analysis (a total welfare standard). The simple reason is that environmental and safety benefits, valued in dollars, rise substantially with income, so the benefits of these regulations accrue disproportionately to high-income individuals, often by much more than the incidence of costs rises with income. Hence, distributive weighting would reduce marginal benefits relative to marginal costs, making weaker regulations optimal.

Nevertheless, as mentioned, a consumer welfare standard is often favored on distributive grounds in discussions of competition policy. This reflects an implicit view that, regardless of the rest of the government's apparatus and the views of other government decision-makers (notably, legislatures), greater redistribution is to be preferred. Actually, as some recognize, this is so even at the expense of lower income individuals because maximizing their well-being would put some weight on producer surplus, particularly in light of its long-run incidence (discussed in section B). Moreover, even though particular merger cases may involve a different incidence—for example, when workers capture some producer surplus and the merger involves luxury goods that are disproportionately consumed by the rich—the pure consumer welfare standard is maintained. These features might be defended on secondary institutional grounds: an across-the-board, pure consumer welfare standard may be easier to implement than may a more nuanced approach and, precisely because competition agencies lack expertise in distributive matters, it is better that these competing considerations be ignored. Hence the appeal of a simple, surrogate objective.

The policy analysis required to justify this approach, however, is not generally discussed in industrial organization research (which by design does not usually attend to distributive matters) or in writing on competition policy. But more explicit justification is required because the aforementioned principle of matching instruments to objectives favors the total welfare criterion, indeed, under any standard social welfare function. Confining redistribution to the income tax and transfer system while setting competition policy to maximize total welfare is a Pareto superior strategy: all income groups can be made strictly better off if competition policy (and other policies, like environmental regulation) aims to maximize total welfare rather than consumer welfare or any other objective. The simple-minded version of the core intuition is that adherence to the total welfare objective maximizes the pie that the government's distributive machinery has available to redistribute, and direct redistribution via the tax and transfer system, although distorting, is the least distortionary way to redistribute income under benchmark assumptions.[5]

---

5. For informal expositions of this public economics framework, see Kaplow (2004, 2020).

This notion, which has long been familiar to economists in rough terms, has received surprisingly little attention in recent decades' shift in favor of a consumer welfare standard. Furthermore, it is not widely appreciated in industrial organization economics or in the overlapping antitrust community that these ideas are well grounded in formal work that grows out of a half-century of research in public economics. To be sure, a complete analysis—beyond the scope of this investigation—is somewhat subtle and, as with any economic modeling, the results depend on various assumptions. That said, the requisite assumptions are somewhat general and—a key point here—their relaxation is largely unrelated to standard views of how to enhance the efficacy of income redistribution, through competition policy or otherwise.

To make the connection across fields explicit, Kaplow (2021b) intersects the standard Mirrlees (1971) problem—choosing the optimal tax and transfer system in light of the effects of redistribution on labor supply—with competition policy, specifically, an abstract instrument that adjusts the strength of competition policy in a manner that affects prices and thus consumer welfare in familiar ways. That model, importantly, allows markups to have any distributive incidence on consumers. Moreover, it allows any distribution of profits as a function of income, including any degree of upward skew, wherein most or all profits are earned by the highest-income individuals. The model also allows for the income tax and transfer system as well as these markups to have any effect on labor supply at each level of income. The main result is that moving competition policy in the direction favored by a total welfare standard can always be implemented in a manner (that combines adjustments to the income tax and transfer system) that generates a strict Pareto improvement: individuals at all income levels are strictly better off. Therefore, society can move from a consumer to a total welfare standard so as to raise everyone's utility and thus the utility of all consumers in particular.

The analysis draws on decades of work in public economics. The underlying idea traces to Atkinson and Stiglitz's (1976) famous paper on how, in the basic case, optimal commodity taxes are uniform; in particular, employing higher taxes on luxuries or lower taxes on necessities is a dominated distributive strategy. Continuing to oversimplify, the core idea is that such indirect means of redistribution cause the same degree of distortion of labor supply as direct redistribution does (for any given degree of redistribution), but they also cause additional allocative inefficiency in individuals' consumption choices. If earning more income means that an individual spends less on necessities and more on luxuries, then the posited differential taxation has the result that effective consumption—specifically, utility from consumption—does not rise as rapidly with earned income as it does when commodity taxes are uniform (at the same average rate for the population as a whole). The resulting suppression of labor supply is the same as that which would result from instead employing a somewhat more redistributive income tax and transfer system that redistributed to the same extent as under the system that differentially taxes luxuries and necessities.

To proceed, if one swapped a slightly more redistributive income tax and transfer system for the differential commodity tax system—in a way that left individuals at every income level with the same disposable income—government revenue would be the same but each individual, now facing different relative commodity prices, would adjust consumption and, by revealed preference, be better off. The formal argument is a bit more subtle, but the basic conclusion holds.[6] Indeed, as shown in Kaplow (2006), nothing in the argument depends on whether the preexisting income tax and transfer system is optimal, whether the commodity tax reform is in the neighborhood of the optimum, or whether one is considering marginal or discrete reforms. There are qualifications, to be sure (Kaplow 2004, 2008), but these are largely orthogonal to typical considerations regarding redistribution.[7] For example, as already noted, Kaplow (2021b) shows that the

---

6. Briefly, the formal argument constructs a distributively offsetting adjustment to the income tax and transfer system that holds the utility of individuals at all income levels constant when combined with the reform that reduces differentiation in commodity taxation. Because of the efficiency gain from consumption reallocation, this adjustment raises more revenue from all types of individuals, generating a surplus that can be rebated, for example, pro rata. Before the final rebate, it is further shown that, with weak separability of labor in individuals' utility functions, there is no effect on labor supply from the reform package that combines the total-surplus-increasing change to commodity taxes (or to competition policy) and the distributively offsetting income tax adjustment. (Nonseparability is addressed in the next footnote.)

7. The most familiar qualification, tracing to Corlett and Hague (1953), is that it is efficient to tax (subsidize) leisure complements (substitutes) to some degree because that boosts labor supply, which is distorted downward by income taxation. On that ground, supracompetitive prices for streaming services or novels may enhance the efficiency of income redistribution, but higher prices for work clothes would be

results hold regardless of the incidence of markups in the sector targeted by competition regulation and regardless of the distribution of firm ownership and thus of the beneficiaries of supracompetitive profits.[8]

This chapter, like the rest of this book, sets political economy considerations to the side. If one had to make a conjecture, however, one might suppose that the extent of redistribution overall at any point in time reflects a prevailing political equilibrium, in which case a rational legislature, as well as competing factions, would tend to benefit from achieving any degree of redistribution in the most efficient manner. But there are many potential complications. A legislature might favor more or less redistribution than its constituents want and hence attempt to hide some redistribution (in its preferred direction) in the activities of regulatory bodies, even if the result is a less favorable distribution of income for a given overall redistributive cost. Or an egalitarian public may fail to appreciate that redistribution being confined to the tax and transfer system has advantages not only of institutional specialization but also of enabling greater equality at a given efficiency cost. Hence, the populace may favor a government in which each agency "does its part" in the redistributive enterprise, even if that means— which they do not see—that there will be less redistribution overall for a given cost, or greater cost for a given degree of redistribution. Finally, there may be agency problems with competition regulators, wherein they may

---

additionally inefficient on this ground. Even then, it tends to be optimal to implement such second-best adjustments through differential taxes and subsidies rather than through regulatory means that raise production costs. In any event, even though such subtle considerations may constitute the best economic arguments for adjusting competition policy in light of society's broader distributive objectives, they obviously are not what proponents in the competition policy space have in mind; rather clearly, they are not a reason to favor a consumer welfare standard. For example, this third-best adjustment to competition policy (excise taxes and subsidies being the second-best instruments) may favor cartels and anticompetitive mergers of book publishers and suppliers of components for televisions and game consoles but err against potentially consumer-welfare-reducing mergers of firms that create software that makes it easier to work from home.

8. In the extension in Kaplow (2021b), it is shown that the results hold when some or all of the ex post supracompetitive profits constitute returns on ex ante investments, whether productive or rent-seeking ones. As explored in section B, a case of interest is that in which, on an ex ante risk-adjusted basis, there are no long-run profits (beyond competitive returns to capital and risk-bearing), in which case the consumer and total welfare standards converge.

prefer to pursue more or less redistribution than does their principal, often a legislature, hoping to fly under the radar screen in their efforts.

A useful analogy in this regard concerns the widely recognized efficiency benefits of pollution taxes or tradeable permit systems in reducing pollution. It took decades for these economic ideas to (partially) penetrate public debate and there is still substantial demand for much less efficient command-and-control regulations, often because their costs are hidden. For example, higher gasoline prices may be traced more directly to government policy when there is a steep carbon tax than are higher auto prices that result from complex regulations that are costly to satisfy. That said, economic analysis contributes to the policy debate by explaining how we can achieve more stringent pollution control at lower cost. Likewise, economics contributes to policy debate when it shows how we can achieve greater redistribution at a lower efficiency cost.

B. Short Run versus Long Run

Equilibrium producer surplus is zero in many standard economic models (Dixit and Stiglitz 1977; Mankiw and Whinston 1986; Aghion and Howitt 1992; Hopenhayn 1992; Ericson and Pakes 1995; Melitz 2003). Profits constitute quasi-rents that recover the costs of prior investments, including fixed entry costs, research and development, other innovative activity, and rent-seeking.[9] See Schumpeter (1947) and Demsetz (1973), and, on rent seeking in particular, Tullock (1967), Krueger (1974), Posner (1975), and Fudenberg and Tirole (1987). Some of these models are static but may best be interpreted as describing the long-run equilibrium of some dynamic process. The literature discussed in chapter 5 on entry, some revisited here, includes both types of models.

This long-run equilibrium view tends to render the choice between consumer and total welfare standards moot because the difference between the two—whether to include producer surplus—vanishes (Roberts and Salop 1996; Katz and Shelanski 2007b).[10] At any given moment, a short-run policy

---

9. Hall and Woodward's (2010) empirical analysis suggests that entrepreneurs funded by venture capital approximately break even on an ex ante, risk-adjusted basis.
10. This claim should not be confused with the argument that a laissez-faire policy is desirable in significant part because the market tends to erode market power in

Objectives

can extract quasi-rents that are returns to prior investment, but such a practice is unlikely to be beneficial in the long run except when it targets returns to inefficient rent-seeking activity. There are other models in which certain factors, such distinctive human capital, may earn pure rents. Even competitive returns on some individuals' labor effort may be quite high, although this source of inequality is probably best understood as that which underlies the optimal income tax problem discussed in section A and hence is best addressed with redistributive income taxation. Other rents might be associated with scarce natural resources, like land, although current owners often paid prior owners market prices that reflected the expected value of the resource at the time of purchase. In any event, here as well a tax—famously, on the value of land—is the best targeted instrument.

These brief observations about quasi-rents and the long run are basic to the functioning of a market economy, including one with significantly imperfect competition in many sectors. Nevertheless, they are typically set to the side in applications of industrial organization economics to competition policy. That is so despite the fact that this perspective is featured in prominent work in the field, including some of that discussed in chapter 5 on entry, and is regarded to be central to the understanding of competition policy and innovation more broadly.

Pragmatic considerations may favor a short-run framing when competition agencies examine particular merger proposals because time and other resources are scarce and the ability to predict the future beyond a few years is quite limited. Although these points are well taken, there are some qualifications. First, agencies should employ general rules and other protocols that are conducive to long-run welfare maximization, even if the most useful proxies and shortcuts do not involve undertaking anywhere near a complete long-run analysis. Second and relatedly, many of the most important effects of merger decision-making do not materialize immediately, so a short time frame can be incomplete and even misleading. For example, if a permissive

---

the long run. The transition path is important with any discounting and, moreover, some anticompetitive effects involve undermining or delaying that very process. In a wide range of models, competition remains imperfect in the long run, and competition policy has the potential to reduce these imperfections. The point advanced here, by contrast, is that, in the long run, the consumer and total welfare standards tend to converge with respect to which competition regulations are superior.

policy stifles innovation, that effect is unlikely to be important early on; likewise if a policy enhances innovation. Indeed, all investment looks undesirable in the very short run because costs are front-loaded whereas benefits often do not begin immediately and are mostly further into the future. As a consequence, some areas of competition law, notably, the regulation of exclusionary practices by dominant firms, seek to prohibit acts that may be neutral or beneficial to consumers in the short run (like predatory pricing) but are harmful in the long run. Truncating the time frame in that domain would usually miss the point of the investigation. Relatedly, an important rationale for permitting a firm with market power to charge a supracompetitive price is that the prospect of such profits induces ex ante investment that tends to raise consumer welfare in the long run. Ignoring this basic point in formulating policy could have highly detrimental consequences.

Turn now to some particular questions addressed in earlier chapters where the difference between a short- and long-run analysis is likely to be important. Beginning with anticompetitive effects, in the Cournot model of unilateral effects in homogeneous goods markets, it was explained that there often will be none in the short run and that many such mergers will not be profitable for the merging parties. This model is more plausibly applicable when capacity is set in an initial period and quantities are produced and sold subsequently. Anticompetitive effects arise from the merging firms choosing a smaller quantity, but if their plants are already in place, the fixed costs are sunk, so they may not reduce output anytime soon. However, over time, they would reinvest less to maintain those plants or choose to build smaller ones for the next generation. Berry and Pakes (1993) show that many Cournot mergers that are unprofitable from a static view become profitable in the future (and sufficiently so to be profitable at the time of the merger) precisely because of falling postmerger investment. A short time frame would ignore such anticompetitive effects. Likewise, an agency taking such a view—seeing no short-run anticompetitive effects and therefore finding the merger to be unprofitable—might reason from the merging firms' rationality constraint that there must be efficiencies when in fact there are none and the profitability arises instead from future anticompetitive effects caused by subsequent drops in the merging firms' investments.

For coordinated effects, agencies' ability to predict how a given merger may make them more or less likely is quite limited. That said, in some cases future coordination may take time, yet again because of investments (perhaps in sufficient capacity to punish defectors, or to diminish capacity to make cheating less profitable) and also because learning to coordinate may involve a trial and error process.

Efficiencies and entry, which receive less attention from competition agencies, often tend to be longer-run phenomena. Indeed, this may contribute to their being downplayed, a tendency criticized by Katz and Shelanski (2007b). Many forms of efficiencies, whether having to do with economies of scale in production or economies of scope in organizing many activities of a firm, take years to materialize. The few merger retrospectives discussed in section 6.B that address efficiencies tend to find that prices rose in the short run but then fell a few years after the merger when the efficiencies were realized. Hence, even though efficiencies are quite difficult to analyze, confining attention to the very short run would be inappropriate.

Another important issue with efficiencies is the requirement in many jurisdictions that they be passed on to consumers if they are to be credited against potential anticompetitive effects. Hence, they must be variable cost efficiencies.[11] However, in the long run all fixed costs are variable, and in many of the aforementioned models, the long-run market equilibrium has price equal to average total cost. See, for example, the analysis of fixed and variable cost efficiencies in Kaplow's (2023a) analysis of efficiency effects in a model with free entry and exit. Furthermore, as a practical matter, many more costs are variable over a period of a few years than can be adjusted immediately. As mentioned at the outset of section A, the pass-through requirement in many modern merger guidelines is the primary instantiation of the embrace of a consumer welfare standard, so this point goes to the core of the choice of welfare standards for the review of horizontal mergers.

Chapter 5 explores how both ex post and ex ante entry are cast in a different light when one takes an equilibrium view of the subject.[12] Regarding ex post entry, the market equilibrium both pre- and postmerger implies

---

11. It is often said that attention must also be devoted to the pass-through rate. However, as explained in subsection 3.B.2, one can determine net upward pricing pressure in a unilateral effects model by, in essence, subtracting marginal cost reductions from gross upward pricing pressure. More precisely, one feeds the marginal cost reductions into the model and computes the resulting (net) upward or downward pricing pressure from the merger. The pass-through rate is, however, required to translate that net pressure into a price effect, if such is required.

12. Moreover, ex post entry usually takes some time (Hilke and Nelson 1993; Geroski 1995), making a very short-run perspective inappropriate regardless of how such entry is then analyzed.

that merger-induced entry does not fully offset a merger's anticompetitive effects, except in the limit as entry becomes extremely easy. Nevertheless, entry affects the analysis via inference from the merging firms' rationality constraint, where the relevant consideration is how postmerger entry, whenever it occurs, affects the present discounted value of anticipated profits through price increases. Moreover, ex post entry as such may make a merger more or less efficient than otherwise because entry incentives in imperfectly competitive markets can be socially inadequate or excessive. Again, attention to equilibrium, which generally involves a longer-term perspective, casts the matter in a different light even if one does not seek to determine the entire time path of subsequent entry.

Additional qualitative differences were seen with respect to ex ante entry, that induced by the prospect of subsequent buyouts. As explained, in some settings the long-run dynamic equilibrium involves socially costly and excessive entry under a lenient merger policy. Interestingly, the stricter policy is a bit worse for consumer welfare because, although it may be favorable in the short run, it discourages ex ante (socially excessive) entry that temporarily dampens prices before buyouts occur. When additional ex ante entry would be socially desirable, by contrast, a more permissive merger policy is favored. But this is not because allowing the merger currently before the agency raises consumer or total welfare; it may do the opposite in the short run. Instead, the anticipated policy affects ex ante incentives, so the benefits of permitting a perhaps anticompetitive merger today would lie in increased variety or other innovation tomorrow. Essentially all ex ante welfare effects of merger policy on entry—which may be favorable to tougher merger regulation in some settings and to more lenient regulation in others—lie in the longer run, from anticipation of the stringency of the merger regime. As explained, taking a nascent firm's recent entry and capabilities as given omits what may be the most important effects of merger policy in this domain. Indeed, the very decision to scrutinize incumbents' acquisitions of nascent firms with respect to their future potential to disrupt the industry reflects appropriate attention to long-run considerations rather than confining the analysis of a merger's effects to the short run.

More broadly, as already noted, effects of competition policy on innovation (in either direction) manifest themselves in the long run. Long-run welfare, including consumer welfare, depends largely on an economy's dynamism. An important purpose of competition policy is to preserve and enhance dynamism, not to reduce it. However difficult these effects may be to determine, simply ignoring them in formulating rules may produce choices that reduce welfare, perhaps greatly.

We can see that, although it may be quite difficult to predict mergers' likely effects beyond short time horizons, many of mergers' most important consequences, for better and for worse, lie in the future. As mentioned, even if the particulars cannot plausibly be predicted with much reliability in a given investigation, it is optimal to formulate protocols and proxies with these longer-run effects in mind.[13] And sometimes the longer run may be easier to predict because equilibrium forces are sometimes clear even if it is difficult to say precisely when and how they will manifest themselves.[14]

C. Single-Sector Partial Equilibrium versus Multisector General Equilibrium

Most theoretical and empirical research in industrial organization economics, including that applied to competition policy, undertakes single-sector partial equilibrium analysis. This approach is often formalized, particularly in empirical work, through the use of an outside good (Lancaster 1980; Berry 1994) that is implicitly taken to be sold in a perfectly competitive

---

13. For example, some have suggested that a consumer welfare standard may be optimal in the short run because it may better promote total welfare in the long run. As discussed in section 2.B, in models with endogenous merger proposals, a policy of prohibiting marginally beneficial mergers will tend to lead prospective merging firms to propose socially preferable mergers that are less profitable to the merging parties. As a consequence, giving somewhat greater weight to consumer surplus, which prospective merging firms ignore, and correspondingly less to producer surplus, which is their focus, may be socially beneficial. Relatedly, it is sometimes suggested that a consumer welfare standard better promotes overall welfare than does a total welfare standard because a consumer welfare standard is tougher—which is socially optimal in the long run—and the competition agency faces a commitment problem. However, it is unclear why an agency known to favor total welfare would be unable to commit to that standard but nevertheless be able to commit to a short-run consumer welfare standard. Political economy considerations may provide an answer in some instances.
14. For example, it may be easier to have a sense that one or another merger rule would significantly encourage or discourage entry of a broad type than to assess whether the prospect of permitting or prohibiting the specific merger before the agency would, in anticipation, have discouraged that particular target firm from entering.

market with price equal to marginal cost.[15] It is also used, for example, in the modeling of entry (Mankiw and Whinston 1986). The motivation for the single-sector partial equilibrium approach is, of course, tractability.

Yet perfect competition is not a good approximation for many sectors of the economy or as an average for the rest of the economy as a whole. See, for example, De Loecker, Eeckhout, and Unger (2020) and Hall (2018), as well as the discussions in Basu (2019) and Syverson (2019). This recognition was an important inspiration for Lipsey and Lancaster's (1956) article on the general theory of the second best, which warned against policy prescriptions aimed at correcting a particular imperfection while ignoring others in the economy. Relatedly, Scitovsky (1954) addressed how pecuniary externalities due to general equilibrium effects, which are typically regarded to be irrelevant to total social welfare, can matter when there are other distortions in the economy. For the last half-century, however, concern about the welfare implications of markups in nontargeted sectors has largely vanished from industrial organization economics, including its application to competition policy.[16]

Kaplow (2023a) examines the effects of competition policy aimed at a targeted sector in a simple multisector general equilibrium model. Sectors may each have different demand functions, cost functions, competitive interactions, and competition policies, and these features jointly determine equilibrium expenditures, numbers of firms, and markups in each sector.[17] Beginning with a single sector (using the device of an outside good), the

---

15. It is typically further assumed that this marginal cost is constant and that the outside good is additively separable in individuals' utility functions, so there are no income effects. This latter restriction can be important when analyzing sectors like housing, automobiles, and gasoline that constitute a significant portion of individuals' budgets, but that concern is orthogonal for present purposes.

16. It has been considered more recently in some literature on international trade and macroeconomics (Bilbiie, Ghironi, and Melitz 2019; Epifani and Gancia 2011; Holmes, Hsu, and Lee 2014).

17. A key simplification for present purposes is that the model takes the firms within each sector of the economy to be symmetric, in part for expositional convenience when representing all the other, nontargeted sectors. As explained at the end of this section (and as noted in Kaplow 2023a), the best way to apply the analysis is to use the conclusions regarding the rest of the economy (all sectors except that in which the proposed merger occurs)—which are most of the results in the analysis—while employing a customized analysis of the targeted sector, including of the merging firms themselves.

effects of entry and exit, the focus of section 5.A, can be analyzed as in Mankiw and Whinston (1986) and other work. But when the outside good is replaced with other, imperfectly competitive sectors, and consumers reallocate their purchases across these sectors when prices and varieties change in the targeted sector (and, through general equilibrium effects, in other sectors), overall welfare consequences differ qualitatively and can be of opposite sign.

First, suppose that there is no entry or exit in the other sectors (which can be formalized by the planner's use of entry taxes and subsidies that are adjusted to keep the number of firms constant).[18] This leaves only cross-sector expenditure reallocations by consumers. By individuals' envelope condition, marginal changes have no direct effect on their utility.[19] Nevertheless, they have first-order effects on producers' surplus in other sectors.

Consider a decision to prohibit a merger that would have raised prices in the targeted sector. Relative to the benchmark of allowing the merger, prices will be lower. To focus on interpretations for standard cases, those lower prices induce consumers to move expenditures from other sectors into the targeted sector. Each dollar moving into the targeted sector raises total welfare by the difference between price and marginal cost, the standard welfare benefit from improved competition. However, each dollar moving into the targeted sector necessarily flows out of some other sector—really, a weighted average of all other sectors, with the weights corresponding to marginal expenditure shares (akin to cross-sector diversion ratios). To the extent that price exceeds marginal cost in some of those other sectors, deadweight loss rises there.[20]

---

18. To close the model, the revenue effects accrue to the representative individual through a (taken as lump-sum) adjustment to the budget constraint. An implication is that, even in this interim analysis, firms' profits and losses ultimately accrue to individuals, so consumer surplus equals total surplus.

19. For expositional convenience, the text here, following the analysis in Kaplow (2023a), examines marginal changes. This approach can be problematic for mergers, which are discrete events, and also for entry and exit, which may be lumpy. As discussed in section 5.A, this continuous approach is undertaken in some of the literature but is subject to provisos relating to the integer constraint, which can be particularly important when there are very few firms in a sector and when entry and exit need to be large relative to the size of the market.

20. There are further effects from general equilibrium price adjustments in all the sectors as a consequence of these resource flows that will be set to the side here.

What is the net effect? Lerner (1934)—in his famous article giving rise to the Lerner index of monopoly power—briefly but insightfully observed that the economy-wide level of markups is irrelevant to welfare.[21] Their "deviations" are all that matter.[22] The simple intuition is that deadweight loss from price in excess of marginal cost arises from too few resources being spent in the distorted sector; they flow instead to other sectors, where marginal utility is lower relative to production costs. However, if every sector is marked up by the same proportion, resources have nowhere else to go. Put another way, distortion arises when price ratios, which determine consumption allocations, differ from marginal cost ratios. But when all markups are proportional, these price ratios are the same as they would be in an undistorted economy.

Turning to the general case, prohibiting our hypothesized price-increasing merger will raise social welfare if the markup in the targeted sector is higher than a knock-out weighted average of the markups in all other sectors. (And it will reduce social welfare if the markup in the targeted sector is lower.) Intuitively, if the average dollar no longer spent in other sectors involves a smaller average markup than in the targeted sector, the resulting reallocation of consumption expenditures is welfare increasing. And conversely, if those other sectors are more distorted on average. If that were the complete story, the prescription would be for competition agencies to prioritize high-markup sectors, indeed, to limit their interventions to such sectors.[23]

---

21. Lerner further noted (in a two-word parenthetical phrase) that the case of proportional markups that he envisioned included leisure, suggesting an awareness that markups implicitly create a labor wedge. These effects are the focus of Kaplow (2021b), discussed in section A (but are ignored here, as the analysis implicitly takes income and thus labor supply to be fixed).

22. Lerner's statement about deviations is ambiguous and, in important senses, not quite right. No standard measure of dispersion will match the measure of net deadweight loss, which depends on utility and cost functions, but his rough intuition stands.

23. This relates to a point in note 2 in section A, above, that there is a basis for targeting sectors that have high markups, holding constant the effect of a proposed merger on price. As mentioned, section 3.B explains that it is a mystery why so much attention is given to the level of the HHI, which typically is irrelevant to the magnitude of the price increase caused by a merger. If one regards the HHI level to be a crude proxy for the degree of extant market power, then it would to that extent be a rough indicator of which sectors should be targeted under the assumptions maintained in the text here.

Continuing to follow Kaplow (2023a), let us now relax the assumption that the number of firms in all other sectors is held fixed by the planner. Instead, assume free entry and exit, and focus on the resulting equilibrium. This formulation involves the comparison of two worlds in steady state, one with a tougher merger policy for a given sector and one with a more lenient policy in that sector, an exercise that can be undertaken for any or all sectors of the economy.

First, examine the special case in which every other sector involves homogeneous goods, where we know that imperfectly competitive markets feature excessive entry due to the business-stealing externality. Here, the aforementioned inter-sectoral welfare consequences are substantially nullified. Each dollar that flows out of a sector reduces profits in that sector by the difference between price and marginal cost there. The result is that operations in that sector become less profitable, which induces exit. In simple, symmetric models (and focusing on the continuous case), the induced exit saves social resources (the converse of the burn from excessive entry) by precisely the amount of that fall in profits. Hence, when consumers reallocate expenditures away from these other sectors, there is no reduction in social welfare there after all. Consumers impose a negative pecuniary externality on the firms in those sectors, which induces exit that imposes a positive pecuniary externality of the same magnitude on those same (remaining) firms. Hence, even though there may be imperfect competition in every other sector of the economy, and even if the markups elsewhere are high, all these effects offset each other, and the results of single-sector welfare analysis are restored.[24]

This coincidence, however, can be regarded as a polar case. If entry contributes value other than through its effect on price, notably, due to variety or innovation spillovers, then the outflows that induce exit in other sectors reduce social welfare to that extent. The greater this positive externality, the greater the social cost of moving resources out of these other sectors.

---

24. As developed in Kaplow (2023a), the exposition in the text here of the homogeneous goods case oversimplifies by abstracting from the general equilibrium effect on prices in other sectors. When those prices fall as resources move out of those sectors, further exit is induced that, for essentially the reasons given in the text, further raises social welfare.

To better understand this effect of exit, it is helpful to consider an additional focal case: when these variety or innovation spillovers have a magnitude such that the initial equilibrium just happens to have the socially optimal number of firms in every other sector. That is, given demand, cost functions, the nature of competitive interaction, and the state of competition policy in each of those sectors, a social planner would have been indifferent to marginally increasing or reducing the number of firms in any of them. Under this assumption, we would revert to the previous result for when the number of firms in other sectors was held fixed by the planner. After all, our maintained hypothesis is that the marginal effect of exit on social welfare is zero in every other sector, so exit does not at the margin change the welfare consequences from the case in which the exit does not occur.

More broadly, there are intermediate cases as well as cases in which equilibrium entry is socially too low, so that the welfare loss caused by expenditures leaving a sector is even greater than in the case in which the number of firms is taken to be fixed. Furthermore, we would expect the appropriate characterization to vary substantially across sectors, some of which indeed involve homogeneous goods (or close to that) and others in which variety and innovation spillovers are especially important.

As a conceptual matter, it is interesting to reflect on the source and nature of the welfare effects of changes in the strength of competition policy in a multisector economy with free entry and exit. Essentially all these effects are due to pecuniary externalities that are conventionally ignored in welfare analysis. Actual economies feature distortions from imperfect competition in many sectors and also entry and exit decisions in all sectors that generically involve externalities. These effects, moreover, are first order. Indeed, regarding cross-sector effects, the magnitude of outflows from nontargeted sectors is, as an accounting identity, equal to the inflow to the targeted sector, so the welfare effects omitted in single-sector analysis are a priori of similar importance to those that are examined. Hence, unless one believes that most of the economy is almost perfectly competitive, the single-sector approach is quite problematic for welfare analysis. Ubiquitous entry and exit externalities further complicate the story.

What is a competition agency to do? If the objective is total welfare or long-run consumer welfare, then the field's default (implicit) assumption that the rest of the economy is perfectly competitive provides a very poor basis for decision-making.[25] But analyzing these issues in every merger investigation would be wildly impractical.

As a first cut at the problem, it would seem useful for research to attempt to approximate something like an economy-wide average for these effects across all sectors. Such a measure could be used as a stand-in for these multisector general equilibrium effects in most cases, without further analysis. Furthermore, if in a given merger review some other sector(s) involved particularly close substitutes or complements to what is sold in the targeted sector—and one also had an approximation for the relevant sector-specific welfare effects for those sectors—then one could adjust the standard, economy-wide average accordingly.

Echoing a theme of this book as a whole, proper analysis of mergers (or of other matters that competition agencies address) is more complex and subtle than is appreciated. But when there are important additional considerations—indeed, ones that may sometimes be larger than the ones ordinarily examined—treating them all as if they equal zero is not a sound way to proceed. Proxies and shortcuts are required, but these protocols should be designed with an understanding of mergers' full effects in mind. That effort will require the use of averages and approximations. These challenges point to an exciting research agenda for industrial organization economists and also identify the need for competition agencies to think more deeply about the design of their standard operating procedures.

D. Competition as a Process

The promotion of competition as a process is sometimes advanced as a substitute for or complement to effects-based notions of economic welfare as the goal of competition policy. Competition as a process is an appealing objective in many ways. To begin, it would seem almost tautological that promoting competition is the goal of competition policy. This simple point has obvious relevance to the domain and jurisdiction of competition

---

25. Echoing the point in section B about consumer and total welfare being equivalent in the long run in such models, the welfare function in Kaplow (2023a), from which the results described in the text are obtained, is the representative individual's utility function. Analysis compares (long-run) equilibria, in all of which firms' profits are zero.

agencies, as explored in section 7.D. Their task is to advance welfare by promoting competition, not by regulating emissions or dictating safety requirements. Those important problems are assigned to other agencies.[26]

At its core, promoting competition is a means of advancing social welfare. The favorable welfare properties of a market economy derive importantly from how the competitive process allocates resources to their best uses and provides incentives through price signals. Imperfect competition often interferes with these functions, so correcting such imperfections is a means to the end of advancing welfare. That said, perfect competition is infeasible, and policies aimed to approximate it as closely as possible would be highly destructive. In most sectors, truly atomistic firms could not accomplish much of what is done in a modern economy. And if prices never exceeded marginal costs, most investments could never be recovered.

Analysis in the field of industrial organization and in this book, however, looks more directly at the welfare consequences of competition agency actions, such as blocking mergers, rather than at the competitive process itself. But not all competition policy operates in this fashion. For example, monopolization law in the United States does not prohibit a dominant firm from charging a supracompetitive price, even though forcing prices lower would seem to raise both consumer and total welfare. Here, rather than competition agencies undertaking the project of setting all prices in the economy, they defer, even to monopolies, as long as no other, improper conduct is involved in creating or maintaining dominance. An important justification is the dynamic one just noted, that the prospect of quasi-rents incentivizes investment and innovation. In some settings, this phenomenon is referred to as Schumpeterian competition or competition for the

---

26. In the United States, this limitation relating to competition as a process also relates to the sorts of arguments, notably, defenses, that will be considered by the courts. *National Society of Professional Engineers* did not accept as valid the defendant professional society's claim that its restriction on competitive bidding promoted safety. This argument was rejected as a matter of principle—because it was premised on the notion that competition was socially undesirable, an argument that could be made to the legislature but not to the courts seeking to enforce existing competition laws. Underlying this limitation were concerns about jurisdiction and institutional competence, but a further motivation may have been the presumptive view that competing sellers should not be trusted when they proffer a buyer protection rationale for limiting their own competition, particularly direct price competition with each other.

market, a process notion that diverges significantly from textbook depictions of perfect competition. Furthermore, central planners subject to informational constraints and incentive problems often do more harm than good when trying to set prices for much of the economy. Exceptions may be made for certain natural monopolies, whose prices and other actions may best be regulated by specialized commissions. But that type of regulation is not generally regarded to be part of a competition agency's toolkit, and, in any event, such regulation is seen as a substitute for competition rather than as an instantiation of the competitive process.

A broad view of the competitive process also has implications for merger policy that receive little attention. On one hand, a permissive merger policy may facilitate the market for corporate control, particularly if firms engaged in closely related activities are in the best position to identify target firm deficiencies and rectify them. Moreover, acquisitions of assets (which are, in actuality, what so-called merger law covers) are often essential pathways of firm growth and evolution that constitute important features of competitive dynamism. On the other hand, mergers that reduce competitive pressures on the merged firm may increase agency costs and reduce incentives for innovation, generating difficult-to-quantify future dynamic costs (Leibenstein 1966; Hart 1983; Berger and Hannan 1998; Syverson 2004; Bloom and Van Reenen 2007; World Bank Group and OECD 2017).[27] These and other such considerations would benefit from additional research and should, at least at the margin and perhaps more strongly, influence the stringency of merger review, at least in some settings.

Some advance a qualitatively different approach wherein promoting competition as a process would receive much greater weight, even replacing direct assessment of the welfare effects of mergers.[28] One justification, given

---

27. A qualitatively different point, examined briefly in section 2.C, is that agency costs or behavioral biases may lead prospective acquirers to be too willing to merge so that, ceteris paribus, a tougher merger policy may promote efficiency along that dimension. As noted previously, however, reasoning from the merging firms' (now, managers') rationality constraint may lead to the inference that proposed mergers are less likely to be anticompetitive—and less likely to enhance efficiencies—because the profitability constraint has been relaxed, indeed, moved into negative territory.
28. Language throughout the U.S. Merger Guidelines (2023) could be read to suggest an implicit shift along these lines through the almost complete elimination of explicit reference to concrete harms, notably, to customers, and the substitution of references

greater force by much of the analysis in this book, concerns the difficulty of predicting mergers' future effects. Another is that the broader benefits of competition as a process are nearly impossible to quantify but nevertheless quite important.[29]

Although such a perspective may have force in some domains—such as the decision to largely abstain from regulating supracompetitive prices—the implication for mergers could be radical. Competition means rivalry, and horizontal mergers eliminate rivalry between the merging firms. Should we conclude, then, that all horizontal mergers should be illegal from this perspective? Even the highly restrictive U.S. merger policy of the 1960s was not nearly that extreme. Two accountants teaming up to form a partnership would be illegal. Likewise firms' hiring employees who might otherwise have become sole proprietors in the same line of business.[30]

As a fallback, one might embrace something like a rivalry index, wherein a merger (or partnership, which is just a small merger taking a particular legal form) would be illegal if it reduced the value of this index by at least some specified amount. Such an index might fall from the direct elimination of competition but rise to the extent that the merger made the resulting combination a stronger competitive force. But what would be the measure of such strength? And what counts as a competitive force rather than a competitively neutral or anticompetitive one? And how would these features be

---

to harm to competition as such. Nevertheless, a single, strong, more conventional focus on welfare effects appears in the introduction and should perhaps be taken to cast the other passages in a different light. The body of the document gives little indication of what any contemplated alternative set of objectives might be, how their achievement might be measured, or whether the various invocations are internally consistent.

29. One might also advance promotion of the competitive process as an end in itself. Analogy may be made to sports contests, although there the value of competition lies in the quality of the entertainment provided to spectators, a sort of benefit inapplicable in the present setting. This point reinforces the danger of metaphorical invocations of competition as such that do not further specify the purpose of the enterprise.

30. In discussions of protecting competition as a process in the merger context, it is usually forgotten that merger regulation (for good reason) applies to all acquisitions or transactions (so, notably, acquisitions of other firms' assets are covered). Even "internal growth" is usually impossible without such acquisitions, and most transactions acquire or tie up counterparties' resources that could otherwise have been used by other, competing parties.

converted to a common denominator with the direct reduction of rivalry? And how would that rivalry reduction itself be measured?

It is no surprise that economists have not developed such an abstract index of rivalry or competition but instead have focused on the analysis and measurement of effects on welfare, or effects on prices, quality, and other determinants of welfare.[31] Despite some calls for merger policy to focus on competition as a process rather than attempting to predict mergers' effects on welfare, it is hard to understand what is even contemplated.[32] Perhaps such advocacy is best interpreted as frustration with the perceived weakness of merger enforcement and, relatedly, with courts' inability to analyze welfare effects, which may in turn lead to excessively permissive merger decisions. Regardless, even the approximate contours of a process-based regime are obscure.

E. Other Objectives

At various times and in differing jurisdictions, a wide range of other objectives has been advanced, including the integration of national economies, preservation of jobs, avoidance of undue political influence, protection of opportunities for independent entrepreneurs, reduction of inequality, and avoidance of large-sized firms for its own sake. Such possibilities are addressed here only briefly.

To begin, it is useful to identify which alternative objectives, in whole or in part, embody aspects of economic notions of social welfare but ones that may be excluded from conventional analyses. Some of the items on the foregoing list might be viewed as proxies for effects on welfare. For such objectives, the main reason for competition agencies not to advance them explicitly would be that they are better addressed elsewhere. For example,

---

31. Edlin and Farrell (2015) examine the process view and argue that it is advanced by focusing on which practices improve or worsen the situation of counterparties, which seems close to cashing out the idea in terms of welfare. Interestingly, they omit horizontal mergers from their list of applications.

32. Over a half-century ago, McNulty (1968) wrote an article entitled "Economic Theory and the Meaning of Competition," advancing reasons that the concept of competition, taken literally, is often unhelpful or misleading for understanding economic forces as a descriptive matter and, by implication, for guiding policy.

section A on consumer versus total welfare explained why distributive objectives are best met using the tax and transfer system.

Taking another example, concerns about employment and job loss are best addressed through fiscal and monetary policy, job training, and social insurance. Moreover, in a long-run steady state, competition policy likely has little effect on employment. By contrast, some imperfections in labor markets, notably, those due to monopsony, are readily encompassed by standard welfare analysis of competitive effects of mergers and other practices; for that reason, they are already covered by conventional rules and protocols. And many short-run effects are often opposed to efficiency and thus, if they guide policy, are likely to make society, including consumers (many of whom are workers, and vice versa), worse off in the long run. For example, a competition policy narrowly and naively concerned with jobs may favor a merger outcome that stifles pharmaceutical innovation because effective drugs are a substitute for hospitalization that is more labor intensive and, more broadly, may oppose efficient restructuring and all manner of innovation that, viewed broadly, is important to the dynamic functioning of the economy.

Political influence is a more complicated problem because direct regulation may otherwise be prohibited, such as by constitutional provisions in the United States. Concentration-increasing mergers may reduce free-rider problems in a sector, thereby promoting special interest lobbying. That would be a coordinated effect of a horizontal merger, but one manifested in a different domain from that usually considered by competition agencies. In addition, in certain sectors such as media, social networks, or internet search, concentration may be of greater concern due to worries about a small number of firms having excessive influence on the political process.

Other objectives are even further removed or, perhaps more likely, do not appeal to economic welfare at all.[33] Entrepreneurial opportunity promotes innovation, but it may be favored because of a desire to expand life

---

33. Regarding welfarist versus nonwelfarist objectives, Kaplow and Shavell (2001) demonstrate that giving any weight to the latter entails sometimes favoring policies that violate the Pareto principle, that is, under which everyone is strictly worse off. For a broader discussion of nonwelfarist objectives, see Kaplow and Shavell (2002). Of course, many seemingly nonwelfarist notions may be inspired by or be proxies for otherwise neglected aspects of social welfare, as discussed earlier in this section.

choices for prospective entrepreneurs. Of course, individuals are free to operate independent businesses that are not very profitable, earning a lower financial return on their human capital that is more than compensated for by their nonpecuniary utility from being their own bosses. Perhaps society wishes to offer a further subsidy to this way of making a living, deemed valuable for reasons unrelated to those individuals' welfare. Even then, it is likely that small business subsidies—of which there are many—are better instruments than attempts to alter the general direction of competition policy. After all, it is well understood that higher prices and lower quality products are what make life easier for inefficient entrepreneurs, so giving weight to this objective, pursued through this means, may largely reverse standard merger prescriptions and much else in competition law.

Regarding such additional objectives, a rather different concern has to do with the power and accountability of competition agencies. If they were regularly to consider a large number of objectives of unspecified weight, lacking a clear common denominator and often pointing in different directions, they would accordingly have quite broad discretion that may be abused and, relatedly, be difficult to scrutinize. These fears may even be greatest in some areas where serious social problems are present. For example, it may be dangerous to give a government agency the power to engage in broad scrutiny of media, social networks, and internet search firms with a specific focus on political considerations. Threats to exercise or offers to abstain from using this very power may be subject to abuse that itself exerts undue influence on the political process, here under the control of a government agency that may seek to entrench an incumbent administration.

Stepping back, whether various additional objectives should be given weight in competition policy has not been explored in much depth in the literature, including with regard to merger review in particular. Future research along these lines is most likely to be helpful if it clearly identifies just what any proffered objective is taken to mean and addresses why the tools of competition policy—here, decision-making on horizontal mergers—are well suited to advancing the objective, if indeed it is an appealing one for the government to pursue.

9 Conclusion

Industrial organization economics has developed methods for analyzing anticompetitive effects of horizontal mergers that conflict with official protocols and much practice throughout the developed world. Merger efficiencies are regarded to justify allowing most horizontal mergers, yet efficiencies are not usually examined directly and the field does not offer much guidance on how to do so. Entry is primarily addressed because of the possibility that it may defeat price increases caused by mergers, but this formulation does not reflect core economic precepts, and even less attention has been given to how best to analyze how merger policy influences entry and investment that may be induced by the prospect of a subsequent buyout. More broadly, the conduct of merger review conflicts with basic teachings of decision analysis, requires better grounding in evidence and expertise on industries and firms' operations, and often fails to leverage understandings developed in other fields of economics.

Rethinking merger analysis is necessary along almost every relevant dimension despite the great progress that has been made thus far. This book attempts to identify overlooked questions, sharpen our appreciation of existing deficiencies, advance analysis by building on the strengths of what is already known in industrial organization economics and other areas of inquiry, and offer suggestions for further research, policy formulation, and the practice of merger review.

Basic principles of decision analysis, although familiar to economists and many others who analyze horizontal mergers, are contravened in important and unappreciated respects by modern merger protocols and to some extent in competition agencies' merger investigations and court review. Most problematic is the sequential siloing of analysis, starting with anticompetitive effects and only later, when they appear to be established, proceeding to the consideration of efficiencies and entry. The best way to determine which way a balance tips is not to zoom in on one side to the exclusion of the other.

Many particular defects with this approach are identified. To begin, taking the odds ratio formulation of Bayes' rule—and the oversimplified case in which there are two distinct hypotheses, that either anticompetitive effects or efficiencies explain the merger—how can one go about updating based only on consideration of the former? The prior odds are multiplied by the likelihood ratio, which lacks a denominator when only anticompetitive effects are under consideration. Merging firms' rationality constraint further implies that any evidence bearing on one explanation necessarily shifts the conditional likelihood of the other. More practically, much information (say, on firms' cost functions) is obviously pertinent to anticompetitive effects, efficiencies, and entry, and the most probative information to collect next depends on its diagnosticity-to-cost ratio, not the issue that it is most likely to illuminate. Finally, recognizing that the available information often provides a diffuse signal, prior probabilities are all the more important, suggesting the value of additional research and further analysis of the complementary empirical inquiries that already have been conducted as well as agencies' development of broader in-house and on-call expertise in many of the industries they must analyze. In both research and practice, systematic triangulation across issues and sources of information should be the aim.

The analysis of anticompetitive effects that may be generated by horizontal mergers is both a strength of existing methods and one that is directly hampered by existing protocols that focus on market definition, whether using the HMT or otherwise. The striking lack of grounding for the market definition paradigm in industrial organization economics manifests itself in many ways. Most broadly, if the purpose of market definition is to generate a relevant market that, in turn, allows the computation of market shares that purportedly indicate anticompetitive effects, then we should hope that our market definition decision is grounded in our best analysis of a merger's anticompetitive effects. But if we need our best estimate of anticompetitive effects before we can choose the relevant market, why not stop there and use our best estimate? The notion that a structural presumption renders it unnecessary to determine anticompetitive effects is simply false. Much worse,

Conclusion 215

inferences from market shares are highly degraded relative to where we started. The nature and magnitude of this problem is best appreciated by contrasting this approach with our best understanding of how to analyze anticompetitive effects.

Merger analysis of unilateral effects in homogeneous goods industries is grounded in a one-shot quantity-setting Cournot model. The first point is that the analysis and resulting formulas that contain market shares are applicable only in homogeneous goods industries, so the market definition process is not merely unnecessary but, in the event of market redefinition, destroys our ability to proceed. Second, in the simplest cases most favorable to the applicability of such formulas, the HMT/HHI formulations in the U.S. Merger Guidelines would safe harbor some mergers that would cause vastly greater price increases than others that fall in the danger zone. A simple formula for the critical ΔHHI, above which a merger should be challenged, generates differences of more than two orders of magnitude for this threshold, even when constrained to demand elasticities consistent with the HMT choosing the narrow, homogeneous goods market. In any event, it does not appear that many merger investigations involve cases that fit the Cournot homogeneous goods model well.

The correct analysis of mergers in which the firms sell differentiated products is the most developed, and it is widely appreciated that the correct analysis makes no use of market definition. Instead, analysis focuses on the diversion ratios between the merging firms' products and the firms' profit margins on those products. There do exist formulas and estimation methods under which market shares of a sort (within a product cluster) may be probative, either by assumption or as demonstrated by the evidence. But even then, only the shares of the merging firms' products matter, those shares rather than the ΔHHI are the proper sufficient statistics for this element of the analysis, and other information (substitution elasticities) is critical regardless.

Coordinated effects have proved difficult to analyze, particularly regarding prediction of the extent to which any proposed merger would facilitate successful coordination. Market definition, the HHI, and the ΔHHI are unhelpful here as well. Indeed, once one accounts for the number of firms and its reduction from a merger, the HHI is largely irrelevant to most considerations (and has the wrong sign with respect to one of them, the asymmetry among firms), and the ΔHHI has essentially no relationship to any key factor. Finally, the HMT is a particularly odd construction in this setting, which happens to be the one that motivated early merger guidelines that first incorporated this method. It is natural to ask why merger guidelines use a hypothetical *monopolist* test in the first place. For coordinated effects, success involves the firms behaving as if they were a monopolist. But as to that, we should be interested only in the first step of the HMT: how much would a hypothetical monopolist raise price? It would be pointless, with that answer in hand, to ignore it except for purposes of choosing a market and then to proceed instead to calculate market shares in order to match the resulting HHI and ΔHHI against some guideline levels to decide whether the merger is dangerous. Taken together, for all types of anticompetitive dangers from horizontal mergers, the best analysis involves, unsurprisingly, use of the tools designed to address the problem at hand rather than reliance, even in part, on a protocol that deviates, often greatly, from that path of inquiry.

Merger efficiencies pose a qualitatively different set of challenges. On one hand, efficiencies are often taken to be sufficiently ubiquitous to justify allowing most horizontal mergers, but on the other hand, it is often suggested that efficiencies are rarely analyzed in merger investigations. Implicitly, the challenge thresholds for anticompetitive effects are set fairly high, embodying what is sometimes described as a (large) efficiency credit. Then, in mergers that appear to generate significant anticompetitive effects, the merging parties' efficiency proffers are regarded to be inadequate. This state of affairs reflects the unfortunate sequential siloing of anticompetitive effects and efficiencies, but it also arises due to the underdeveloped state of analysis as well as a lack of requisite expertise to scrutinize efficiencies.

Efficiencies must be merger specific if they are to justify an otherwise anticompetitive horizontal merger. Elaboration of this central concept provides needed illumination. First, the concern is really about the nexus between a merger's anticompetitive effects and efficiencies. This point is familiar when a merger of retailers involves modest geographic overlap, enabling the merger to be permitted with appropriate spinoffs, thereby realizing most of the merger's efficiencies but avoiding its anticompetitive effects. But the implications are broader and often more nuanced. Indeed, it is even possible for synergies to be merger specific but not the anticompetitive effects. Moreover, alternatives to a merger that might be able to realize the proffered efficiencies may themselves generate similar anticompetitive effects, unless there is to be intensive regulation of the nonmerger arrangements, which is unlikely to occur.

Second, much greater effort is required to appreciate the core elements and myriad subtleties of pertinent alternatives to merger, which often involve contractual arrangements. Due to increased specialization, some of the most pertinent fields of inquiry—the theory of the firm and contract theory (associated with several Nobel prizes), organizational economics, and more—are not part of the skill set of most industrial organization economists who study competition issues and staff competition agencies. Many of the issues pertain to vertical integration and the use of complements, which are defining features of many firms and pervade often highly complex contractual relationships when activities are outsourced. Economies of scope—which can also be central when the apparent efficiency involves economies of scale—must be understood before they can be assessed in particular cases. To succeed at this endeavor, agencies need to broaden their in-house and on-call expertise to include both academic training in other fields and industry experience as managers, consultants, financiers, and market analysts. Efficiencies often appear inscrutable and thus are relegated to the end of agencies' inquiries or set aside entirely in significant part because there is insufficient research and institutional capacity to consider them properly.

The consideration of entry in modern merger analysis focuses on whether it will be sufficiently likely, timely, and substantial to counteract a merger's anticompetitive effects. Yet, short of fairly extreme cases (a number of which do exist), equilibrium analysis of entry indicates that such an offset is unlikely: higher postmerger prices are required for postmerger entry to be profitable. The correct question is whether the prospect of entry is sufficient to render unprofitable a merger motivated by anticompetitive effects, in which case inference from the merging parties' rationality constraint indicates that efficiencies are a more plausible explanation. In addition, direct welfare effects of postmerger entry have been ignored; they can render a proposed merger even less desirable than otherwise, but they sometimes raise social welfare in other ways that may offset the anticompetitive harms of a merger.

A different channel of entry, that induced by the prospect of a subsequent buyout via merger, has been largely ignored until quite recently, with increasing attention to technology and pharmaceutical incumbents' acquisitions of startups. The existence and capabilities of target firms is often taken as given, whereas the most important social welfare effects of a merger regime in this regard are likely to be on ex ante incentives for entry, investment, and innovation. This poses a significant challenge for merger review, but key channels of influence can be identified. Highly imitative entry motivated by the prospect of a buyout premium tends to be socially excessive, so a tough merger policy tends to be desirable. Interestingly, the social benefit here derives primarily from deterring entry and investment rather than from preserving subsequent competition that may not come about precisely because of the ex ante disincentive. On the other hand, complementary and more innovative entry are often socially insufficient, so the added inducement from a permissive merger regime can be beneficial. More broadly, the question is not just one of the overall toughness of merger review but also the relative stringency across types of acquisitions, which influences the channeling of ex ante investment.

Although the focus of this book has been conceptual—on rethinking merger analysis—attention is also given to empirical evidence and institutional capacity. Both for choosing prior probabilities and for determining likelihood functions to process the information gathered in merger review, it is important to examine existing empirical evidence more deeply. Industry studies, merger retrospectives, merger simulation, and stock market event studies all have notable limitations, but each also offers some illumination, constitutes a realm in which further research may yield rewards, and provides a source for triangulation. There is potential for cross-fertilization among industrial organization researchers, financial economists, other experts, and agencies (who could systematically record their findings and perform follow-up investigations to better learn how to refine their methods and to provide data for researchers). Furthermore, agencies and reviewing courts could enhance their merger review capabilities even given existing knowledge by drawing on a broader range of expertise and using it in additional ways.

Merger analysis and competition policy more broadly are guided by choices of objectives, instruments, and second-best proxies and shortcuts that are needed to undertake investigations with finite time and resources. An agency's objectives are dictated by broad normative decisions as well as considerations of institutional competence and specialization. Regarding the latter, competition agencies largely concern themselves with ills caused

Conclusion

by defective competition rather than problems regarding the environment, national defense, or macroeconomic stability. Hence, cartels are not generally permitted if the conspirators are polluters or need extra profits for added resilience in the event of war.

More controversial is whether competition agencies should design competition rules and undertake their enforcement so as to maximize total welfare, economists' traditionally stated objective, or consumer welfare, a goal often advanced on distributive grounds. On this question, little attention has been given to the teachings of public economics, associated with the Mirrleesian optimal income taxation framework. Long-standing results and recent applications to competition policy show that, in rough but fairly general terms, a total welfare criterion is the dominant target under any standard social welfare function: moving from consumer to total welfare, combined with adjustments to the tax and transfer system, can make all income groups strictly better off.

Another important point regarding the choice of welfare standards is that, in the long run, even in imperfectly competitive economies, prices tend to equal average costs, implying that consumer and total welfare tend to be aligned. This point also has important implications for more familiar topics of merger analysis: in some models, anticompetitive effects are delayed (until existing capacity is retired), and both efficiencies and entry do not tend to materialize immediately. Effects on innovation, whether via incentives for ex ante entry and investment or otherwise, appear only in the longer run. It is familiar in competition law that the long-run consequences of an act, whether a simple investment in a plant or innovation or a strategy of predatory pricing, can be of opposite sign to short-run effects. Analyzing the long-run impact of particular mergers is daunting and thus, in many respects, must be limited in agency review. Nevertheless, protocols and proxies should be chosen with an appreciation for their likely long-run consequences. Similar suggestions are offered regarding general equilibrium effects that are omitted in most industrial organization research and agency analyses of particular mergers but can be quite important in modern economies characterized by significant markups in many sectors.

These final points echo broader themes of this investigation. Rethinking merger analysis is essential. Many key foundations were never laid, and some of them would require impossible feats of engineering. But many of the most important challenges are already significantly addressed by existing research in industrial organization and other fields of economics. Empirical knowledge from the academy has not been fully assimilated, and additional wisdom from related fields is largely untapped. Hence, there are significant prospects for near-term improvement as well as some well-identified research paths worth pursuing. This book aims to articulate the relevant questions, many of which have not been appreciated, and to begin to develop answers and provide directions for further study. Throughout, the analysis seeks to be as candid as possible about the obstacles, for only when they are recognized can we begin to overcome them. Shortcuts are needed, but we need to know where we are headed and to avoid dead ends and other hazards along the way.

References

Aghion, Philippe, and Peter Howitt. 1992. A Model of Growth through Creative Destruction. *Econometrica* 60: 323–51.

Alchian, Armen A., and Harold Demsetz. 1972. Production, Information Costs, and Economic Organization. *American Economic Review* 62: 777–95.

American Bar Association Section of Antitrust Law. 2017. *Presidential Transition Report: The State of Antitrust Enforcement.*

Angrist, Joshua D., and Jörn-Steffen Pischke. 2010. The Credibility Revolution in Empirical Economics: How Better Research Design Is Taking the Con Out of Econometrics. *Journal of Economic Perspectives* 24(2): 3–30.

Ashenfelter, Orley, David Ashmore, Jonathan B. Baker, Suzanne Gleason, and Daniel S. Hosken. 2006. Empirical Methods in Merger Analysis: Econometric Analysis of Pricing in FTC v. Staples. *International Journal of the Economics of Business* 13: 265–79.

Ashenfelter, Orley, and Daniel Hosken. 2010. The Effect of Mergers on Consumer Prices: Evidence from Five Mergers on the Enforcement Margin. *Journal of Law and Economics* 53: 417–66.

Ashenfelter, Orley, Daniel Hosken, and Matthew Weinberg. 2013. The Price Effects of a Large Merger of Manufacturers: A Case Study of Maytag-Whirlpool. *American Economic Journal: Economic Policy* 5(1): 239–61.

Ashenfelter, Orley, Daniel Hosken, and Matthew Weinberg. 2014. Did Robert Bork Understate the Competitive Impact of Mergers? Evidence from Consummated Mergers. *Journal of Law and Economics* 57: S67–S100.

Asker, John, and Volker Nocke. 2021. Collusion, Mergers, and Related Antitrust Issues. In *Handbook of Industrial Organization*, edited by Kate Ho, Ali Hortaçsu, and Alessandro Lizzeri, 5: 177–279. Amsterdam: Elsevier.

Atalay, Enghin, Ali Hortaçsu, Mary Jialin Li, and Chad Syverson. 2019. How Wide Is the Firm Border? *Quarterly Journal of Economics* 134: 1845–82.

Atalay, Enghin, Ali Hortaçsu, and Chad Syverson. 2014. Vertical Integration and Input Flows. *American Economic Review* 104: 1120–48.

Atkinson, Anthony B., and Joseph E. Stiglitz. 1976. The Design of Tax Structure: Direct versus Indirect Taxation. *Journal of Public Economics* 6: 55–75.

Auerbach, Alan J., and David Reishus. 1988. The Effects of Taxation on the Merger Decision. In *Corporate Takeovers: Causes and Consequences*, edited by Alan J. Auerbach, 157–90. Chicago: National Bureau of Economic Research.

Baker, George, Robert Gibbons, and Kevin J. Murphy. 2002. Relational Contracts and the Theory of the Firm. *Quarterly Journal of Economics* 117: 39–84.

Baker, Jonathan B. 1999. Econometric Analysis in *FTC v. Staples*. *Journal of Public Policy & Marketing* 18: 11–21.

Baker, Jonathan B. 2002. Mavericks, Mergers, and Exclusion: Proving Coordinated Competitive Effects under the Antitrust Laws. *New York University Law Review* 77: 135–203.

Baker, Jonathan B., and Timothy F. Bresnahan. 1985. The Gains from Merger or Collusion in Product-Differentiated Industries. *Journal of Industrial Economics* 33: 427–44.

Basu, Susanto. 2019. Are Price-Cost Markups Rising in the United States? A Discussion of the Evidence. *Journal of Economic Perspectives* 33(3): 3–22.

Baumol, William. 1959. *Business Behavior, Value and Growth*. New York: Macmillan.

Ben-David, Itzhak, Utpal Bhattacharya, and Stacey E. Jacobsen. 2022. The (Missing) Relation between Announcement Returns and Value Creation. NBER Working Paper 27976 (revised).

Beneish, M. Daniel, Campbell R. Harvey, Ayung Tseng, and Patrick Vorst. 2022. Unpatented Innovation and Merger Synergies. *Review of Accounting Studies* 27: 706–44.

Berger, Allen, and Timothy Hannan. 1998. The Efficiency Cost of Market Power in the Banking Industry: A Test of the "Quiet Life" and Related Hypotheses. *Review of Economics and Statistics* 80: 454–65.

Bernstein, Lisa. 2015. Beyond Relational Contracts: Social Capital and Network Governance in Procurement Contracts. *Journal of Legal Analysis* 7: 561–621.

Berry, Steven. 1994. Estimating Discrete-Choice Models of Product Differentiation. *Rand Journal of Economics* 25: 242–62.

Berry, Steven, James Levinsohn, and Ariel Pakes. 1995. Automobile Prices in Market Equilibrium. *Econometrica* 63: 841–90.

References

Berry, Steven, and Ariel Pakes. 1993. Some Applications and Limitations of Recent Advances in Empirical Industrial Organization: Merger Analysis. *American Economic Review* 83(2): 247–52.

Berry, Steven, and Peter Reiss. 2007. Empirical Models of Entry and Market Structure. In *Handbook of Industrial Organization*, edited by Mark Armstrong and Robert Porter, 3: 1845–86. Amsterdam: Elsevier.

Bertrand, Marianne, Esther Duflo, and Sendhil Mullainathan. 2004. How Much Should We Trust Differences-in-Differences Estimates? *Quarterly Journal of Economics* 119: 249–75.

Besanko, David, and Daniel F. Spulber. 1993. Contested Mergers and Equilibrium Antitrust Policy. *Journal of Law, Economics, & Organization* 9: 1–29.

Betton, Sandra, B. Espen Eckbo, and Karin S. Thorburn. 2008. Corporate Takeovers. In *Handbook of Empirical Corporate Finance*, edited by B. Espen Eckbo, 2: 291–429. Amsterdam: North-Holland.

Bhattacharya, Vivek, Gastón Illanes, and David Stillerman. 2023. Merger Effects and Antitrust Enforcement: Evidence from US Retail. NBER Working Paper 31123.

Bhattacharyya, Sugato, and Amrita Nain. 2011. Horizontal Acquisitions and Buying Power: A Product Market Analysis. *Journal of Financial Economics* 99: 97–115.

Bilbiie, Florin O., Fabio Ghironi, and Marc J. Melitz. 2019. Monopoly Power and Endogenous Product Variety: Distortions and Remedies. *American Economic Journal: Macroeconomics* 11: 140–74.

Björnerstedt, Jonas, and Frank Verboven. 2016. Does Merger Simulation Work? Evidence from the Swedish Analgesics Market. *American Economic Journal: Applied Economics* 8(3): 125–64.

Bloom, Nicholas, and John Van Reenen. 2007. Measuring and Explaining Management Practices across Firms and Countries. *Quarterly Journal of Economics* 122: 1351–408.

Bork, Robert H. 1978. *The Antitrust Paradox: A Policy at War with Itself*. New York: Basic Books.

Bresnahan, Timothy F., and Peter C. Reiss. 1991. Entry and Competition in Concentrated Markets. *Journal of Political Economy* 99: 977–1009.

Bulow, Jeremy I., John D. Geanakoplos, and Paul D. Klemperer. 1985. Multimarket Oligopoly: Strategic Substitutes and Complements. *Journal of Political Economy* 93: 488–511.

Butters, J. Keith, John Lintner, and William L. Cary. 1951. *Effects of Taxation: Corporate Mergers*. Boston: Harvard Graduate School of Business.

Byrne, David P., and Nicolas De Roos. 2019. Learning to Coordinate: A Study in Retail Gasoline. *American Economic Review* 109: 591–619.

Cabral, Luís. 2021. Merger Policy in Digital Industries. *Information Economics and Policy* 54: 100866.

Callander, Steven, and Niko Matouschek. 2022. The Novelty of Innovation: Competition, Disruption, and Antitrust Policy. *Management Science* 68: 37–51.

Caradonna, Peter, Nathan H. Miller, and Gloria Sheu. 2023. Mergers, Entry, and Consumer Welfare (unpublished manuscript).

Carlton, Dennis W. 2009. Why We Need to Measure the Effect of Merger Policy and How to Do It. *Competition Policy International* 5(1): 77–90.

Chang, Howard F. 1995. Patent Scope, Antitrust Policy, and Cumulative Innovation. *Rand Journal of Economics* 26: 34–57.

Chen, Jiawei. 2009. The Effects of Mergers with Dynamic Capacity Accumulation. *International Journal of Industrial Organization* 27: 92–109.

Chipty, Tasneem, and Christopher M. Snyder. 1999. The Role of Firm Size in Bilateral Bargaining: A Study of the Cable Television Industry. *Review of Economics and Statistics* 81: 326–40.

Coase, R. H. 1937. The Nature of the Firm. *Economica* 4: 386–405.

Collis, David J., and Cynthia A. Montgomery. 2005. *Corporate Strategy: A Resource-Based Approach*. 2nd ed. New York: McGraw-Hill/Irwin.

Compte, Olivier, Frédéric Jenny, and Patrick Rey. 2002. Capacity Constraints, Mergers and Collusion. *European Economic Review* 46: 1–29.

Conlon, Christopher, and Jeff Gortmaker. 2020. Best Practices for Differentiated Products Demand Estimation with PyBLP. *Rand Journal of Economics* 51: 1108–61.

Corlett, W. J., and D. C. Hague. 1953. Complementarity and the Excess Burden of Taxation. *Review of Economic Studies* 21: 21–30.

Craig, Stuart V., Matthew Grennan, and Ashley Swanson. 2021. Mergers and Marginal Costs: New Evidence on Hospital Buyer Power. *Rand Journal of Economics* 52: 151–78.

Cunningham, Colleen, Florian Ederer, and Song Ma. 2021. Killer Acquisitions. *Journal of Political Economy* 129: 649–702.

Dafny, Leemore. 2009. Estimation and Identification of Merger Effects: An Application to Hospital Mergers. *Journal of Law and Economics* 52: 523–50.

Dalkir, Serdar, and Frederick R. Warren-Boulton. 2004. Prices, Market Definition, and the Effects of Merger: Staples–Office Depot (1997). In *The Antitrust Revolution:*

Economics, Competition, and Policy, 4th ed., edited by John E. Kwoka Jr. and Lawrence J. White, 52–72. New York: Oxford University Press.

Dasgupta, Partha, and Joseph Stiglitz. 1980. Uncertainty, Industrial Structure, and the Speed of R&D. *Bell Journal of Economics* 11: 1–28.

Datta, Sudip, Mai Iskandar-Datta, and Kartik Raman. 2001. Executive Compensation and Corporate Acquisition Decisions. *Journal of Finance* 56: 2299–336.

Davidson, Carl, and Raymond Deneckere. 1984. Horizontal Mergers and Collusive Behavior. *International Journal of Industrial Organization* 2: 117–32.

Davidson, Carl, and Raymond Deneckere. 1986. Long-Run Competition in Capacity, Short-Run Competition in Price, and the Cournot Model. *Rand Journal of Economics* 17: 404–15.

De Loecker, Jan, Jan Eeckhout, and Gabriel Unger. 2020. The Rise of Market Power and the Macroeconomic Implications. *Quarterly Journal of Economics* 135: 561–644.

De Loecker, Jan, and Chad Syverson. 2021. An Industrial Organization Perspective on Productivity. In *Handbook of Industrial Organization*, edited by Kate Ho, Ali Hortaçsu, and Alessandro Lizzeri, 4: 141–223. Amsterdam: Elsevier.

Demsetz, Harold. 1973. Industry Structure, Market Rivalry, and Public Policy. *Journal of Law and Economics* 16: 1–9.

Deneckere, Raymond, and Carl Davidson. 1985. Incentives to Form Coalitions with Bertrand Competition. *Rand Journal of Economics* 16: 473–86.

Dixit, Avinash K., and Joseph E. Stiglitz. 1977. Monopolistic Competition and Optimum Product Diversity. *American Economic Review* 67: 297–308.

Donald, Stephen G., and Kevin Lang. 2007. Inference with Difference-in-Differences and Other Panel Data. *Review of Economics and Statistics* 89: 221–33.

Dubé, Jean-Pierre, Jeremy T. Fox, and Che-Lin Su. 2012. Improving the Numerical Performance of Static and Dynamic Aggregate Discrete Choice Random Coefficients Demand Estimation. *Econometrica* 80: 2231–67.

Eckbo, B. Espen. 1983. Horizontal Mergers, Collusion, and Stockholder Wealth. *Journal of Financial Economics* 11: 241–73.

Eckbo, B. Espen, and Peggy Wier. 1985. Antimerger Policy under the Hart-Scott-Rodino Act: A Reexamination of the Market Power Hypothesis. *Journal of Law and Economics* 28: 119–49.

Edlin, Aaron, and Joseph Farrell. 2015. Freedom to Trade and the Competitive Process. In *The Oxford Handbook of International Antitrust Economics*, edited by Roger D. Blair and D. Daniel Sokol, 1: 298–310. Oxford: Oxford University Press.

Eliason, Paul J., Benjamin Heebsh, Ryan C. McDevitt, and James W. Roberts. 2020. How Acquisitions Affect Firm Behavior and Performance: Evidence from the Dialysis Industry. *Quarterly Journal of Economics* 135: 221–67.

Elzinga, Kenneth G. 1969. The Antimerger Law: Pyrrhic Victories? *Journal of Law and Economics* 12: 43–78.

Epifani, Paolo, and Gino Gancia. 2011. Trade, Markup Heterogeneity and Misallocations. *Journal of International Economics* 83: 1–13.

Ericson, Richard, and Ariel Pakes. 1995. Markov-Perfect Industry Dynamics: A Framework for Empirical Work. *Review of Economic Studies* 62: 53–82.

European Commission. 2004. *Guidelines on the Assessment of Horizontal Mergers under the Council Regulation on the Control of Concentrations between Undertakings*. Official Journal C 031.

European Union. 1997. *Commission Notice on the Definition of Relevant Market for Purposes of Community Competition Law*. Official Journal C 372.

Fabra, Natalia, and Massimo Motta. 2018. Assessing Coordinated Effects in Merger Cases. In *Handbook of Game Theory and Industrial Organization*, edited by Luis C. Corchón and Marco A. Marini, 2: 91–122. Cheltenham: Edward Elgar.

Fan, Joseph P. H., and Larry H. P. Lang. 2000. The Measurement of Relatedness: An Application to Corporate Diversification. *Journal of Business* 73: 629–60.

Fan, Ying. 2013. Ownership Consolidation and Product Characteristics: A Study of the US Daily Newspaper Market. *American Economic Review* 103: 1598–628.

Fan, Ying, and Chenyu Yang. 2020. Competition, Product Proliferation, and Welfare: A Study of the US Smartphone Market. *American Economic Journal: Microeconomics* 12(2): 99–134.

Farrell, Joseph, and Michael L. Katz. 2006. The Economics of Welfare Standards in Antitrust. *Competition Policy International* 2(2): 3–28.

Farrell, Joseph, and Carl Shapiro. 1990. Horizontal Mergers: An Equilibrium Analysis. *American Economic Review* 80: 107–26.

Farrell, Joseph, and Carl Shapiro. 2001. Scale Economies and Synergies in Horizontal Merger Analysis. *Antitrust Law Journal* 68: 685–710.

Farrell, Joseph, and Carl Shapiro. 2008. How Strong Are Weak Patents? *American Economic Review* 98: 1347–69.

Farrell, Joseph, and Carl Shapiro. 2010. Antitrust Evaluation of Horizontal Mergers: An Economic Alternative to Market Definition. *B.E. Journal of Theoretical Economics: Policies and Perspectives* 10(1): article 9.

Federal Trade Commission and U.S. Department of Justice. 2006. *Commentary on the U.S. Merger Guidelines.*

Fee, C. Edward, and Shawn Thomas. 2004. Sources of Gains in Horizontal Mergers: Evidence from Customer, Supplier, and Rival Firms. *Journal of Financial Economics* 74: 423–60.

Focarelli, Dario, and Fabio Panetta. 2003. Are Mergers Beneficial to Consumers? Evidence from the Market for Bank Deposits. *American Economic Review* 93: 1152–72.

Friedman, James W. 1971. A Non-cooperative Equilibrium for Supergames. *Review of Economic Studies* 38: 1–12.

Friedman, James W. 1988. On the Strategic Importance of Prices versus Quantities. *Rand Journal of Economics* 19: 607–22.

Fu, Fangjian, Leming Lin, and Micah S. Officer. 2013. Acquisitions Driven by Stock Overvaluation: Are They Good Deals? *Journal of Financial Economics* 109: 24–39.

Fudenberg, Drew, and Jean Tirole. 1987. Understanding Rent Dissipation: On the Use of Game Theory in Industrial Organization. *American Economic Review* 77: 176–83.

Gandhi, Amit, Luke Froeb, Steven Tschantz, and Gregory J. Werden. 2008. Post-Merger Product Repositioning. *Journal of Industrial Economics* 56: 49–67.

Garmon, Christopher. 2017. The Accuracy of Hospital Merger Screening Methods. *Rand Journal of Economics* 48: 1068–102.

Garvey, Gerald T. 1995. Why Reputation Favors Joint Ventures Over Vertical and Horizontal Integration: A Simple Model. *Journal of Economic Behavior & Organization* 28: 387–97.

Gautier, Axel, and Joe Lamesch. 2021. Mergers in the Digital Economy. *Information Economics and Policy* 54: 100890.

Gaynor, Martin, Kate Ho, and Robert J. Town. 2015. The Industrial Organization of Health-Care Markets. *Journal of Economic Literature* 53: 235–84.

Gaynor, Martin, and Robert J. Town. 2012. Competition in Health Care Markets. In *Handbook of Health Economics*, edited by Mark V. Pauly, Thomas G. McGuire, and Pedro P. Barros, 2: 499–637. Amsterdam: Elsevier.

Geroski, Paul A. 1995. What Do We Know about Entry? *International Journal of Industrial Organization* 13: 421–40.

Gibbons, Robert. 2005. Four Formal(izable) Theories of the Firm? *Journal of Economic Behavior & Organization*: 58: 200–45.

Gibbons, Robert, and John Roberts. 2013. *The Handbook of Organizational Economics.* Princeton: Princeton University Press.

Gilbert, Richard J. 2020. *Innovation Matters: Competition Policy for the High-Technology Economy*. Cambridge, MA: MIT Press.

Gilbert, Richard J., and Michael L. Katz. 2022. Dynamic Merger Policy and Pre-Merger Product Choice by an Entrant. *International Journal of Industrial Organization* 81: 102812.

Goppelsroeder, Marie, Maarten Pieter Schinkel, and Jan Tuinstra. 2008. Quantifying the Scope for Efficiency Defense in Merger Control: The Werden-Froeb-Index. *Journal of Industrial Economics* 56: 778–808.

Gowrisankaran, Gautam. 1999. A Dynamic Model of Endogenous Horizontal Mergers. *Rand Journal of Economics* 30: 56–83.

Gowrisankaran, Gautam, Aviv Nevo, and Robert Town. 2015. Mergers When Prices Are Negotiated: Evidence from the Hospital Industry. *American Economic Review* 105: 172–203.

Green, Edward J., and Robert H. Porter. 1984. Noncooperative Collusion under Imperfect Price Information. *Econometrica* 52: 87–100.

Grossman, Sanford J., and Oliver D. Hart. 1986. The Costs and Benefits of Ownership: A Theory of Vertical and Lateral Integration. *Journal of Political Economy* 94: 691–719.

Hall, Robert E. 2018. New Evidence on the Markup of Prices over Marginal Costs and the Role of Mega-Firms in the US Economy. NBER Working Paper 24574.

Hall, Robert E., and Susan E. Woodward. 2010. The Burden of the Nondiversifiable Risk of Entrepreneurship. *American Economic Review* 100: 1163–94.

Halonen, Maija. 2002. Reputation and the Allocation of Ownership. *Economic Journal* 112: 539–58.

Harford, Jarrad. 1999. Corporate Cash Reserves and Acquisitions. *Journal of Finance* 54: 1969–97.

Harford, Jarrad, Mark Humphery-Jenner, and Ronan Powell. 2012. The Sources of Value Destruction in Acquisitions by Entrenched Managers. *Journal of Financial Economics* 106: 247–61.

Harrington, Joseph E., Jr. 2013. Evaluating Mergers for Coordinated Effects and the Role of "Parallel Accommodating Conduct." *Antitrust Law Journal* 78: 651–68.

Harrington, Joseph E., Jr. 2017. *The Theory of Collusion and Competition Policy*. Cambridge, MA: MIT Press.

Hart, Oliver. 1983. The Market Mechanism as an Incentive Scheme. *Bell Journal of Economics* 14: 366–82.

References

Hart, Oliver. 1995. *Firms, Contracts, and Financial Structure*. Oxford: Oxford University Press.

Hart, Oliver. 2009. Hold-Up, Asset Ownership, and Reference Points. *Quarterly Journal of Economics* 124: 267–300.

Hart, Oliver. 2011. Thinking about the Firm: A Review of Daniel Spulber's *The Theory of the Firm*. *Journal of Economic Literature* 49: 101–13.

Hart, Oliver. 2017. Incomplete Contracts and Control. *American Economic Review* 107: 1731–52.

Hart, Oliver, and Bengt Holmstrom. 2010. A Theory of Firm Scope. *Quarterly Journal of Economics* 125: 483–513.

Hart, Oliver, and John Moore. 1990. Property Rights and the Nature of the Firm. *Journal of Political Economy* 98: 1119–58.

Hart, Oliver, and John Moore. 2008. Contracts as Reference Points. *Quarterly Journal of Economics* 123: 1–48.

Hemphill, C. Scott, and Nancy L. Rose. 2018. Mergers That Harm Sellers. *Yale Law Journal* 127: 2078–109.

Heyer, Kenneth. 2006. Welfare Standards and Merger Analysis: Why Not the Best? *Competition Policy International* 2(2): 29–54.

Heyer, Kenneth. 2007. Predicting the Competitive Effects of Mergers by Listening to Customers. *Antitrust Law Journal* 74: 87–127.

Hilke, John C., and Philip B. Nelson. 1993. The Economics of Entry Lags: A Theoretical and Empirical Overview. *Antitrust Law Journal* 61: 365–85.

Ho, Kate, and Robin S. Lee. 2017. Insurer Competition in Health Care Markets. *Econometrica* 85: 379–417.

Hoberg, Gerard, and Gordon Phillips. 2010. Product Market Synergies and Competition in Mergers and Acquisitions: A Text-Based Analysis. *Review of Financial Studies* 23: 3773–811.

Hoberg, Gerard, and Gordon Phillips. 2016. Text-Based Network Industries and Endogenous Product Differentiation. *Journal of Political Economy* 124: 1423–65.

Holmes, Thomas J., Wen-Tai Hsu, and Sanghoon Lee. 2014. Allocative Efficiency, Mark-Ups, and the Welfare Gains from Trade. *Journal of International Economics* 94: 195–206.

Holmstrom, Bengt. 1999. The Firm as a Subeconomy. *Journal of Law, Economics, & Organization* 15: 74–102.

Holmstrom, Bengt, and Paul Milgrom. 1994. The Firm as an Incentive Scheme. *American Economic Review* 84: 972–91.

Holmstrom, Bengt, and John Roberts. 1998. The Boundaries of the Firm Revisited. *Journal of Economic Perspectives* 12(4): 73–94.

Holmstrom, Bengt, and Jean Tirole. 1991. Transfer Pricing and Organizational Form. *Journal of Law, Economics, & Organization* 7: 201–28.

Hopenhayn, Hugo A. 1992. Entry, Exit, and Firm Dynamics in Long Run Equilibrium. *Econometrica* 60: 1127–50.

Hunter, Graeme, Gregory K. Leonard, and G. Steven Olley. 2008. Merger Retrospective Studies: A Review. *Antitrust* 23(1): 34–41.

Jaffe, Sonia, and E. Glen Weyl. 2013. The First-Order Approach to Merger Analysis. *American Economic Journal: Microeconomics* 5(4): 188–218.

Jensen, Michael C. 1986. Agency Costs of Free Cash Flow, Corporate Finance, and Takeovers. *American Economic Review* 76(2): 323–29.

Jensen, Michael C., and William H. Meckling. 1976. Theory of the Firm: Managerial Behavior, Agency Costs and Ownership Structure. *Journal of Financial Economics* 3: 305–60.

Jin, Ginger Zhe, Mario Leccese, and Liad Wagman. 2023. How Do Top Acquirers Compare in Technology Mergers? New Evidence from an S&P Taxonomy. *International Journal of Industrial Organization* 89: 102891.

Joskow, Paul L. 1991. The Role of Transaction Cost Economics in Antitrust and Public Utility Regulatory Policies. *Journal of Law, Economics, & Organization* 7: 53–83.

Kahle, Kathleen M., and Ralph A. Walkling. 1996. The Impact of Industry Classifications on Financial Research. *Journal of Financial and Quantitative Analysis* 31: 309–35.

Kamepalli, Sai Krishna, Raghuram Rajan, and Luigi Zingales. 2022. Kill Zone. NBER Working Paper 27146 (revised).

Kaplow, Louis. 1984. The Patent-Antitrust Intersection: A Reappraisal. *Harvard Law Review* 97: 1813–92.

Kaplow, Louis. 2004. On the (Ir)relevance of Distribution and Labor Supply Distortion to Government Policy. *Journal of Economic Perspectives* 18(4): 159–75.

Kaplow, Louis. 2006. On the Undesirability of Commodity Taxation Even When Income Taxation Is Not Optimal. *Journal of Public Economics* 90: 1235–50.

Kaplow, Louis. 2008. *The Theory of Taxation and Public Economics*. Princeton: Princeton University Press.

Kaplow, Louis. 2010. Why (Ever) Define Markets? *Harvard Law Review* 124: 437–517.

References

Kaplow, Louis. 2011a. Market Definition and the Merger Guidelines. *Review of Industrial Organization*: 39: 107–25.

Kaplow, Louis. 2011b. Market Share Thresholds: On the Conflation of Empirical Assessments and Legal Policy Judgments. *Journal of Competition Law & Economics* 7: 243–76.

Kaplow, Louis. 2011c. On the Optimal Burden of Proof. *Journal of Political Economy* 119: 1104–40.

Kaplow, Louis. 2012a. Market Definition Alchemy. *Antitrust Bulletin* 57: 915–52.

Kaplow, Louis. 2012b. On the Choice of Welfare Standards in Competition Law. In *The Goals of Competition Law*, edited by Daniel Zimmer, 3–26. Cheltenham: Edward Elgar.

Kaplow, Louis. 2013a. *Competition Policy and Price Fixing*. Princeton: Princeton University Press.

Kaplow, Louis. 2013b. Market Definition: Impossible and Counterproductive. *Antitrust Law Journal* 79: 361–79.

Kaplow, Louis. 2017. On the Relevance of Market Power. *Harvard Law Review* 130: 1303–407.

Kaplow, Louis. 2019. Balancing versus Structured Decision Procedures: Antitrust, Title VII Disparate Impact, and Constitutional Law Strict Scrutiny. *University of Pennsylvania Law Review* 167: 1375–462.

Kaplow, Louis. 2020. A Unified Perspective on Efficiency, Redistribution, and Public Policy. *National Tax Journal* 73: 429–72.

Kaplow, Louis. 2021a. Efficiencies in Merger Analysis. *Antitrust Law Journal* 83: 557–619.

Kaplow, Louis. 2021b. Market Power and Income Taxation. *American Economic Journal: Economic Policy* 13(4): 329–54.

Kaplow, Louis. 2022. Replacing the Structural Presumption. *Antitrust Law Journal* 84: 565–627.

Kaplow, Louis. 2023a. Competition Policy in a Simple General Equilibrium Model. *Journal of Political Economy Microeconomics* 1: 80–114.

Kaplow, Louis. 2023b. Entry and Merger Analysis. *Antitrust Law Journal* 85: 103–46.

Kaplow, Louis. 2024. The 2023 Merger Guidelines and Market Definition: Doubling Down or Folding? *Review of Industrial Organization* 65 (forthcoming).

Kaplow, Louis, and Carl Shapiro. 2007. Antitrust. In *Handbook of Law and Economics*, edited by A. Mitchell Polinsky and Steven Shavell, 2: 1073–225. Amsterdam: North-Holland.

Kaplow, Louis, and Steven Shavell. 2001. Any Non-welfarist Method of Policy Assessment Violates the Pareto Principle. *Journal of Political Economy* 109: 281–86.

Kaplow, Louis, and Steven Shavell. 2002. *Fairness versus Welfare*. Cambridge, MA: Harvard University Press.

Katz, Michael L. 2021. Big Tech Mergers: Innovation, Competition for the Market, and the Acquisition of Emerging Competitors. *Information Economics and Policy* 54: 100883.

Katz, Michael L., and Howard A. Shelanski. 2007a. Merger Analysis and the Treatment of Uncertainty: Should We Expect Better? *Antitrust Law Journal* 74: 537–74.

Katz, Michael L., and Howard A. Shelanski. 2007b. Mergers and Innovation. *Antitrust Law Journal* 74: 1–85.

Kellogg, Ryan. 2011. Learning by Drilling: Interfirm Learning and Relationship Persistence in the Texas Oilpatch. *Quarterly Journal of Economics* 126: 1961–2004.

Kim, E. Han, and Vijay Singal. 1993. Mergers and Market Power: Evidence from the Airline Industry. *American Economic Review* 83: 549–69.

Klein, Benjamin, Robert G. Crawford, and Armen A. Alchian. 1978. Vertical Integration, Appropriable Rents, and the Competitive Contracting Process. *Journal of Law and Economics* 21: 297–326.

Klein, Benjamin, and Andres V. Lerner. 2008. The Firm in Economics and Antitrust Law. In *Issues in Competition Law and Policy*, edited by Wayne Dale Collins, 1: 249–71. Chicago: American Bar Association.

Knittel, Christopher R., and Konstantinos Metaxoglou. 2014. Estimation of Random-Coefficient Demand Models: Two Empiricists' Perspective. *Review of Economics and Statistics* 96: 34–59.

Kreps, David M., and José A. Scheinkman. 1983. Quantity Precommitment and Bertrand Competition Yield Cournot Outcomes. *Bell Journal of Economics* 14: 326–37.

Krueger, Anne O. 1974. The Political Economy of the Rent-Seeking Society. *American Economic Review* 64: 291–303.

Kwoka, John. 2014. *Mergers, Merger Control, and Remedies: A Retrospective Analysis of U.S. Policy*. Cambridge, MA: MIT Press.

Kwoka, John. 2017. The Structural Presumption and the Safe Harbor in Merger Review: False Positives or Unwarranted Concerns? *Antitrust Law Journal* 81: 837–72.

Kwoka, John. 2019. Mergers, Merger Control, and Remedies: A Response to the Vita-Osinski Critique. *Antitrust Law Journal* 82: 741–61.

Kwoka, John, and Chengyan Gu. 2015. Predicting Merger Outcomes: The Accuracy of Stock Market Event Studies, Market Structure Characteristics, and Agency Decisions. *Journal of Law and Economics* 58: 519–43.

References

Lafontaine, Francine. 1992. Agency Theory and Franchising: Some Empirical Results. *Rand Journal of Economics* 23: 263–83.

Lancaster, Kelvin. 1980. Competition and Product Variety. *Journal of Business* 53(3): S79–S103.

Leibenstein, Harvey. 1966. Allocative Efficiency vs. "X-Efficiency." *American Economic Review* 56: 392–415.

Lerner, A. P. 1934. The Concept of Monopoly and the Measurement of Monopoly Power. *Review of Economic Studies* 1: 157–75.

Letina, Igor, Armin Schmutzler, and Regina Seibel. 2023. Killer Acquisitions and Beyond: Policy Effects on Innovation Strategies. University of Zurich Department of Economics Working Paper 358.

Levin, Dan. 1990. Horizontal Mergers: The 50-Percent Benchmark. *American Economic Review* 80: 1238–45.

Li, Sophia, Joe Mazur, Yongjoon Park, James Roberts, Andrew Sweeting, and Jun Zhang. 2022. Repositioning and Market Power after Airline Mergers. *Rand Journal of Economics* 53: 166–99.

Lipsey, R. G., and Kelvin Lancaster. 1956. The General Theory of Second Best. *Review of Economic Studies* 24: 11–32.

Loertscher, Simon, and Leslie M. Marx. 2021. Coordinated Effects in Merger Review. *Journal of Law and Economics* 64: 705–44.

Loury, Glenn C. 1979. Market Structure and Innovation. *Quarterly Journal of Economics* 93: 395–410.

Magelssen, Catherine. 2020. Allocation of Property Rights and Technological Innovation within Firms. *Strategic Management Journal* 41: 758–87.

Malmendier, Ulrike, Enrico Moretti, and Florian S. Peters. 2018. Winning by Losing: Evidence on the Long-Run Effects of Mergers. *Review of Financial Studies* 31: 3212–64.

Malmendier, Ulrike, and Geoffrey Tate. 2008. Who Makes Acquisitions? CEO Overconfidence and the Market's Reaction. *Journal of Financial Economics* 89: 20–43.

Mankiw, N. Gregory, and Michael D. Whinston. 1986. Free Entry and Social Inefficiency. *Rand Journal of Economics* 17: 48–58.

Manuszak, Mark D., and Charles C. Moul. 2008. Prices and Endogenous Market Structure in Office Supply Superstores. *Journal of Industrial Economics* 56: 94–112.

March, James G., and Herbert A. Simon. 1958. *Organizations*. New York: Wiley.

Mariuzzo, Franco, and Peter L. Ormosi. 2019. Post-Merger Price Dynamics Matters, So Why Do Merger Retrospectives Ignore It? *Review of Industrial Organization* 55: 403–29.

Marris, Robin. 1964. *The Economic Theory of "Managerial" Capitalism*. London: Palgrave Macmillan.

Marshall, Robert C., and Leslie M. Marx. 2012. *The Economics of Collusion: Cartels and Bidding Rings*. Cambridge, MA: MIT Press.

Maskin, Eric, and Jean Tirole. 1987. A Theory of Dynamic Oligopoly, III: Cournot Competition. *European Economic Review* 31: 947–68.

Masten, Scott E. 1988. A Legal Basis for the Firm. *Journal of Law, Economics, & Organization* 4: 181–98.

Mathewson, G. Frank, and Ralph A. Winter. 1985. The Economics of Franchise Contracts. *Journal of Law and Economics* 28: 503–26.

Mazzeo, Michael J., Katja Seim, and Mauricio Varela. 2018. The Welfare Consequences of Mergers with Endogenous Product Choice. *Journal of Industrial Economics* 66: 980–1016.

McAfee, R. Preston, and Michael A. Williams. 1988. Can Event Studies Detect Anticompetitive Mergers? *Economics Letters* 28: 199–203.

McAfee, R. Preston, and Michael A. Williams. 1992. Horizontal Mergers and Antitrust Policy. *Journal of Industrial Economics* 40: 181–87.

McNulty, Paul J. 1968. Economic Theory and the Meaning of Competition. *Quarterly Journal of Economics* 82: 639–56.

Melitz, Marc J. 2003. The Impact of Trade on Intra-Industry Reallocations and Aggregate Industry Productivity. *Econometrica* 71: 1695–725.

Mermelstein, Ben, Volker Nocke, Mark A. Satterthwaite, and Michael D. Whinston. 2020. Internal versus External Growth in Industries with Scale Economies: A Computational Model of Optimal Merger Policy. *Journal of Political Economy* 128: 301–41.

Miller, Nathan H., Marc Remer, Conor Ryan, and Gloria Sheu. 2016. Pass-Through and the Prediction of Merger Price Effects. *Journal of Industrial Economics* 64: 683–709.

Miller, Nathan H., Marc Remer, Conor Ryan, and Gloria Sheu. 2017. Upward Pricing Pressure as a Predictor of Merger Price Effects. *International Journal of Industrial Organization* 52: 216–47.

Miller, Nathan H., and Matthew C. Weinberg. 2017. Understanding the Price Effects of the MillerCoors Joint Venture. *Econometrica* 85: 1763–91.

Mirrlees, James A. 1971. An Exploration in the Theory of Optimum Income Taxation. *Review of Economic Studies* 38: 175–208.

Morck, Randall, Andrei Shleifer, and Robert W. Vishny. 1990. Do Managerial Objectives Drive Bad Acquisitions? *Journal of Finance* 45: 31–48.

References

Motta, Massimo, and Martin Peitz. 2021. Big Tech Mergers. *Information Economics and Policy* 54: 100868.

Motta, Massimo, and Helder Vasconcelos. 2005. Efficiency Gains and Myopic Antitrust Authority in a Dynamic Merger Game. *International Journal of Industrial Organization* 23: 777–801.

Nevo, Aviv. 2000. Mergers with Differentiated Products: The Case of the Ready-to-Eat Cereal Industry. *Rand Journal of Economics* 31: 395–421.

Nevo, Aviv. 2001. Measuring Market Power in the Ready-to-Eat Cereal Market. *Econometrica* 69: 307–42.

Nevo, Aviv, and Michael D. Whinston. 2010. Taking the Dogma Out of Econometrics: Structural Modeling and Credible Inference. *Journal of Economic Perspectives* 24(2): 69–81.

Nocke, Volker, and Michael D. Whinston. 2010. Dynamic Merger Review. *Journal of Political Economy* 118: 1200–51.

Nocke, Volker, and Michael D. Whinston. 2013. Merger Policy with Merger Choice. *American Economic Review* 103: 1006–33.

Nocke, Volker, and Michael D. Whinston. 2022. Concentration Thresholds for Horizontal Mergers. *American Economic Review* 112: 1915–48.

Ottaviani, Marco, and Abraham L. Wickelgren. 2011. Ex Ante or Ex Post Competition Policy? A Progress Report. *International Journal of Industrial Organization* 29: 356–59.

Panzar, John C., and Robert D. Willig. 1981. Economies of Scope. *American Economic Review* 71(2): 268–72.

Pautler, Paul A. 2003. Evidence on Mergers and Acquisitions. *Antitrust Bulletin* 48: 119–222.

Perry, Martin K., and Robert H. Porter. 1985. Oligopoly and the Incentive for Horizontal Merger. *American Economic Review* 75: 219–27.

Peters, Craig. 2006. Evaluating the Performance of Merger Simulation: Evidence from the U.S. Airline Industry. *Journal of Law and Economics* 49: 627–49.

Phillips, Gordon, and Alexei Zhdanov. Forthcoming. Venture Capital Investments, Merger Activity, and Competition Laws around the World. *Review of Corporate Finance Studies*.

Pittman, Russell. 2007. Consumer Surplus as the Appropriate Standard for Antitrust Enforcement. *Competition Policy International* 3(2): 205–24.

Porter, Robert H. 2020. Mergers and Coordinated Effects. *International Journal of Industrial Organization* 73: 102583.

Posner, Richard A. 1975. The Social Costs of Monopoly and Regulation. *Journal of Political Economy* 83: 807–27.

Prado, Tiago S., and Johannes M. Bauer. 2022. Big Tech Platform Acquisitions of Start-Ups and Venture Capital Funding for Innovation. *Information Economics and Policy* 59: 100973.

Rasmusen, Eric. 1988. Entry for Buyout. *Journal of Industrial Economics* 36: 281–99.

Rhodes-Kropf, Matthew, and S. Viswanathan. 2004. Market Valuation and Merger Waves. *Journal of Finance* 59: 2685–718.

Roberts, Gary L., and Steven C. Salop. 1996. Efficiencies in Dynamic Merger Analysis: A Summary. *World Competition* 19(4): 5–18.

Roll, Richard. 1986. The Hubris Hypothesis of Corporate Takeovers. *Journal of Business* 59: 197–216.

Röller, Lars-Hendrik, Johan Stennek, and Frank Verboven. 2006. Efficiency Gains from Mergers. In *European Merger Control*, edited by Fabienne Ilzkovitz and Roderick Meiklejohn, 84–201. Cheltenham: Edward Elgar.

Rose, Nancy L., and Jonathan Sallet. 2020. The Dichotomous Treatment of Efficiencies in Horizontal Mergers: Too Much? Too Little? Getting It Right. *University of Pennsylvania Law Review* 168: 1941–84.

Rubin, Paul H. 1978. The Theory of the Firm and the Structure of the Franchise Contract. *Journal of Law and Economics* 21: 223–33.

Salant, Stephen W., Sheldon Switzer, and Robert J. Reynolds. 1983. Losses from Horizontal Merger: The Effects of an Exogenous Change in Industry Structure on Cournot-Nash Equilibrium. *Quarterly Journal of Economics* 98: 185–99.

Salop, Steven C. 2010. Question: What Is the Real and Proper Antitrust Welfare Standard? Answer: The True Consumer Welfare Standard. *Loyola Consumer Law Review* 22: 336–53.

Savor, Pavel G., and Qi Lu. 2009. Do Stock Mergers Create Value for Acquirers? *Journal of Finance* 64: 1061–97.

Scherer, F. M. 1991. Comment on Robert D. Willig, Merger Analysis, Industrial Organization Theory, and Merger Guidelines. *Brookings Papers on Economic Activity: Microeconomics* 1991: 323–27.

Schmalensee, Richard. 1987. Ease of Entry: Has the Concept Been Applied Too Readily? *Antitrust Law Journal* 56: 41–51.

Schmalensee, Richard. 2012. "On a Level with Dentists?" Reflections on the Evolution of Industrial Organization. *Review of Industrial Organization* 41: 157–79.

Schmitt, Matt. 2017. Do Hospital Mergers Reduce Costs? *Journal of Health Economics* 52: 74–94.

Schumpeter, Joseph A. 1947. The Creative Response in Economic History. *Journal of Economic History* 7: 149–59.

Scitovsky, Tibor. 1954. Two Concepts of External Economies. *Journal of Political Economy* 62: 143–51.

Shahrur, Husayn. 2005. Industry Structure and Horizontal Takeovers: Analysis of Wealth Effects on Rivals, Suppliers, and Corporate Customers. *Journal of Financial Economics* 76: 61–98.

Shapiro, Carl. 2012. Competition and Innovation: Did Arrow Hit the Bull's Eye? In *The Rate and Direction of Inventive Activity Revisited*, edited by Josh Lerner and Scott Stern, 361–410. Chicago: University of Chicago Press.

Sheen, Albert. 2014. The Real Product Market Impact of Mergers. *Journal of Finance* 69: 2651–88.

Shleifer, Andrei, and Robert W. Vishny. 2003. Stock Market Driven Acquisitions. *Journal of Financial Economics* 70: 295–311.

Sidak, J. Gregory. 2013. Court-Appointed Neutral Economic Experts. *Journal of Competition Law & Economics* 9: 359–94.

Simon, Herbert A. 1991. Organizations and Markets. *Journal of Economic Perspectives* 5(2): 25–44.

Simpson, John, and David Schmidt. 2008. Difference-in-Differences Analysis in Antitrust: A Cautionary Note. *Antitrust Law Journal* 75: 623–35.

Spence, Michael. 1976. Product Selection, Fixed Costs, and Monopolistic Competition. *Review of Economic Studies* 43: 217–35.

Stiebale, Joel, and Florian Szücs. 2022. Mergers and Market Power: Evidence from Rivals' Responses in European Markets. *Rand Journal of Economics* 53: 678–702.

Stigler, George J. 1950. Monopoly and Oligopoly by Merger. *American Economic Review* 40(2): 23–34.

Stigler, George J. 1964. A Theory of Oligopoly. *Journal of Political Economy* 72: 44–61.

Stillman, Robert. 1983. Examining Antitrust Policy towards Horizontal Mergers. *Journal of Financial Economics* 11: 225–40.

Stinchcombe, Arthur L. 1990. *Information and Organizations*. Berkeley: University of California Press.

Sullivan, Sean P. 2016. What Structural Presumption? Reuniting Evidence and Economics on the Role of Market Concentration in Horizontal Merger Analysis. *Journal of Corporation Law* 42: 403–44.

Syverson, Chad. 2004. Product Substitutability and Productivity Dispersion. *Review of Economics and Statistics* 86: 534–50.

Syverson, Chad. 2019. Macroeconomics and Market Power: Context, Implications, and Open Questions. *Journal of Economic Perspectives* 33(3): 23–43.

Teece, David J. 1980. Economies of Scope and the Scope of the Enterprise. *Journal of Economic Behavior and Organization* 1: 223–47.

Tirole, Jean. 1988. *The Theory of Industrial Organization*. Cambridge, MA: MIT Press.

Traina, James. 2018. Is Aggregate Market Power Increasing? Production Trends Using Financial Statements. Stigler Center for the Study of the Economy and the State Working Paper 17.

Tullock, Gordon. 1967. The Welfare Costs of Tariffs, Monopolies, and Theft. *Western Economic Journal* 5: 224–32.

U.S. Department of Justice. 1968. *Merger Guidelines*.

U.S. Department of Justice and Federal Trade Commission. 2010. *Horizontal Merger Guidelines*.

U.S. Department of Justice and Federal Trade Commission. 2023. *Merger Guidelines*.

Varian, Hal R. 2019. Recent Trends in Concentration, Competition, and Entry. *Antitrust Law Journal* 82: 807–34.

Vasconcelos, Helder. 2005. Tacit Collusion, Cost Asymmetries, and Mergers. *Rand Journal of Economics* 36: 39–62.

Vita, Michael, and F. David Osinski. 2018. John Kwoka's *Mergers, Merger Control, and Remedies*: A Critical Review. *Antitrust Law Journal* 82: 361–88.

Weinberg, Matthew C. 2011. More Evidence on the Performance of Merger Simulations. *American Economic Review* 101(3): 51–55.

Weinberg, Matthew C., and Daniel Hosken. 2013. Evidence on the Accuracy of Merger Simulations. *Review of Economics and Statistics* 95: 1584–600.

Werden, Gregory J. 1996. A Robust Test for Consumer Welfare Enhancing Mergers among Sellers of Differentiated Products. *Journal of Industrial Economics* 44: 409–13.

Werden, Gregory J. 2007. Monopsony and the Sherman Act: Consumer Welfare in a New Light. *Antitrust Law Journal* 74: 707–37.

Werden, Gregory J. 2015. Inconvenient Truths on Merger Retrospective Studies. *Journal of Antitrust Enforcement* 3: 287–301.

Werden, Gregory J., and Luke M. Froeb. 1994. The Effects of Mergers in Differentiated Products Industries: Logit Demand and Merger Policy. *Journal of Law, Economics, & Organization* 10: 407–26.

Werden, Gregory J., and Luke M. Froeb. 1998. The Entry-Inducing Effects of Horizontal Mergers: An Exploratory Analysis. *Journal of Industrial Economics* 46: 525–43.

Wernerfelt, Birger. 1984. A Resource-Based View of the Firm. *Strategic Management Journal* 5: 171–80.

Whinston, Michael D. 2003. On the Transaction Cost Determinants of Vertical Integration. *Journal of Law, Economics, & Organization* 19: 1–23.

Whinston, Michael D. 2006. *Lectures on Antitrust Economics*. Cambridge, MA: MIT Press.

Whinston, Michael D. 2007. Antitrust Policy toward Horizontal Mergers. In *Handbook of Industrial Organization*, edited by Mark Armstrong and Robert Porter, 3: 2369–440. Amsterdam: North-Holland.

Wickelgren, Abraham L. 2005. Managerial Incentives and the Price Effects of Mergers. *Journal of Industrial Economics* 53: 327–53.

Wickelgren, Abraham L. 2021. Optimal Merger Standards for Potential Competition: The Effect of Ex Ante Investment Incentives (unpublished manuscript).

Williamson, Oliver E. 1968. Economies as an Antitrust Defense: The Welfare Tradeoffs. *American Economic Review* 58: 18–36.

Williamson, Oliver E. 1974. The Economics of Antitrust: Transaction Cost Considerations. *University of Pennsylvania Law Review* 122: 1439–96.

Williamson, Oliver E. 1975. *Markets and Hierarchies: Analysis and Antitrust Implications*. New York: Free Press.

Williamson, Oliver E. 1977. Economies as an Antitrust Defense Revisited. *University of Pennsylvania Law Review* 125: 699–736.

Williamson, Oliver E. 1985. *The Economic Institutions of Capitalism*. New York: Free Press.

Williamson, Oliver E. 2002. The Theory of the Firm as Governance Structure: From Choice to Contract. *Journal of Economic Perspectives* 16(3): 171–95.

Willig, Robert D. 1991. Merger Analysis, Industrial Organization Theory, and Merger Guidelines. *Brookings Papers on Economic Activity: Microeconomics* 1991: 281–312.

Wollmann, Thomas G. 2018. Trucks without Bailouts: Equilibrium Product Characteristics for Commercial Vehicles. *American Economic Review* 108: 1364–406.

Wollmann, Thomas G. 2019. Stealth Consolidation: Evidence from an Amendment to the Hart-Scott-Rodino Act. *American Economic Review: Insights* 1: 77–94.

Wollmann, Thomas G. 2021. How to Get Away with Merger: Stealth Consolidation and Its Effects on US Healthcare. NBER Working Paper 27274 (revised).

World Bank Group and OECD. 2017. *A Step Ahead: Competition Policy for Shared Prosperity and Inclusive Growth*. Washington, DC: World Bank.

Index

Agencies. *See also* Competition policy; Courts
  choice of market definition by, 148
  commitment to standards by, 20 and n8, 181, 182, 183n
  competition agencies compared to others, 11, 171, 184–186, 189 and n4, 205–206, 218–219
  and coordinated effects of mergers, 70n46, 97, 173, 177, 196
  early acquisitions, assessment of, 133
  efficiencies, consideration of, 97, 103, 108 and n29, 110, 112–113, 173–174, 176–177, 217
  entry, consideration of, 124–125, 132–133
  and ex ante effects, 20, 132–133
  expertise needed in, 10–11, 20n7, 112–113, 170, 171, 172–177, 214, 217
  fines and damages, use of, 180n
  and industry-specific expertise, 8, 11, 20n7, 112–113, 170, 174, 175, 214
  information available to, 10–11, 18, 19, 25n16, 36, 39, 137, 141, 144, 148n8, 158, 162–163, 181–182, 218
  institutional capacity of, 10–11, 20n7, 27, 79, 80, 112–113, 138, 158–159, 170, 171–177, 184–186 and n10, 180, 190, 211, 217, 218
  internal evidence, use of, 18, 169, 172, 176, 182
  jurisdiction of, 11, 25 and n16, 184–186 and n10, 189, 205–206, 209, 210, 211, 218–219
  long-run vs. short-run analysis by, 114–115, 195–196
  and the market definition paradigm, 34–35n2, 41n, 75, 79–80
  merger guidance by, 1, 16, 21, 25, 34–35n2, 75, 78–79
  merger proposals and agencies' expected decisions, 22, 147
  merger retrospectives, use of, 158, 175
  merger review by, 10–11, 15, 19, 27, 34–35n2, 36, 108, 158, 162–163, 179, 181–184, 186, 205, 218
  merger simulations, use of, 159–160
  methods, choice of, 158, 162–163, 205
  models, use of, 60, 112, 174
  non-neoclassical merger motives, assessment of, 26–27
  protocols used by, 16 and n2, 49, 115, 195, 205, 219
  rationality constraint, reasoning from, 124, 196
  reverse-engineering by, 41n, 80, 148

Agencies (cont.)
  screening of proposals, 25–26n16, 36, 39, 79, 108, 141, 143, 147, 148n, 172
  static analysis by, 27
  welfare standards of, 20n8, 25, 32, 189–190, 195, 199n13, 204–205, 219
Agency problems and merger motives, 24, 25n15, 123n10, 165 and n24, 207n27
Alternatives to merger, 1, 7, 81, 83–84, 85, 100, 101–103, 104, 167n2, 216–217
Analytical methods. *See also* Competition policy; Information; Market definition paradigm; Rationality constraint
  articulation of explanations in, 18–19n6
  decision analytic perspective, 15–16, 137, 213–214
  deficiencies in, 1–2, 3–4, 27, 74–76, 79–80, 107–108, 110–111
  dynamic vs. static analysis, 27, 59–60, 128–129, 194
  evolution of, 77–79
  information sources and processing, 137, 139–140, 149, 218
  integrated vs. siloed approaches, 3–4, 8, 17–18, 23, 81, 107–113, 125n, 213–214
  long-run vs. short-run analysis, 4, 12, 28–29, 113–115, 157, 187, 194–199, 219
  market definition paradigm, 1, 33–46, 64–66, 76–80
  of merger review, 3–4, 12–13, 137, 218
  models in analysis, 47, 48, 57–58, 60–61, 112, 128, 129, 139, 145, 159, 173, 174, 191, 194, 200
  new questions and proposals for, 2–3, 12–13, 27, 29, 30–31, 79–80, 88–89, 108–109, 112–113, 137–141, 159, 213–220
  proxies in, 3, 13, 27, 34, 45, 65, 76, 78, 113, 115, 138, 141, 142, 195, 199, 205, 209, 218, 219
  reverse engineering in, 4, 10, 16n2, 34n3, 41 and n9, 43, 64n36, 80, 148
  single-sector partial equilibrium vs. multi-sector general equilibrium analysis, 199–205
  stress points in, 48
  targeted-sector vs. cross-sector analysis, 30–31
  triangulation in, 3, 8, 109, 137, 155, 163, 214
  uncertainty and, 22n11, 29, 97, 103
  welfare standard, choice of, 188–194, 199n13, 219
Anticompetitive effects
  barriers to entry, 95n
  coordinated effects and, 68
  direct analysis of, 79–80
  downstream and upstream, 33
  and efficiencies, 7, 17, 19, 23 and n13, 24, 81, 82–85, 97–98, 100, 104, 107–113, 130, 177, 216, 217
  information on, 109, 144, 214
  in integrated vs. siloed analysis, 17, 19, 23, 107–113, 213–214, 216
  long-run vs. short-run analysis of, 196, 219
  in market definition paradigm, 34, 36, 214–215
  merger specificity of, 82–85
  postmerger entry and, 8, 23, 118, 121, 124
  probability analysis of, 16
  and profitability, 22
  in protocols, 3, 214
  structural presumption about, 140, 141, 214

Index

Bayes' rule, 16n1. *See also* Prediction of merger effects; Probabilities
  odds ratio formulation of, 4, 18, 109, 137, 140, 214
  and updating of probabilities, 17, 109, 137, 214
Behavioral problems and merger motives, 24, 25n15, 123n10, 165, 207n27
Bertrand model, 57, 58n28, 60, 61, 64, 67, 77, 146, 159

Canadian merger guidelines, 31, 188
Commitment in legal systems, 20 and n8
Competition and competitors. *See also* Bertrand model; Competition policy; Cournot model
  asset sharing between competitors, 7, 81, 104–107
  Bertrand competition, 57, 61, 63n35, 66, 77, 146
  contracting between competitors, 102, 104
  as process, compared to outcome, 12, 187, 205–209
  quantity competition, 50, 57, 58–59
  as rivalry, 208
  social welfare, effect on, 194–195n10, 206
Competition policy, 11–12. *See also* Analytical methods; Competition; Merger regulation
  consumer vs. total welfare in, 4, 11, 12, 187, 188–191, 194–195n10, 219
  and innovation, 198–199
  issues outside scope of, 209–211, 219
  market power in, 44 and n10
  market share thresholds in, 44
  match of instruments to policies, 11, 187, 189, 218–219
  multi-sector general equilibrium approach, 187, 200
  objectives of, 4, 11–12, 184–185, 187–188, 198–199, 205–206, 218–219
  other economic issues and, 189, 209–210
  partial vs. general equilibrium analysis in, 4, 199–205
  process compared to outcomes in, 12, 187, 205–209
  redistribution and, 189–191
  short-term vs. long-term analysis in, 4, 12, 187, 194–199
  single-sector partial vs. multisector general equilibrium approach, 12, 187, 199–205
  and social welfare calculus, 4, 11–12, 184–185, 188–194
  specialization of agencies responsible for, 184–186 and n10
  and tax and transfer system, 191, 219
Consumer welfare. *See also* Total (or social) welfare
  and assessment of efficiencies, 31, 104, 108, 188n1
  choice of welfare standard, 4, 11–12, 20n8, 31–32, 82 and n2, 108, 119n4, 187, 188–190, 199n13, 204, 219
  convergence of consumer and total welfare, 12, 31–32, 187, 194 and n10, 199n13, 219
  defined, 189
  long-run and short-run, 20n8, 31–32, 113, 198, 199n13
  in merger guidelines, 31, 113, 188, 197
  vs. total welfare, 4, 11–12, 15, 20n8, 31–32, 57, 119n4, 187, 188–194, 199n13, 219
Contracts and contracting
  between competitors, 102, 104
  contractual practice, 11
  merger vs., 1, 7, 81, 83, 85–86, 88–89, 92, 93, 102, 103–104, 173n2, 217

Contracts and contracting (cont.)
  for sharing of assets, 104–107
  in the theory of the firm, 85, 86, 92, 98, 103
Coordinated effects of mergers. *See also* Price effects of mergers
  analysis of, 49, 68–73, 74, 77, 160, 172, 177, 196–197, 215
  competition policy on, 68 and n42
  difficulties in coordination, 71–73
  long-run vs. short-run analysis of, 196–197
  in merger guidelines, 70 and n46, 78
  paradoxes in, 68–69 and n43
  and postmerger entry, 121n
  prediction of, 6, 68, 71, 77, 160, 173, 184, 196–197, 215–216
  rationality constraint and, 73
  structural features of markets and, 71
Cournot model, 5–6, 27–28, 44, 50, 53, 56, 57–61, 64, 65, 66, 67, 77, 146, 157, 196, 215
Courts. *See also* Agencies; U.S. Supreme Court
  on competition as a process, 206n
  coordinated effects, treatment of, 70n46
  efficiencies, consideration of, 108 and n29, 188n1
  expert magistrates and witnesses in, 11, 75n52, 141, 171, 177–178
  information, limits of, 141, 177–178
  institutional capacity of, 138, 171, 177–180, 218
  jurisdiction of, 25
  litigation reform, 177–180
  market definition paradigm, reliance on, 34, 43, 62n, 64, 75, 76, 153–154
  merger guidance by, 1, 16 and n2, 34
  merger review by, 11, 15, 23, 34, 75, 80, 141, 171, 177–180, 218
  monitoring of agencies by, 180
  probabilities, focus on, 140
  reasonable probability standard of, 16n3
  reverse engineering by, 16n2, 41n, 80

Decision analysis, 4, 15, 213
  and expectations about agency decisions, 22n12
  and mechanism design approach, 15–16 and n1
  in prediction of merger effects, 9, 15, 213–214
  and sequential siloed analysis, compared, 213–214
  welfare effect in, 15, 21
Decision-making (by agencies and courts)
  and courts' expertise, 177–180
  expected values compared to probabilities in, 16
  fundamental elements for, 15, 31
  information collection and, 19
  reverse engineering in, 41n
  structural presumption and, 137
  under uncertainty, 3, 140
  and use of experts, proposal for, 178–179
  welfare as objective function, 31
Differentiated products mergers, unilateral effects with. *See also* Bertrand model
  analysis of, 49, 61–68, 74, 78, 171, 215
  models of, 61
  rationality constraint in, 56
Dynamic analysis, 6, 9, 27, 28, 29, 59–60, 68, 128

Economies of scale or scope. *See under* Efficiencies
Efficiencies
  agencies' expertise about, 11, 25, 112–113, 173–174, 176–177

Index

analysis of, 7–8, 17, 19, 25, 66–67, 81–82, 89, 94, 97, 107–108, 112, 173–174, 176–177, 216
and anticompetitive effects, 7, 17, 19, 23 and n13, 24, 81, 82–85, 97–98, 100, 104, 107–113, 130, 177, 216, 217
asset sharing, 7, 81, 104–107
claims of, in merger proposals, 19
and consumer welfare standard, 31, 104, 188n1
and coordination, 73
economies of scale, 7, 81, 84, 95–101, 103, 125, 130, 170, 197, 217
economies of scope, 7, 81, 94n16, 101–104, 130, 170, 197, 217
effect of price changes on, 66–67
efficiency credit, 7, 17n4, 110–112, 176, 216
and entry analysis, 125n, 130–131
ex ante effects on, 82n1
information on, 109–111, 173–174
integrated vs. siloed analysis of, 17, 19, 23, 81, 107–113, 213–214, 216
long-run perspective on, 81–82, 113–115, 197, 219
in merger guidelines, 82, 107n, 108, 125n
and merger vs. contract choice, 81, 83–84, 85, 88–89, 92
merger-specificity of, 1, 6, 21n9, 81, 82–83, 84–86, 94n18, 96, 100, 101, 104, 131, 173, 216
negative, 22n11
and postmerger entry, 8, 23
postponement of, 182
and profitability, 22, 56
in protocols, 3
synergies as, 94–95 and n18, 170, 173, 216
in the theory of the firm, 87, 88, 89, 93–94, 98
uncertainty about, 7, 19, 97, 103, 112
and vertical arrangements, 85, 94–95, 98
welfare standards for, 82n, 83, 104, 108

Entry. *See also* Ex ante entry; Ex post entry
agencies' consideration of, 124–125, 132–133
analysis of, 2, 8–9, 11, 15, 17, 117–118, 132–135, 197–198, 217–218
and anticompetitive effects and efficiencies, 118, 119, 120, 124, 217
barriers to, 95n, 117n
early acquisitions by incumbents, 133–135, 217–218
ex ante entry, 2, 8–9, 11, 118, 126–135, 197, 198
ex post entry, 2, 8, 11, 23, 117–118, 119–126, 197–198, 217
free entry in market economy, 4, 27
in homogeneous goods industries, 8, 9, 118, 127, 129, 135, 203
and imperfect competition, 15, 203
and innovation, 117, 119, 122, 126, 129, 203
integrated vs. siloed analysis of, 17–18, 213–214
in merger guidelines, 8, 117–118 and n2, 123, 125 and n12, 126
merger regime and, 21–22
and profitability, 123–124, 217
in protocols, 3
uncertainty about, 120
variety- or complementarity-enhancing, 8, 117, 119, 122, 129, 130, 134, 203
welfare effects of, 2, 8, 118, 119 and n4, 122–123, 125, 126, 128, 129, 217–218

Equilibrium
Cournot equilibrium, 57
dynamic vs. static analysis of, 27, 28, 29, 194

Equilibrium (cont.)
  equilibrium analysis, 2, 8, 12, 27, 47, 113–114, 199–205
  equilibrium entry behavior, 119–120, 130, 217
  equilibrium price, 50
  long-run vs. short-run analysis of, 2, 4, 6, 27–29, 113–114, 194–199, 219
  multi-sector distortions in, 29–31
  single-sector partial equilibrium vs. multisector general equilibrium, 2, 4, 12, 187, 199–205
European Union (EU)
  consumer welfare standard in, 188
  coordinated effects, focus on, 70n46
  efficiencies, consideration of, 108n29
  merger guidelines in, 15, 31, 34n2, 82, 117, 125 and n12, 141n, 188
  research on mergers in, 166n
  Treaty on the Functioning of the European Union (TFEU), 44, 106n
Ex ante entry. *See also* Entry; Ex ante incentives and investment; Ex post entry
  agencies' expertise about, 175
  analysis of, 2, 8–9, 118, 126–135, 174–175, 198, 217–218
  benefits for innovation, synergies, and variety, 22, 118, 126, 129, 131, 198, 218
  and buyout premium, 117, 118, 126, 127–128, 130–131, 134, 218
  defined, 118
  early acquisitions by incumbent firms, 133–135, 174–175
  to generate synergies, 130–131
  and investment, 8–9, 118, 126, 129–130 and n18, 131, 133, 218
  long-run vs. short-run perspective on, 198
  welfare effects of, 118, 126, 129, 198

Ex ante incentives and investment, 8–9, 20. *See also* Ex ante entry
  buyout premiums and, 20, 117, 126, 129 and n18, 218
  effects on efficiency, 82n1
  effects of merger review, 16
  to generate synergies, 131
  merger regime and, 21–22, 131–132
Exit
  and economies of scale, 96, 97, 99
  and imperfect competition, 15
  in market economy, 4, 27
  prospective buyouts and, 117
  and welfare effect of inter-sector flows, 203–204
Ex post effects, 16, 23
Ex post entry. *See also* Entry; Ex ante entry
  analysis of, 8, 117–118, 119–126, 197–198, 217
  and anticompetitive effects, 8, 23, 118, 121, 124, 197–198
  defined, 117
  effect on price increases, 2, 8, 118, 120–121, 123–124
  long-run vs. short-run perspective on, 197n12
  in merger guidelines, 8, 117, 125
  and parties' rationality constraint, 118, 123, 174, 217
  welfare effects of, 8, 118, 119 and n4, 122, 198–199, 217, 218
Ex post merger review. *See under* Merger review

Federal Trade Commission (FTC), 13, 185
Firms. *See* Theory of the firm

Herfindahl-Hirschman Index (HHI). *See also* Hypothetical Monopolist Test
  HHI, 5, 6, 34, 36, 39, 42, 44, 49, 50, 51, 52, 53, 55, 57, 62, 65, 66 and

n38, 69, 70, 71–72 and n48, 74,
76 and n53, 140, 141, 142, 147,
202n23, 215, 216
ΔHHI, 1, 5, 6, 34, 36, 39, 40, 42, 44,
45, 48, 49, 51, 52, 53, 55, 66n38,
69, 70, 72 and n48, 74, 76, 140,
141, 142, 146, 147, 151, 215, 216
and coordinated effects of mergers, 6,
69, 70, 215–216
in differentiated products mergers,
62, 65
in homogeneous goods mergers,
51–53, 215
in market definition paradigm, 34
and n1, 36, 40, 42, 45, 49, 70, 74
in merger guidelines, 1, 5, 34 and
n1, 36, 44, 49, 52, 53, 70, 74, 142,
188n2, 215
as proxy for market power, 76n,
188n2, 202n23
in structural presumption, 141, 142,
147
Homogeneous goods industries and
markets, 196. *See also* Cournot
model
coordinated effects in, 70 and n45
entry in, 8. 9, 118, 127, 129, 135, 203
as focus of analysis, 5, 44, 49, 60, 215
price effects in, 5, 50–61, 74
Horizontal mergers
as the focus of study, 3, 12, 30, 33,
81, 112, 119, 159, 208, 213
identification of, 19, 164 and n22
literature on, 87
and vertical arrangements, 94–95 and
n19, 101
and vertical mergers, distinguished,
164–165 and n23
Hypothetical Monopolist Test (HMT), 1,
5, 34, 36, 39, 40, 43, 48, 49, 51, 52,
53, 55, 62, 65, 69, 70, 74, 76, 141,
142, 147, 214, 215, 216. *See also*
Herfindahl-Hirschman Index;
Market definition paradigm

Industrial organization economics
compared to official protocols, 48,
213, 214
experts in, 20n7, 172, 217
research in, 3, 4, 12, 27, 30, 33, 60,
139, 159, 171, 172, 176n, 190, 195,
206, 214, 218, 219, 220
single-sector partial equilibrium
approach in, 12, 187, 199–200
Industry expertise, 10, 137, 149, 163,
169–170, 172, 175
Industry studies, 10, 137, 149–155, 218
Information
agencies' use of, 10, 18, 19, 25n16,
39, 141, 143–144, 158, 159,
162–163, 181–182, 214
asymmetric information, 102, 134
complementarity of, 10, 149, 163,
169
diagnosticity–cost ratio of, 19, 109,
111, 214
firms' internal evidence, 18, 110, 163,
169 and n27, 172, 176, 182
industry expertise, 10, 137, 149, 163,
169–170, 172, 175
industry studies, 10, 137, 149–155,
218
limitations of, 10, 79, 137, 141, 158,
164, 214
in market definition paradigm, 36–37,
39, 79
merger retrospectives, 10, 137, 147,
148n, 149, 152, 155–159, 163, 175,
182, 197
merger simulations, 10, 11, 59, 61,
121, 128, 137, 146, 147, 149, 152,
155, 159–163, 172, 218
order of gathering and analyzing, 19,
109
for predicting mergers' effects, 10, 18,
23, 79, 137, 139, 149–170
processing of, to update priors, 137,
139
sources of, 10, 110, 137, 149–170, 218

Information (cont.)
    stock market event studies, 10, 137, 140, 149, 163–168, 218
    for updating probabilities, 17, 23, 109, 137
Innovation
    entry and, 117, 118, 119, 122, 126, 129 and n18, 198, 203
    as factor in merger analysis, 115, 122, 126, 129, 198
    incentives for, 22, 129n18, 206, 218, 219
    long-run perspective on, 115, 198–199, 210, 219
    and price effects, 33
Institutions. See Agencies; Courts
Investment
    ex ante, 8–9, 21–22, 27, 117, 118, 126, 129–131 and n18, 218
    externalities of, 28
    to generate synergies, 131
    and imperfect competition, 15, 28
    incentives for, 8–9, 21–22, 27, 32, 117, 129–130, 206, 218
    postmerger, effects of, 6, 28
    short-run and long-run effects of, 32

Legal rules. See U.S. legal rules
Litigation reform. See under Courts

Market definition paradigm
    composite functions of, 35, 39–43
    courts' reliance on, 34, 43, 62n, 64, 75, 76, 153–154
    elements and logic of, 34, 35–39
    evolution of, 77–79
    Herfindahl-Hirschman Index in, 34 and n1, 36, 40, 42, 45, 49, 70, 74
    and market power, 4, 39, 40 and n8, 42, 43, 44 and n10, 45, 46, 52, 77
    market shares in, 34, 35, 36, 39, 41–42, 43–47, 49, 55, 77–78, 214
    merger guidelines and, 34, 40, 43, 49, 52–53, 66, 70, 74, 78
    not used in modern merger analysis, 4, 6, 33, 35, 62, 214
    relevant market issue in, 40, 45, 65, 70, 75, 79, 214
    and reverse engineering in analysis, 4, 10, 35n3, 41 and n9, 43, 64n36, 80
    structural presumption and, 9–10, 141–148, 214
    weaknesses of, 4–5, 35–36, 38, 45, 49–50, 64–65, 70, 74–76, 79–80, 147–148, 214–215
Market power
    Lerner index of, 29, 50, 77, 202
    market definition paradigm and, 4, 39, 40 and n8, 42, 43, 44 and n10, 45, 46, 52, 77
    market shares and, 44, 45 and n11, 46, 62, 77
    under merger guidelines threshold, 40, 52, 188–189n2
    proxy for, 76n, 188–189n2, 202n23
    uncertainty about, 40, 44 and n10, 45 and n11
Market shares. See also Herfindahl-Hirschman Index
    correct analysis of, 47, 65
    industry studies and, 150, 152
    inferences from, 34, 35, 36, 39, 43–47, 55, 77–78, 214–215
    in market definition paradigm, 34, 35, 36, 39, 41–42, 43–47, 49, 55, 77–78, 214
    and market power, 44, 45 and n11, 46, 62, 77
    in structural presumption, 9, 141
Mechanism design, 4, 15, 137
    and decision analytic perspective, 15–16 and n1
    and ex ante effects, 20–22
Merger guidelines
    by agencies, 1, 78
    Canadian guidelines, 31, 188
    competition per se emphasized in, 207–208n28

Index

consumer welfare standard in, 31, 113, 188, 197
by courts, 1, 43, 75
effect of courts' expertise on, 179
efficiencies in, 82, 107n, 125n
entry in, 8, 117–118 and n2, 123, 125 and n12, 126
European guidelines, 15, 31, 34n2, 82, 117, 125 and n12, 141n, 188
Herfindahl-Hirschman Index in, 1, 5, 34 and n1, 36, 44, 49 and n17, 52, 53, 70, 74, 142, 188n2, 215
Hypothetical Monopolist Test in, 1, 5, 34, 36, 43, 49, 52, 53, 74, 142, 215, 216
and market definition paradigm, 34, 40, 43, 46, 49, 52–53, 66, 70, 74, 78, 142
market shares, inferences from, 44, 78n56
omissions in, 2, 15, 23 and n13, 40 and n8, 43, 60, 87, 126, 207n28
protocols in, 1, 15, 16, 43, 49
structural presumptions in, 44, 49 and n17, 69n44, 141
thresholds in, 1, 5, 39, 40, 44, 52, 53 and n20, 69n44, 74–75, 78
U.S. Merger Guidelines, 1, 5, 13, 15, 31, 34, 46, 49, 52, 60, 70, 78, 82, 141, 188, 215 (*for details see* U.S. Merger Guidelines)
Merger proposals
costs of, 22n11–12
effect of agency standards on, 21, 22, 147
effect of courts' expertise on, 179
efficiencies in, 19, 108–109
future proposals, 21
and merger retrospectives, 158
non-neoclassical motives for, 24 and n14, 25n15
screening of, 25–26n16, 27, 36, 39, 79, 108, 141, 172

Merger regulation. *See also* Competition policy
effects on social welfare, 2, 126, 132, 184–185, 204
ex ante and ex post review compared, 180, 181
ex ante effects of, 21–22, 132
merger retrospectives and, 158–159
models used in, 48
and regulation of interfirm contracts, 106n
scope of, 208n30
and short-run vs. long-run analysis, 12
Merger retrospectives, 10, 137, 147, 148n, 149, 152, 155 159, 163, 175, 182, 197, 218
Merger review
by agencies, 10–11, 15, 16 and n2, 19, 23, 27, 34–35n2, 36, 108, 158, 162–163, 171–177, 179, 181–184, 186, 205, 218
analytical steps in, 3–4, 17–20
Cournot model in, 5–6
by courts, 11, 15, 23, 34, 75, 80, 141, 171, 177–180, 218
evidence and information for, 10, 18, 137, 149–170, 218
ex post, 11, 171, 180–184
integrated vs. siloed analysis in, 3–4, 17–18, 23, 109
long-term vs. short-term perspective in, 2, 113–115
proposals for, 12–13, 19, 112–113, 205, 218
screening stage in, 19–20, 36, 108
static vs. dynamic analysis in, 27
uncertainty in, 3, 181, 184
Merger simulations, 10, 11, 59, 61, 121, 128, 137, 146, 147, 149, 152, 155, 159–163, 172, 218
Merger vs. contract, 1, 7, 81, 83, 85–86, 88, 89, 92, 93, 102, 103–104, 173n2, 217

Neoclassical merger motives, 22–23, 56
Non-neoclassical merger motives, 24
  and n14, 25n15, 26–27, 165n24,
  207n27

Organizational economics, 7, 11, 85,
  173, 217

Postmerger entry. *See* Ex post entry
Prediction of merger effects, 9, 33, 48,
  77, 79, 125. *See also* Information;
  Probabilities
  challenges of, 138, 141, 171, 180,
    182, 208
  of coordinated effects, 6, 68, 71, 77,
    173, 184, 196–197, 215–216
  decision analytic perspective of, 9, 137
  focus on probabilities and
    magnitudes, compared, 140
  functions for, 39, 43–44
  information sources for, 9, 39, 137,
    139, 149–170
  long-run perspective on, 28–29,
    195–196, 199
  in market definition paradigm, 35–43,
    142
  and market shares, analysis of, 46–47
  overview of, 137–141
  structural presumption and, 9,
    46n12, 137, 141–148
  uncertainty in, 29, 180, 181, 184
Premerger entry. *See* Ex ante entry
Price effects of mergers. *See also*
    Coordinated effects of mergers;
    Differentiated products mergers;
    Homogeneous goods industries
    and markets
  analysis of, generally, 4–5, 6, 8, 9, 33,
    47, 48–50, 53n21
  coordinated effects, 49, 68–73, 74,
    215–216
  and diversion ratios of firms' products,
    6, 62, 63, 64, 172

marginal costs and, 54
in market definition paradigm, 4–5,
  33–34, 36–39, 41–42, 44, 76
and market shares, analysis of, 43–47,
  62
as stand-in for quality and
  innovation, 33
unilateral effects with differentiated
  products, 49, 56, 61–68, 74, 160,
  172
unilateral effects with homogeneous
  goods, 5, 49, 50–61, 74
and welfare effects, compared, 57
Probabilities
  of anticompetitive effects and
    benefits, optimal weighting of, 16
  Bayes' rule for, 4, 16n1, 17, 18, 109,
    137, 140, 214
  and likelihood ratio, 4, 9, 109,
    111n34, 137–138, 139, 214, 218
  and magnitudes, compared, 140
  in prediction of merger effects, 9,
    137–141
  prior and posterior probabilities, 4, 9,
    137–138, 140, 214, 218
  prior probabilities, choice of, 17,
    111n34, 138–139, 218
  reasonable probability standard,
    16n3
  updating of, 16n1, 17, 23, 109,
    111n34, 149, 214
Profitability
  from anticompetitive effects and
    efficiencies, 22, 123n10
  as assumed merger motivation, 22,
    123n10, 165
  effect of postmerger entry on, 23,
    123–124, 174
  of merging vs. nonmerging firms, 56
  prices or efficiencies as factors in, 56
  as rationality constraint, 2, 3, 22, 56,
    109, 123 and n10, 140, 174
  threshold of, 24

Index

Protocols, 13, 205
  anticompetitive effects in, 3
  disconnect between protocols and analysis, 1, 3, 15, 16, 43, 49, 213, 214
  efficiencies in, 3
  entry in, 3
  focus on probabilities in, 140
  and industrial organization economics, compared, 48, 49, 213
  integrated vs. siloed analysis in, 3, 8
  market definition in, 43, 64, 214
  in merger guidelines, 1, 15, 16, 43, 49
  short-run and long-run perspectives and, 2, 4, 115, 195, 199, 219
Public economics, 11
  optimal tax system, 191, 219

Quality, price effects and, 33

Rationality constraint, 19, 56
  agencies' consideration of, 26, 124, 196
  coordinated effects and, 73
  effect of postmerger entry on, 8, 118
  efficiencies and, 56, 67, 73, 217
  inferences from, 2, 8, 15, 22, 56, 73, 118, 169, 174, 207n27, 217
  profitability expectation as, 2, 3, 22, 56, 109, 123 and n10, 140, 174
  and updating in analysis, 23, 214
Redistribution
  and competition policy, 189–190, 219
  regulation as instrument for, 32 and n21
  and tax and transfer system, 191–194, 210, 219
Relevant market, in analysis, 34, 40, 45, 48, 65, 70, 75, 79, 142, 214. *See also* Market definition paradigm
Reverse engineering in analysis, 4, 10, 16n2, 34n3, 41 and n9, 43, 64n36, 80, 148

Social welfare. *See* Total (or social) welfare
Static analysis, 27, 29
Stock market event studies, 10, 137, 140, 149, 163–168, 218
Structural presumption, 10, 44, 46n12, 49n17, 69n44, 137, 138, 140, 141–148, 177, 214
Structure-conduct-performance paradigm, 46, 78n55, 145, 151, 171

Tax and transfer system, and redistribution, 191–194, 210, 219
Tax savings and merger motives, 24, 25n15, 123n10
Theory of the firm, 1, 7, 11
  legal and functional notions of firms compared, 85–86 and n5–6, 88–89
  literature on, 85–94, 173
  and merger vs. contract, 1, 7, 81, 85–86, 88–89, 92, 93, 103–104, 217
Thresholds
  challenge thresholds, 1, 216
  for efficiency credit, 112
  long-run effects considered in, 21
  in merger guidelines, 1, 5, 39, 40, 44, 49, 52, 53 and n20, 69n44, 74–75, 78, 141n
  profitability threshold, 24
  stringency threshold, 20, 21
  structural presumption threshold, 141, 146
Total (or social) welfare. *See also* Consumer welfare
  and assessment of efficiencies, 82n2, 108
  choice of welfare standard, 4, 11–12, 20n8, 31–32, 82 and n2, 108, 119n4, 187, 188–190, 199n13, 204, 219
  consumer-surplus-neutral merger and, 88

Total (or social) welfare (cont.)
  vs. consumer welfare, 4, 11–12, 20n8, 31–32, 57, 119n4, 187, 188–194, 199n13, 219
  convergence of consumer and total welfare, 12, 31–32, 187, 194 and n10, 219
  effect of competition on, 206
  effects of entry on, 2, 8, 118, 119 and n4, 122–123, 125, 126 128, 129, 217–218
  effects of inter-sector flows on, 203–204
  effects of merger regulation on, 2, 126, 132, 184–185, 204
  as goal of multiple agencies, 185
  long-run and short-run merger effects on, 2, 12, 20n8, 31–32, 60, 113
  and non-welfarist objectives, compared, 210–211 and n33
  as objective function of decision-making, 31
  price effects and, 30, 57
  proxies for, 195, 209, 210n
  redistribution and competition policy distinguished for, 190
  short-run vs. long-run standards of, 12, 20n8, 31–32, 198
  tax and transfer system and, 190, 191

U.S. Department of Justice, 13
U.S. legal rules
  emphasis on probabilities in, 16 and n3, 140
  on use of experts, 75n52, 177–178
U.S. Merger Guidelines, 1, 145. *See also* Merger guidelines
  Commentary on Merger Guidelines (2006), 60, 70n46
  competition per se emphasized in, 207–208n28
  consumer welfare standard in, 31, 188
  coordinated effects in, 70 and n46, 78
  and Cournot analysis, 60 and n31
  efficiencies in, 82, 107n, 125n
  entry in, 117–118 and n2, 125n
  HMT and HHI formulations in, 5, 34 and n1, 49 and n17, 70, 215
  legal analysis in, 13n
  market definition paradigm in, 34 and n2, 49, 70, 78
  market shares, inferences from, 44, 49, 78 and n56
  Merger Guidelines (1968), 78
  Merger Guidelines (1982 and 1984), 46, 49, 78
  Merger Guidelines (1992), 70
  Merger Guidelines (2010), 5, 13, 34n2, 40n, 49 and n15–16, 52, 53 and n20, 60, 62n, 82, 107n, 117, 125, 141n
  Merger Guidelines (2023), 5, 13 and n1, 35n2–3, 44, 49n15 and 17, 53n20, 60n, 62n, 69n44, 73n, 78n56, 82, 108n28, 117–118 and n2, 125, 141, 143n, 207n28
  omissions in, 15, 40n, 60, 125n, 207n28
  price effects in, 49
  structural presumptions in, 40n, 44, 49n17, 69n44, 141
  thresholds in, 1, 5, 44, 49, 52, 53 and n20, 69n44, 74–75, 78, 141n
U.S. Supreme Court. *See also* Courts
  consumer welfare standard and, 188n1
  merger decisions by, 34, 44, 45, 78, 141, 188n1

Variety, as benefit of entry, 8, 9, 22, 117, 118, 119, 122, 129, 198, 203
Vertical arrangements, 85, 98, 101, 217
  and horizontal arrangements, compared, 94–95 and n19, 101
Vertical mergers and horizontal mergers, distinguished, 164–165 and n23

Welfare. *See* Consumer welfare; Total (or social) welfare

Cases

Alcoa: United States v. Aluminum Co. of America, 148 F.2d 416 (2d Cir.1945), 46n11
Brown Shoe: Brown Shoe Co. v. United States, 370 U.S. 294 (1962), 45, 78, 79n, 188n1
Clorox: Federal Trade Commission v. Procter & Gamble Co., 386 U.S. 568 (1967), 188n1
General Dynamics: United States v. General Dynamics Corp., 415 U.S. 486 (1974), 45, 79n
National Society of Professional Engineers: National Society of Professional Engineers v. United States, 435 U.S. 679 (1978), 206n
Philadelphia Bank: United States v. Philadelphia National Bank, 374 U.S. 321 (1963), 34 and n1, 35n2, 44, 46, 73n, 78, 141, 142, 143n, 145
Staples: Federal Trade Commission v. Staples, 970 F. Supp. 1066 (D.D.C. 1997), 154

Statutes

Clayton Act, 16n3, 100n, 181
Sherman Act, 44, 77, 105n
Treaty on the Functioning of the European Union (TFEU), 44, 106n